Aram Hajian, Wolfram Luther, A. J. Han Vinck (Eds.)

Collaborative Technologies and Data Science
in Smart City Applications

**International Workshop at the American University of Armenia,
September 12 to September 15, 2018**

Revised contributions

Volume Editors

Aram Hajian
American University of Armenia, College of Science and Engineering
40 Marshal Baghramyan Ave, Yerevan 0019, Armenia
Email: ahajian@aua.am

Wolfram Luther
University of Duisburg-Essen
Scientific Computing, Computer Graphics, and Image Processing Group
Lotharstraße 63, 47057 Duisburg, Germany
E-mail: wolfram.luther@uni-due.de

A. J. Han Vinck
University of Duisburg-Essen, Institute of Digital Signal Processing
Bismarckstrasse 81, 47057 Duisburg, Germany
E-mail: han.vinck@uni-due.de

Bibliographic information published by the Deutsche Nationalbibliothek
The Deutsche Nationalbibliothek lists this publication in the Deutsche Nationalbibliografie; detailed bibliographic data are available on the Internet at http://dnb.d-nb.de .

ACM Subject Classification (1998): H.1.1, H.1.2, H.5.2, H.5.3, I.2.x, I.6, J.1, J.5

ISBN 978-3-8325-4734-9

Logos Verlag Berlin GmbH
Comeniushof, Gubener Str. 47,
10243 Berlin
Tel.; +49 (0)30 42 85 10 90
Fax: +49 (0)30 42 85 10 92
INTERNET: https://www.logos-verlag.de

PREFACE

Since many years, two partnerships have been well established by researchers from the Faculty of Engineering at the University of Duisburg-Essen (UDE) and Armenian research scientists: first, the long-term cooperation between Prof. W. Luther, Dr. D. Biella, Dr. B. Weyers and the Armenian scientist Prof. N. Baloian, visiting professor at the American University of Armenia (AUA) and professor at the University of Chile and his colleagues of the Department of Computer Sciences; and second the collaboration between Prof. A. J. Han Vinck, Dr. Y. Chen and Armenian scientists Prof. G. Khachatryan, Prof. M. Haroutunian, Dr. A. Harutyunyan and Dr. A. Ghazaryan. The success of both cooperations becomes visible through a large number of joint publications, completed master theses, realized research networks in specific topics and funded research projects. All these activities have paved the way for the young people to face new research challenges and explore new forms of collaboration.

Recently, two research networks crossed their paths at the *Armenian-German Fact Finding Mission Tradition and Smart Living* funded by the German Academic Exchange Service (DAAD). Mutual visits were organized at the universities of Yerevan on Sept. 6th-13th, 2017 and at UDE on December 4th-10th 2017. A memorandum of cooperation between both faculties of engineering at AUA and UDE has been concluded. The first of several collaboration-building activities is an exploratory bilateral Workshop in Armenia on Sept. 12-15, 2018, entitled Collaborative Technologies and Data Science in Smart City Applications.

The society, technologies, and sciences undergo a rapid and revolutionary transformation towards Ambient Intelligence (AmI). Systems that technologies design, create and utilize are growing in their smart capabilities and ease collaboration among people while learning and working for benefits of the human being (cf. the Internet of Things (IoT), Cloud Computing, Smart Grids, etc.). Mobile systems could enhance the possibilities available for designers and practitioners. However, a number of requirements must be fulfilled and complexities resolved before such systems generate reliable, accurate and timely information which is really trusted and appreciated by users. The main source and asset for making smart systems is data which our information age made easily accessible. The next main challenge we face is to effectively and efficiently extract knowledge from huge amounts of data from heterogeneous sources to make the systems self-contained and autonomous. To ensure data quality, accurate results and reliable (visual) analysis support in human-centered artificial intelligence applications, additional collaboration issues, privacy and security requirements should be addressed within a throughout verification and validation management. Major industrial domains are on the way to perform this tectonic shift based on Big Data, Collaborative Technologies, Smart Environments (SmE) supporting Virtual and Mixed Reality Applications, Multimodal Interaction and Reliable Visual Analytics.

Research in AmI and SmE in Urban and Rural Areas presents great challenges: AmI depends on advances in sensor networks, artificial intelligence, ubiquitous and persuasive computing, knowledge representation, spatial and temporal reasoning.

SmE builds upon embedded systems, smart integration, and an increasing fusion of real and virtual objects in the IoT. Customized sensor networks are used to detect human behavior and activities, evaluation logic and process mining are needed to replace people's cognitive abilities in Ambient Assisted Living (AAL) applications, detecting recurring activities without being noticed and hurting their privacy. As digitization has become an integral part of everyday life, data collection has resulted in the accumulation of huge amounts of data that can be used in various beneficial application domains. Effective analysis, quality assessment and utilization of big data are key factors for success in many business and service domains, including the smart systems domain. However, a number of challenges must be overcome to reap the benefits of big data. As big data handles large amounts of data with varying data structures and real-time processing, one of the most important challenges is to maintain data security and adopt proper data privacy policies. In general, there is a strong need to gain information of interest from big data analysis and, at the same time, prevent misuse of data so that people's trust in digital channels is not broken. To ensure data quality, accurate results and reliable analysis support in health care applications, additional collaboration issues, privacy and security requirements are addressed within a throughout verification and validation management.

This workshop has attracted paper submissions which deal with the challenges mentioned above. The studies are in specialized areas and show novel solutions. Especially interesting are approaches based on existing theories suitably applied.

The succeeding talks in this volume are organized thematically. The first contribution dealing with collaborative technologies *A Conversational Agent that Uses Turn-taking Rules for Supporting a Non-native Speaker* is written by Tomoo Inoue and Zixuan Guo. In this paper, the authors propose a conversational agent to support a non-native speaker in second language conversations. The agent joins the conversation, makes a script-based intervention on the turn-taking rule and gives the next turn to the non-native speaker.

Exploring Cooperation within a Virtual Khatchkar Museum resumes the actual work schedule developed and realized within the *Digitization of Khachkars: Establishing a Virtual Museum in Armenia* project by its participating three universities and persons in charge: Nelson Baloian, Wolfram Luther, and Daniel Biella.

Gustavo Zurita, Nelson Baloian, Sergio Peñafiel, José A. Pino, Wolfram Luther, and Aram Hajian propose *Collaborative Hyper Storytelling to Support Learning of Cultural Heritage* and report on a virtual museum dedicated to the Armenian cross-stones or Khatchkars. They describe a method and a software tool to make collaborative descriptions of archeological artifacts or sites. Learners can explore 3D models of selected Khatchkars and their surroundings and create their own exhibitions.

The Institute for Informatics and Automation Problems (IIAP) of the National Academy of Sciences of the Republic of Armenia operates the Academic Scientific Research Computer Network of Armenia (ASNET-AM), the National Grid Initiative (ArmNGI), and provides computational and networking facilities and advanced services to users. Hrachya Astsatryan, Wahi Narsisian, Vladimir Sahakyan and Yuri Shoukourian, members of the IIAP, present research and development of a collaborative cloud-computing infrastructure in Armenia.

Under the title *A Batching Location Cloaking Algorithm for Location Privacy Protection,* Guillermo Tobar et al. are facing technical challenges for smart environments. They consider the problems of efficient construction of location cloaking areas when a trusted anonymizer needs to provide location privacy protection for heterogeneous Location Based Services (LBS) clients and to limit the cost of processing many location-cloaked queries at the LBS. Their key observation is to build shared cloaking regions for LBS users located nearby each other and having similar privacy concerns. Several batching approaches for building proper cloaking regions are proposed.

When embedded systems are connected to the Internet of Things they have to become dynamic systems that can be changed flexibly at runtime. Gregor Schiele presents his current approach towards a platform combining adaptive (system) software with reconfigurable hardware and discusses its use for lightweight authentication and on-device machine learning in the paper *Reconfigurable Hardware and Adaptive Software for the Internet of Things: How Runtime Flexibility Changes Embedded Systems.*

The contribution *A survey of resource positioning strategies* addresses the indoor and outdoor position problem. Daniel Moreno, Sergio Ochoa and Nelson Baloian describe the main positioning techniques and methods and determine their overall performance in outdoor scenarios based on a proposed set of metrics.

Within the Smart Human Centered Computing track, Laura Pilz identifies and discusses problems of *scientific paper recommender systems* and addresses them by describing several metrics to clearly define and improve different recommendation tasks.

Benjamin Weyers presents an ongoing development of a conceptual framework for the characterization of *Reliability in Visual Analytics.* The term is characterized by means of three major dimensions: visual integrity, user interface, and the interaction process as well as three quality criteria, namely accuracy, adequacy and efficiency and a set of measures to rate the reliability criteria.

In a more general approach Ekaterina Auer and Wolfram Luther introduce *human-centered paradigms into a formal Verification and Validation Assessment* (VVA) within a workflow for designing, modeling, and implementing various real life processes and AmI environments. The new proposal includes not only code and result verification, uncertainty management, validation and evaluation assessment, but also tailored user interaction, recommender techniques and reliable visual analytics.

Nelson Baloian et al. report on a *Preliminary Assessment of Public Transportation Routes using free available Cloud Services and Belief Routes.* The authors propose to use existing crowdsourced data to support a transportation network decision making process. The method uses the *Dempster-Shafer Theory* and provides a framework to model transportation demand based on maps obtained from *Google Maps,* information about facilities located near the route from *OpenStreetMap* and information about the traffic from *Waze.* With this information the Belief Route and the Belief Congestion can be computed.

Together with another author group, Nelson Baloian addresses the topic *Data Science in e-Health: Two Examples from Japan.* Based on the patient's symptoms, the first example uses Bayesian networks for recommending medical exams to be applied on patients arriving at an urgency unit of a hospital in order to have a more accurate diagnosis. The second one uses a combination of machine learning and expert system based on the *Dempster-Shafer* plausibility theory for predicting the patient's risk of having a stroke in the near future.

A Japanese author group headed by Tomoo Inoue presents the paper *Chat Bot Improves the Motivation Toward Using a Self-Guided Mental Healthcare Course*. Digital content of a self-guided mental healthcare course based on the Structured Association Technique counseling method and a system using a chat bot have been developed to improve the user's motivation and convenience as an important issue.

A. J. Han Vinck opens the *Data Science and Information Theory* track. His lecture deals with *Smart Networking and Memory Systems:* Error correcting codes improve the performance with respect to the life time of a memory. Special coding techniques are required to optimize storage capacity. The author considers this problem from an information-theoretic point of view and discusses the use of different types of memory systems.

Thoughts on Information-Theoretic Aspects of Several Problems in Data Science offer Ashot Harutyunyan, Yanling Chen, and A. J. Han Vinck. Largely motivated by intelligent and data-driven cloud management tasks in industry, they specify several problem areas in view of information theory fundamentals which can have also interesting algorithmic implications for those data science problems.

Design and Security Analysis of Novel White Box Encryption is an extended abstract written by Gurgen Khachatrian and Sergey Abrahamyan. It resumes a paper structure concerning a modified white-box encryption based on SAFER+ algorithm and showing that it is secure against different types of attacks including those that have been successfully used against AES white-box implementations.

Yanling Chen, O. Ozan Koyluoglu, and A. J. Han Vinck ask a question about *Secrecy in Communication Networks: Being Cooperative or Competitive?* The authors focus on the multiple access channel where several transmitters communicate to a common receiver in the presence of an external eavesdropper. The goal is to explore the cooperative competition (coopetition) between the transmitters in order to obtain an efficient communication under a certain reliability and security guarantee.

Mariam Haroutunian, Karen Mkhitaryan, and Josiane Mothe deal with *f-Divergence Measures for Evaluation in Community Detection*. In this paper, the authors highlight the usual evaluation measures used for community detection evaluation. Then they review the properties of *f*-divergence measures and propose a selection that can serve for community detection evaluation. Preliminary experiments show the advantage of these measures in the case of large number of communities.

Ashot Harutyunyan et al. are responsible for *Learning Baseline Models of Log Sources*. The author team focuses on learning the baseline model of log sources in terms of the distribution of log event types generated by VMware's software solution vRealize Log Insight. Applying the algorithms to different data sets, they identify the expected normal discrepancy from such a baseline that the log source exhibits.

Mariam Haroutunian making a team with Evgueni Haroutunian, Parandzem Hakobyan, and Hovsep Mikayelyan present a further paper entitled *Logarithmically Asymptotically Optimal Testing of Statistical Hypotheses in Steganography Applica-*

tions. The problem of such a testing of statistical hypotheses for the steganography model with a passive counterpart is solved by the technical method of types which gives the functional dependence of the error probability exponents of the first and the second kind errors.

The organizers Aram Hajian, Wolfram Luther and A.J. Han Vinck would like to express their gratitude to the German Research Foundation (DFG) for funding our common activities. Finally, we want to thank Nelson Baloian, José A. Pino, Yanling Chen, and Ashot Harutyanyan for their ongoing encouragement and support and all participants for their presentations and contributions to the workshop and this proceedings volume.

Yerevan, Duisburg, September 2018

The Editors: Aram Hajian, Wolfram Luther, and A. J. Han Vinck

CONTENTS

A Conversational Agent that Uses Turn-taking Rules for Supporting a Non-native Speaker

Tomoo Inoue[1] and Zixuan Guo[1]

[1] University of Tsukuba, Tsukuba, Japan
inoue@slis.tsukuba.ac.jp

Abstract. When a non-native speaker talks with a native speaker, a non-native speaker sometimes feels hard to take speaking turns due to language proficiency. The resulting imbalanced conversation between a non-native speaker and a native speaker is not always productive. In this paper, we propose a conversational agent to support a non-native speaker in his/her second language conversation. The agent joins the conversation and makes intervention by a simple script based on the turn-taking rule for taking the agent's turn, and gives the next turn to the non-native speaker. Initial evaluation of the proposed agent suggested that the number of turn-taking was increased in front of the agent regardless of the intervention by the agent.

Keywords: Conversational Agent, Turn-taking, Second Language Communication Support, Non-native Speaker.

1 Introduction

We often face with the situation that people with different mother tongues talk together. However, when a non-native speaker (NNS) uses a second language (L2) to talk to a native speaker (NS), NNS has disadvantage in language proficiency and sometimes has difficulty in presenting what he/she would like fully. Moreover, NS tends to become dominating the conversational floor due to the difference of language fluency between NS and NNS. Thus in the L2 conversation, a mechanism that enables NNS to participate in the conversation equally is desired in order to achieve more cooperative and productive communication between NS and NNS.

In this paper, we propose a conversational agent system to support NNS in L2 conversation. Based on the existing turn-taking rules, the agent intervenes the conversation to prompt NNS's utterance. We expect that the agent's intervention alleviates the imbalance between NS and NNS.

2   Related Work

2.1   Second Language Conversation Support

Various methods have been studied to support NNS in L2 conversation. Using automatic speech recognition (ASR) to convert utterances into text and present it to NNS in real time is an example. Gao et al.[1] focused on conversational grounding and establishing mutual knowledge in L2 conversation. They signaled potential grounding problems to NS by displaying how NNS use automated transcripts and bilingual dictionaries, which showed increased mutual understanding between NNS and NS. Hautasaari et al. [2] reported that highlighting keywords in ASR transcripts reduced the cognitive load of NNS and helped him/her catching up in audio conferences. Hanawa et al. [3] proposed a system for NS to input keywords during conversation and share it with NNS. It was then verified that mutual understanding and knowledge sharing between two speakers increased. Ye et al. [4] proposed a speech rate awareness system which recognized the speech rate of NS in real time and warned when the speech rate got too fast for the NNS. While most studies focus on NNS's understanding of conversation or shared knowledge in L2 conversation, this paper focuses on NNS 's problem in turn–taking, and proposes to support it by a conversational agent.

2.2   Conversation Support by Agent

Studies of using conversational agents or robots in multi-party conversation have been increasing. These agents or robots actively communicate with participants and play an important role in achieving collaborative multi-party conversation. Kutsuwada et al. [5] proposed a system that recognized conversation groups in real time, and provided topics for conversation to those who did not participate for a while. Takase et al. [6] implemented a conversational robot system that could estimate each participant's conversational dominance and participation role, and produce attentional behaviors and intervene in the conversation in a proper timing. These studies aimed to coordinate and cooperate conversation among participants where all the participants were assumed as equal. In contrast, the agent in this paper aims to coordinate L2 conversation where language proficiency is different by participant, and supports NNS to achieve equal turn-taking.

2.3   Structure of Participation and Model of Face-to-face Conversation

In a face-to-face conversation among three or more participants, the participant speaking is called a speaker, the listener is referred to as an addressee, and the participant who does not receive the speaker's speech is regarded as a side-participant. Turn-taking occurs among the speaker and the addressee, but the side-participant can also join the conversation. In this way, it is possible for a third participant to moderate and control the conversation.

In a conversation between two participants, the two participants exchange the roles of the speaker and the addressee. The turn-taking and context are understood by each other during the conversation [9]. In a conversation among the three participants, the speaker and the addressee constitute the core of the conversation, but a side-participant can actively participate in the conversation in some cases. As a result, the side-participant may change the relationship between the speaker and the addressee, taking turns to speak and controlling the conversation.

In a conversation where the turn is not allocated successfully, if there is a third participant who plays a part in adjusting the imbalanced turn-taking, it will actively improve the participation relationship between NNS and NS.

3 Proposed System

3.1 Overview

The proposed agent detects the speech of the two speakers in real time and decides whether or not to intervene in the conversation. If both NS and NNS were silent for a certain time, the agent decides what to speak according to the decided statement and speak it to NNS by a speech synthesis engine, so that the next turn is moved to NNS.

3.2 Design of the Agent

Agent Utterance
Sacks et al. [10] presented four types of turn-allocation techniques for the current speaker to select the next speaker.

In this study, we designed agent utterances using the following two techniques.

(a) Select a participant as the next speaker by asking a question and give him/her the turn.

(b) Based on the utterance of the last speaker, select him/her as the next speaker by using "tag question" [10].

Table 1 shows the utterances of the agent. Proposed agent uses these four utterances at random to speak to NNS. All utterances start with "Mr./Ms. [speaker's name]" to specify the NNS.

Table 1. Agent Utterances

No.	Selection technique	Agent Utterances
1	(a)	Mr./Ms. [speaker's name], how do you think?
2	(a)	Mr./Ms. [speaker's name], how about you?
3	(b)	Mr./Ms. [speaker's name], don't you think so?
4	(b)	Mr./Ms. [speaker's name] thinks so too, don't you?

Intervention Timing

To decide the intervention timing, we consider the turn-taking rules by Sacks et al [10]. According to the rules, if a current speaker does not select the next speaker, and if other participants do not take turns, the current speaker may take a turn again. According to Nakano et al. [11], more than two seconds of silence divides the speaker's turn.

Therefore, we decide that the agent intervenes in the conversation when more than two seconds of silence occurs in this system (Fig. 1.).

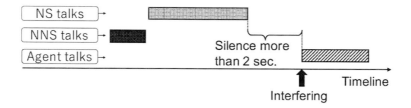

Fig. 1. Intervention by the proposed agent.

3.3 Implementation

MMD Agent

We built a multiple conversational agent using MMD agent [12], which is an open-source toolkit. In this system, a 3D character is used for the agent, which has a basic function to perform language and non-verbal interaction with people, The appearance of the agent is shown in Fig. 2. By adding a socket plugin-in to MMD Agent, we were able to control agents with a Python program.

Fig. 2. Appearance of the proposed agent.

Speech Detection

To acquire speech data in real-time, we use PyAudio[13], which is the one of audio I/O library using Python. In this system, we get the data as 16-bit PCM (Pulse Code Modulation). Normally the volume of a conversation reaches almost 60 dB that equals to 1500 of PCM amplitude. So the agent judges that speakers talk if the speech amplitude surpasses 1500.

Speech synthesis
MMD Agent uses TTS system Open JTalk which speaks Japanese text. Open JTalk [14] provides the voice of a female speaker model called the "May" character. MMD agent building Open JTalk can synthesize fluently voice and emit sound which is similar with human voice. Our agents use "May (normal)" voice.

Configuration
As shown in Fig.3, two PCs detect speakers' voice by a voice detect module. PC1 is equipped with MMD agent and a control module to decide the intervention of the agent. When intervening, one of four types of utterances is randomly selected. Finally, the control module sends command to MMD agent to synthesize voice and then the agent speaks.

4 Experiment

4.1 Participants

There are 24 participants, including 12 Japanese NS and 12 Japanese NNS. Each pair had the same gender so as to reduce the influence from gender. [15]

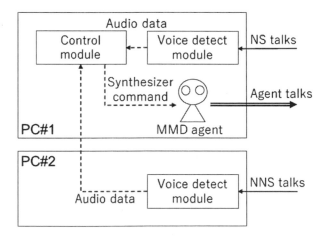

Fig. 3. System configuration.

5

4.2 Equipment

Two laptops were used for speech detection. The proposed agent was controlled by one of them. Two single-directional microphones were used for speech detection. Panasonic 42 inch digital LCD TV (width 957 mm × height 619 mm, and screen resolution is 1920 px ×1080 px) was used to display the agent. Video recording of the experiment was done by 2 video cameras.

4.3 Procedure

Each participant sat on a chair, wore a pin microphone, and had free conversation for 8 minutes. He/she experienced 3 conditions.

4.4 Condition

In order to investigate how the existence and intervention of the agent affects the conversation, comparison was made among the following three conditions:
  1) Speech agent condition
Proposal agent intervenes in the conversation.
  2) Non-speech agent condition
Proposal agent does not speak but only displayed.
  3) Non-agent condition
Without proposal agent, participants just take face-to-face conversations.

4.5 Environment

The experiment was conducted in a laboratory. The environmental noise was 40 db. The distance between two speakers was 1 m. The setup of the experiment is shown in Fig. 4.

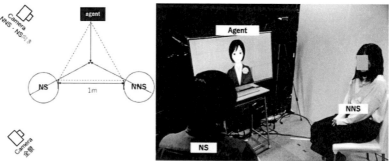

Fig. 4. Experiment setup.

5 Result

Seven minutes which excluded the first one minute because it included many greetings etc., was used for the analysis. The results of the number of utterances, the number of turn-taking, the number of turns, and the ratio of utterance and silence are reported.

5.1 Number of Utterances

The number of utterances of NS, NNS, and the agent were acquired with the silence interval of 300 ms as a threshold.

As shown in Fig.5, in the speech agent condition, the number of utterances was 94.3 for NS, 109.2 for NNS, and 2.5 for agent. In the non-speech agent condition, the number of utterances was 95.5 for NS and 128.8 for NNS, and in the non-agent condition, the number of utterances was 109.2 for NS and 112.7 for NNS.

As a result of comparing the speech agent condition and the non-agent condition, NS tends to decrease the number of utterances under the speech agent condition, and NNS does not show much difference.

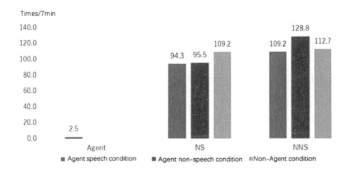

Fig. 5. Number of Utterances.

5.2 Turn-taking

The number of turn-taking among NNS, NS and agent [10] was totalized.

As shown in Fig. 6, the number of turn-taking was 48.3 in the speech agent condition, 54.5 in the non-speech agent condition, and 34.8 in the non-agent condition.

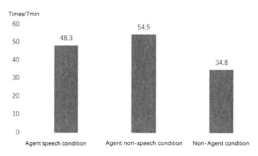

Fig. 6. Number of Speaking Turns.

Both the speech agent condition and the non-speech agent condition were higher than the non-agent condition.

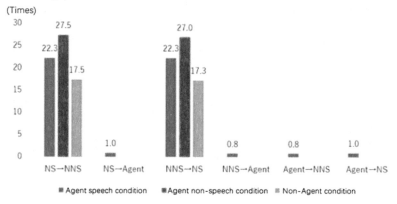

Fig. 7. : Directions of Turn-taking.

As shown in Figure. 7, the number of turns from NNS to NS were 22.3 in the speech agent condition, 27.0 in the non-speech agent condition, and 17.3 in the non-agent condition. The number of turns from NS to NNS were 22.3 in the speech agent condition, 27.5 in the non-speech agent condition, and 17.5 in the non-agent condition. The number of turns from NS to Agent, NNS to Agent, Agent to NS, and Agent to NNS were 1.0, 0.8, 1.0, and 0.8 respectively.

6 Conclusion

In this paper, a conversational agent to prompt NNS to speak in L2 conversation has been proposed. The behavior of the agent is based on the turn-taking rules in multi-party conversation.

Three conditions, the speech agent condition, the non-speech agent condition, and the non-agent condition were compared in the lab study. It is interesting that both the speech agent condition and the non-speech agent condition were higher than the non-agent condition in the number of speaking turns. Although not many turn-taking were directly mediated by the agent, the influence of the agent was observed as the difference in the number of turn-taking.

More detailed analysis will be conducted in the future.

References

1. Ge Gao, Naomi Yamashita, Ari M.J. Hautasaari, and Susan R. Fussell: Improving Multilingual Collaboration by Displaying How Non-native Speakers Use Automated Transcripts and Bilingual Dictionaries. In: Proceedings of the 33rd Annual ACM Conference on Human Factors in Computing Systems (CHI '15), pp. 3463–3472. ACM, New York, USA (2015).
2. Hautasaari Ari, Naomi Yamashita: Catching up in audio conferences: highlighting keywords in ASR transcripts for non-native speakers. In: Proceedings of the 5th ACM international conference on Collaboration across boundaries: culture, distance & technology, pp. 107-110. ACM (2014).
3. Hanawa Hiromi, Xiaoyu Song, Tomoo Inoue: Key-Typing on Teleconference: Collaborative Effort on Cross-Cultural Discussion. In: International Conference on Collaboration Technologies. CCIS 647, pp. 74-88. Springer, Singapore (2016).
4. Jing Ye, Tomoo Inoue: A Speech Speed Awareness System for Non-Native Speakers .In: Proceedings of the 19th ACM Conference on Computer Supported Cooperative Work and Social Computing Companion, pp. 49-52. ACM (2016).
5. Shinji Kutsuwada, Tomoo Inoue: Toward a system for facilitating multi-party conversation based on dynamic group recognition. In: IPSJ SIG Technical Report 2009-GN-72(6), pp. 1-6 (2009).
6. Yutaka Takase, Takashi Yoshino, Yukiko I. Nakano: Conversational Robot with Conversation Coordination and Intervention Functionality in Multi-party Conversations. IPSJ Journal 58(5), pp. 967-980 (2017).
7. Bono Mayumi, SUZUKI Noriko, Katagiri Yasuhiro: Conversation: Do Interaction Behaviors Give Clues to Know Your Interest? Cognitive studies 11(3), pp. 214-227 (2004).
8. E. Goffman: Forms of Talk. University of Pennsylvania Press (1981).
9. Iwao Akiba, Yoichi Matsuyama, Tetsunori Kobayashi: Procedures of Obtaining Initiatives for Multiparty Conversation Facilitation Robots. Information Processing Society of Japan (IPSJ) SIG-SLP 97(10), pp. 1-8 (2013).
10. Sacks, Harvey, Emanuel A. Schegloff, and Gail Jefferson: A Simplest Systematics for the Organization of Turn-Taking for Conversation. Language 50(4), pp. 696-735 (1974).
11. Nakano Yukiko, Yuki Fukuhara: Estimating conversational dominance in multiparty interaction. In: Proceedings of the 14th ACM international conference on Multimodal interaction, pp.77-84 (2012).
12. MMDAgent Homepage, http://www.mmdagent.jp/, last accessed 2018/02/01.
13. Pyaudio Homepage, https://people.csail.mit.edu/hubert/pyaudio/docs/, last accessed 2018/02/01.
14. OpenJTalk Homepage, http://open-jtalk.sp.nitech.ac.jp/, last accessed 2018/02/01.
15. Rubin, J.: A review of second language listening comprehension research. The modern language journal 78(2), pp.199-221 (1994).

Exploring Cooperation within a
Virtual Khatchkar Museum

Nelson Baloian[1], Daniel Biella, Wolfram Luther[2]

[1] Department of Computer Science, Universidad de Chile UCH, Santiago, Chile
nbaloian@dcc.uchile.cl
[2] Centre for Information and Media Services, Computer Sciences
and Applied Cognitive Science, University of Duisburg-Essen UDE, Germany
{daniel.biella, wolfram.luther}@uni-due.de

Abstract. The DiKEViMA project aims at developing a virtual khachkar museum with the aid of engaged volunteers. Visitors explore khachkars in their surroundings and historical context, curators as well as laymen may arrange their own personalized exhibitions taking objects, which are originally located in different places and putting them together in a simulated virtual environment to convey a particular message to the audience. The khachkar, a fundamental symbol of Armenia, the oldest Christian nation, is a relief sculpture with a variety of floral and geometric motifs, ancient symbols, ornaments of flowers and trees, birds and grapevines, biblical scenes and imagery. To create a digital instance of a Khachkar, we need sophisticated techniques to bring the complex surfaces structures into a three-dimensional model and a 3D immersive environment that inspires creativity and engagement of the visitors[1]. In this extended abstract we report on ongoing work and the stage of development of the Khatchkar museum at the American University of Armenia, UCH and UDE.

Keywords: Virtual museum · Armenian Khatchkar Museum · Co-curation

The DiKEViMA Project

In the context of the DAAD project *Tradition and Smart Living: Armenian-German Fact Finding Mission,* a memorandum of cooperation has been concluded between the American University of Armenia (AUA) and the University of Duisburg-Essen to complement a similar memorandum between UCH and UDE in order to extend the already existing effective and mutually beneficial cooperation to develop academic exchange in education and research. The newly started *Digitization of Khachkars: Establishing a Virtual Museum in Armenia* (DiKEViMA) project together with N. Baloian (University of Chile, UCH), D. Biella (UDE), P. Donabédian (Laboratoire d'Archéologie Médiévale et Moderne en Méditerranée LA3M, France), N. Hitschfeld (UCH), N. Karapetyan (AUA), W. Luther (UDE), J.A. Pino (UCH)) aims at developing a virtual khachkar museum presenting about hundred cross stones in their surroundings with the aid of student auxiliary staff under the guidance of professors and experts. Due to its complexity, contributed work in different categories of tasks by student assistants and experts was indispensable to realize the virtual museum.

---

1 Cf.: http://www.vimedeas.com/wordpress/?page_id=203

This work includes: Publishing a call with project description, instruction material and list of khachkars (The consortium traveled in 2016 to Armenia from May 16 to 27 to launch the project), as well as digitizing and creating virtual 3D exhibits and their context, i.e. cross stones, their surroundings and architectural context (done in 2017 by students at the AUA).

Providing metadata, name, creator (master), motive for erection, first and actual location, material, style, ornaments, significance, link to contextual frame following LIDO and ViMCOX standard (done at Yerevan by members of the consortium, student workers and experts of LA3M and RAA (Research on Armenian Architecture)).

Realizing room and landscape design to receive the content (done at UCH by students and members of the consortium).

Assembling the museum, defining learning scenarios and tours, acting as test persons, and contributing to information material and catalogues [1-4].

We will organize a minisymposium within the CODASSCA workshop and discuss the following topics:

- Definition of a Khatchkar feature vector based on the ViMCOX-LIDO description of cross stones and their environment;
- Development of appropriate similarity measures to compile a collection of related Khatchkars on demand;
- How users can build their own Khatchkar with the aid of the structural pattern from the Khatchkar database and an activity tool to assemble the stone by defining and selecting dimensions, material, content, motifs and inscription via framing, borders, cross type, ornaments and composition type?
- An interdisciplinary challenge consists in finding out and documenting the exhibit's history through the past centuries to enable the story telling.

We plan to place QR codes near the Khatchkars allowing visitors to access to the digitized item and its metadata via their smartphones. Alternatively, visitors can use GPS technology to locate items or find the item taking a photo and constructing a feature vector using image recognition algorithms.

References

1. D. Sacher, B. Weyers, T. W. Kuhlen, and W. Luther, An Integrative Tool Chain for Collaborative Virtual Museums in Immersive Virtual Environments. Collaboration and Technology, in Proceedings 21st International Conference, CRIWG 2015, Yerevan, Armenia, September 22—25. Springer International Publishing (2015) 86–94
2. D. Sacher, A generative approach to virtual museums using a new metadata format. A curators', visitors' and software engineers' perspective, PhD thesis 2017, University of Duisburg-Essen. Logos Berlin, ISBN 978-3-8325-4627-4
3. D. Biella, T. Pilz, D. Sacher, B. Weyers, W. Luther, N. Baloian, and T. Schreck, Crowd-sourcing and Co-curation in Virtual Museums: A Practice-driven Approach, Journal of Universal Computer Science 22 (10) (2016) 1277–1297
4. N. Baloian, W. Luther, D. Biella, N. Karapetyan, J. A. Pino, T. Schreck, A. Ferrada, N. Hitschfeld, Exploring Collaboration in the Realm of Virtual Museums. 2017, in C. Gutwin, S. Ochoa J. Vassileva, T. Inoue (eds), Collaboration and Technology, CRIWG 2017, Lecture Notes in Computer Science 10391, Springer, Cham (2017) 252-259

Collaborative Hyper Storytelling to Support Learning of Cultural Heritage

Gustavo Zurita[1], Nelson Baloian[2], Sergio Peñafiel[2], José A. Pino[2] Wolfram Luther[3], and Aram Hajian[4]

[1] Department of Information Systems and Management Control, Faculty of Economics and Business, Universidad de Chile, Diagonal Paraguay 257, Santiago, Chile.
gzurita@fen.uchile.cl
[2] Department of Computer Science, Universidad de Chile, Beauchef 851, Santiago, Chile.
{nbaloian, spenafie, jpino}@dcc.uchile.cl
[3] Computer Sciences and Applied Cognitive Science, University of Duisburg-Essen, Germany.
luther@inf.uni-due.de
[4] College of Science and Engineering, American University of Armenia, Yerevan, Armenia.
ahajian@aua.am

Abstract. Storytelling has been used as a powerful methodology to design learning activities. By producing their own stories, students learn while developing artifacts which can share with other peer learners generating a rich collaborative learning environment based on constructivism. Digital media, and especially hypermedia, has been successfully used to support storytelling in learning contexts since it eases the collaborative authoring process and allows creating stories with parallel threads and multiple versions, supporting various viewpoints of the same narrative. Inspired by the context of learning the cultural heritage of the Armenian cross-stones or Khatchkars, we developed a tool in which students can create their own hyper-stories for telling different aspects of them. The tool reflects the inherent association of a Khatchkar to a geographical location by offering a map on which learners can present the location of the stones. Another important aspect of this tool is that learners can explore 3D models of the Khatchkars in a virtual museum where they can create their own exhibitions by co-locating and assembling stones which are far apart in the real world.

Keywords: Hyper Storytelling, Collaboration, Cultural Heritage, Khatchkars.

1   Introduction

Tangible cultural heritage (ruins, ancient churches, vestiges of certain original cultures, etc.) are scattered across various geographical places around the world. Most of them remain in physical locations where they were originally created, and have not been moved to museums for various reasons. Some are impossible or very difficult to relocate, there is absence of a systematic work to "discover" and classify them, or even the lack of knowledge of their existence. In some cases, aside from local denizens, no one is aware of their existence. In many cases, the geographical context is important to give meaning to the information and knowledge of the historical facts associated with these patrimonies.

Since these heritage sites cannot be taken to museums, a computational tool that is able to take the museum to the geographical origins where they are located would contribute to learn more about these locales. Our proposed method is to use hyper storytelling to make collaborative descriptions of these locales, where participants can generate a unique narrative, interpret their stories from various points of view and comprise a collection of multiple narratives which together account for a more realistic and vivid depiction. The developed computational tool will be used to collaboratively describe places of cultural heritage value, as such as been done in similar scenarios applied in other contexts of Storytelling activities, [1-4, 18].

The heritage sites around which stories can be created correspond to archaeological sites and the objects they contain. For example, in the archaeological site of Noratus, Armenia it is possible to find patrimonial objects called Khatchkars. In Tiahuanaco, Bolivia there are archaeological vestiges of vessels or containers scattered in the area; they have not been registered yet, classified, and little or nothing is known about them. Videos, photos (from the internet or taken in the same place), links to web pages with complementary information, virtual 3D representations of objects (virtual museums), and geo-locations of the places where they are located may be used to describe patrimonial objects.

Authors in [5, 6] have identified what has become known as the problem of "getting lost in hyperspace," which is basically the user's difficulty in building a map or a systematic representation of the structure of the hypertext program and, by extension, the structure of the information it contains. Therefore, in our approach we will include the geo-localization over maps as a central scaffold to solve the sense of being "lost in space."

Several tools for supporting storytelling activities for learning have been developed in the past for students of basic and middle school [1, 7-10]. Most of them implement linear stories instead of non-linear ones (hyper-stories) [9, 11]. These include European history for children [9], Australian history [3], natural history of America in Chicago and New York [5]; or for increasing the intercultural awareness in higher education [12]. Narratives can also be used within the design of new technologies to support lifelong learning in a cultural setting [4]. In [4] authors present a tool which comes close to the idea presented in this work [2] which is a media integrated Storytelling platform for non-linear digital storytelling which can be used as a cultural heritage learning platform. However, they do not consider the location factor, but just descriptions.

2   Hyper Storytelling as a Support of Cultural Heritage

Digital storytelling is a powerful teaching tool in the cultural and educational field [13-15], which facilitates the presentation of ideas, communication or knowledge transmission, through the integration and organization of multimedia resources on technological platforms of various kinds, including Web 2.0 tools [2, 3]. Digital Storytelling, takes advantage of the contributions of content generated by students, through a simple procedure consisting of selecting a topic, performing a research about it, write a script, and develop a story that can have various purposes: descriptive, informative, creative, etc. [13].

The construction and elaboration of stories generates attractive scenarios for learning, in which each student adopts the role of multimedia content producer [14]. This implies applying the narrative, descriptive and creative capacity of the authors, taking as a starting point the design of an initial script or storyboard. It also implies the development of digital narratives that promote new forms of writing and interpretation of multimedia messages, thus training specific digital skills needed to interact in a technological environment, known as digital literacy of the 21st century [15, 16].

Web 2.0 allows generating collaborative spaces enabling users to produce information pills, digital stories and all kinds of stories that can be shared among them through different social network platforms, using narrative formulas and simple technological tools capable of integrating multimedia resources with great impact, expressiveness and communicative value. From the technical point of view, digital stories are constructed using hypermedia language, which can lead to complex histories, which require careful elaboration of a literary and technical script that integrates the optionality and alternatives that hypertext allows. Increasingly, educational units at basic, medium, college and graduate levels, use activities focused on the construction of stories from this perspective, given their characteristics and educational potential, obtaining interesting results [10].

There exists a classification of the most relevant approaches for managing digital storytelling processes in the literature [14, 16], as presented below.

a) Linear vs. non-linear storytelling types are differentiated based on action sequences of media occurring in the story. Non-linearity enables storytellers to tell more complex stories with different storylines within the same story [5, 9, 11], i.e. Hyper Storytelling. Different points of view on individual media could affect the normal flow of a story. Non-linear stories may be told in several versions with various content sequences [10]. The interactive storytelling process enables storytellers as well as story listeners to make their own decisions actively to determine the later course of the storyline. Dynamic narratives are created by which users can interact at each part.

b) Collaborative/social storytelling process can help design the active experience. In particular reference is made to typical web 2.0 environments for narration to define and design multimedia pathways using social features (annotation, collaborative writing, video-sharing, etc.) enabling a continuous improvement of the narrative structure [2].

c) Mobile/ubiquitous storytelling takes place in a physical environment where the digital natives actually move around and interact with digital content as well as with others using mobile devices and communication technologies. Mobile storytelling is considered a part of the transmedia storytelling, the process where key elements of narration are spread out from different devices like smartphones, tablets, etc. [17].

3 Tool Design Requirements

Based on the previous discussion, we now present the requirements for the tool that can support the construction of hyper-stories based on geo-referenced archeological artifacts. We will exemplify the requirements by a hyper-story constructed around the topic of Khatchkars (Armenian cross stones).

R1. Archeological artifacts or sites are the base for the building blocks of the hyper-stories. Users build a story by adding description, comments, multimedia material, including their 3D representation in a virtual environment and links to other building blocks. In order to make an association with a film telling a story we are going to call each building block a "scene" of the hyper-story, which has a scenario (the 3D environment) and a (geographic) location where it develops. In our example the core of a scene might be a single or a group of Khatchkars.

R2. Each scene should be geo-referenced in the place where the artifact they are currently located or where they were originally found. The geo-referencing of the archeological objects can be done while the users are in the same place, using mobile computing devices with positioning capabilities, or it can be done remotely on a desktop computer. In our example the scene might be geo-referenced at the place where the Khatchkar(s) it contains is/are located or were originally found.

R3. Archeological artifacts or sites within a scene should have a digital multimedia representation (pictures, videos, animations, etc.) and a 3D model with metadata which describe them. In our example there is a virtual 3D model of the stone and metadata describing important information like the year of creation, the sculptor who carved it, important ornamental elements it contains, etc.

R4. In order to implement a hyper-story with multiple scenes, each scene may have zero or many links to other scenes which are related to it and may continue the topic, or introduce a new the hyper-story. Links may be labelled with a text in order to describe the relation between the two scenes it links. Links might be one or bi-directional.

R5. Descriptions of the objects and archaeological sites will be carried out collaboratively among the participants. Collaborative work can develop synchronously, as well as asynchronously. The use of tags and colors will allow sorting, classifying and grouping the described historical objects and places.

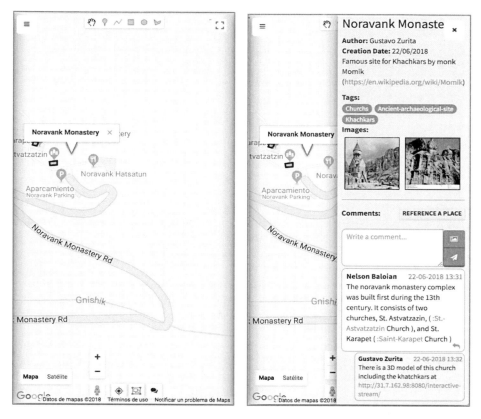

Fig. 1. Views from a mobile phone with the geolocation of two historical sites. "Novarank Monastery" is described in the right side view, labeled "Churches", "Ancient-archaeological-site", and "Khatchkars"; also with commentary that builds the hyperlinking among the users.

4   Tool Description

Fig. 1 and 2 show some of the main interfaces of the tool. Various sessions can be created where users can contribute. Please see "Armenian Cultural Heritage" session at the left hand side of Fig. 2.

In order to implement the R1 requirement, the tool presents as central view the world map taken from GoogleMaps (see the left hand side view of Fig. 1), on which points, or geometric figures corresponding to archaeological sites are geo-referenced for which a description that corresponds to the construction of the story is given, see the right view of Fig 1. For each geo-referencing, users must specify a title, plus the digital artifacts indicated in the R2 requirement. Each created geo-reference can be commented in the description of the story of each geo-referencing or in the comments area, which extends the story in a linear and non-linear way; users can add various digital contents specified in the R3 requirement, such as photos, descriptions that complement the story, links to other web pages (Wikipedia, YouTube, etc.), other related geo-localizations, and virtual 3D representations of objects in virtual Museums. For example, the view on the right of Fig. 2, corresponding to a virtual 3D representation of the church of "St. Astvatzatzin Church "entered by the user "Gustavo Zurita " in the view of Fig. 1 (right).

Any user can create a geo-referencing, or various users can together create one. The generated stories can be constructed based on the comments that users make to each geo-referencing, thus allowing collaborative work that corresponds to the R5 requirement, see Fig. 1 (right).

In the description and comments associated to each geo-location, other locations can be geo-referenced, which allows the creation of hyper-stories as stated in the R4 requirement; Thus, e.g., the geo-referencing "Noravank Monastery", which can be seen in Fig. 1 (right), is associated with the geo-locations "Saint Karapet Church" and "St. Astvatzatzin Church". Please see comment from user "Nelson Baloian".

Geo-locations can be organized by colors and tags, to allow users to track and characterize the descriptions of the historical places of several sites at the same time, or to generate multiple stories of the same archaeological objects or places. At the left of Fig. 2, a list of geo-locations is shown, where the first two in red ("Bjni" and "Noratus Cementery") correspond to ancient Cemeteries, and the next four in blue ("Echmiadzin Cathedral", "Novarank Monastery", "Saint Kaparet Church", and "St. Astvatzatzin Church") correspond to places where Churches are located. In this way the geo-locations in red allow to build a story associated with the churches, and the blue ones correspond to another story associated with the cemeteries.

5 Conclusions and Further Work

The developed tool allows "taking the museum" to the geographical places where archaeological objects belonging to different cultural patrimonies are located through the hyper-storytelling. It also allows users to create linear and nonlinear historical descriptions in a collaborative way, focused on the location of archeological artifacts.

According to the reviewed literature, there is no other proposal similar to ours in which collaborative hyper-stories can be performed by users based on geo-referencing, associated with cultural historical sites.

With the proposed tool, you can also describe intangible heritage objects, which are associated with specific historical places. For example, the reasons why the Khatchkars were built with certain characteristics can be described for certain regions of Armenia, although their vestiges are no longer present.

According to [1], using a tool which supports hyper-storytelling like the one presented in this work can a) enhance collaborative storytelling, b) support collaborative work, and c) ensure a sense of authorship of the stories in a mobile scenario.

Our further work is to refine the requirements R1 to R5 for new features:

- Options to select artifacts, single cross stones or Khatchkar groups by navigating and pointing in the virtual museum, by their GPS coordinates, using typical features recommended by other users or by the system,
- Crowdsourced objects and their metadata submitted using appropriate forms to build a long-term Khatchkar database,

- A workbench for users to create their own cross stones via drag and drop from a toolbox which provides crosses, geometric motifs, ornaments, borders etc.

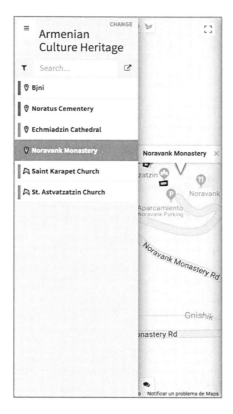

Fig. 2. Left: a list of six archeological sites already created by the used. The first two are in blue color; they correspond to sites where ancient churches are located. At the right hand side there is a 3D view of the artifact of a scene, in this case the Noravank church and its Khatchkars, which are shown at the right hand side of Fig. 1.

References

1. Liu, C.-C., et al., *Collaborative storytelling experiences in social media: Influence of peer-assistance mechanisms.* Computers & Education, 2011. **57**(2): p. 1544-1556.
2. Cao, Y., R. Klamma, and A. Martini. *Collaborative storytelling in the web 2.0.* in *Proceedings of the First International Workshop on Story-Telling and Educational Games (STEG 2008) at ECTEL.* 2008. Citeseer.
3. Smeda, N., E. Dakich, and N. Sharda, *Digital storytelling with Web 2.0 tools for collaborative learning*, in *Collaborative Learning 2.0: Open Educational Resources.* 2012, IGI Global. p. 145-163.

4. Mulholland, P. and T. Collins. *Using digital narratives to support the collaborative learning and exploration of cultural heritage*. in *Database and Expert Systems Applications, 2002. Proceedings. 13th International Workshop on*. 2002. IEEE.
5. McLellan, H., *Hyper stories: Some guidelines for instructional designers*. Journal of research on computing in education, 1992. **25**(1): p. 28-49.
6. Conklin, J., *Hypertext: An Introduction and Survey*. J. Computer, 1987. **20**(9): p. 17-41.
7. Garzotto, F., E. Herrero, and F. Salgueiro. *One Tool-Many Paradigm: Creativity and Regularity in Youngsters' Hyperstories*. in *Joint International Conference on Interactive Digital Storytelling*. 2010. Springer.
8. Dreon, O., R.M. Kerper, and J. Landis, *Digital storytelling: A tool for teaching and learning in the YouTube generation*. Middle School Journal, 2011. **42**(5): p. 4-10.
9. Garzotto, F. and M. Forfori. *Hyperstories and social interaction in 2D and 3D edutainment spaces for children*. in *Proceedings of the seventeenth conference on Hypertext and hypermedia*. 2006. ACM.
10. Soffer, Y., et al., *The effect of different educational interventions on schoolchildren's knowledge of earthquake protective behaviour in Israel*. Disasters, 2010. **34**(1): p. 205-213.
11. Spaniol, M., et al. *Web-based learning with non-linear multimedia stories*. in *International Conference on Web-Based Learning*. 2006. Springer.
12. PM Ribeiro, S., *Developing intercultural awareness using digital storytelling*. Language and Intercultural Communication, 2016. **16**(1): p. 69-82.
13. Niemi, H., et al., *Digital storytelling for 21st-century skills in virtual learning environments*. Creative Education, 2014. **5**(9): p. 657.
14. Gaeta, M., et al., *A methodology and an authoring tool for creating Complex Learning Objects to support interactive storytelling*. Computers in Human Behavior, 2014. **31**: p. 620-637.
15. Robin, B.R., *Digital storytelling: A powerful technology tool for the 21st century classroom*. Theory into practice, 2008. **47**(3): p. 220-228.
16. Cao, Y., R. Klamma, and M. Jarke, *The Hero's Journey-Template-Based Storytelling for Ubiquitous Multimedia Management*. Journal of Multimedia, 2011. **6**(2).
17. Jenkins, H., *Transmedia storytelling and entertainment: An annotated syllabus*. Continuum, 2010. **24**(6): p. 943-958.
18. Antunes, P., Simoes, D., Carrico, L., Pino, J.A., *An end-user approach to business process modeling*. J. of Network and Computer Applications, 2013, 36(6): 1466-1479.

Collaborative Cloud Computing in Armenia: Challenges and Opportunities

Hrachya Astsatryan, Wahi Narsisian, Vladimir Sahakyan, Yuri Shoukourian

Institute for Informatics and Automation Problems of the National Academy of
Sciences of the Republic of Armenia, Yerevan, Armenia
{hrach,wahi,svlad,shouk}@sci.am

Abstract. The Institute for Informatics and Automation Problems (IIAP) of the
National Academy of Sciences of the Republic of Armenia is the only state-
supported structure for software, hardware, and brainware technologies in Armenia. The institute is responsible for Armenia's National research and education network (Academic Scientific Research Computer Network of Armenia,
ASNET-AM) and the National Grid Initiative (ArmNGI), and provides computational and networking facilities and advanced services to users. The article
presents research and development of a collaborative cloud-computing infrastructure in Armenia. The e-infrastructure offers services for inter-disciplinary
e-science applications using the networking resources of ASNET-AM and
computational resources of ArmNGI.

Keywords: Cloud computing, ASNET-AM, ArmNGI, Openstack, SaaS, IaaS.

1 Introduction

Due to a rapid increase in the amount of scientific data, there is a need for storing and
processing this data. Scientists are nowadays searching for new ways for handling the
output of their experiments. Data generation and analysis using computational methods are at the heart of all modern science and technology. New e-science research
methods are using advanced computational resources, data collections and scientific
instruments [1]. The ICT infrastructure for science is a fundamental building block of
the e-Science. It is an environment, where research resources (hardware, software,
and content) can be shared more efficiently, and can be accessed whenever there is a
need for better and more effective research tools. Such environment integrates networks, computational resources, experimental workbenches, data repositories, tools,
instruments, and other operational support that enables global virtual research collab-
orations.

Cloud services based on data storage and data processing facilities are increasingly
popular to deal with such requirements. The main aim of the article is to introduce the
challenges and opportunities of collaborative cloud framework available in Armenia.
The current State of e-infrastructures in Armenia is presented in Section 2 and the
further activities to strengthen the scientific computing capacity in Armenia can be
found in Section 3. Finally, the conclusion and directives for future research are
drawn in the conclusion section.

2 Collaborative Cloud Computing Infrastructure in Armenia

The Armenian e-infrastructure is a complex national IT infrastructure consisting of both communication and distributed computing infrastructures. IIAP plays a key role at national level in the fields of networking and distributed and large-scale research infrastructures (Grid, HPC, Cloud) as a developer and operator of ASNET-AM and ArmNGI [2].

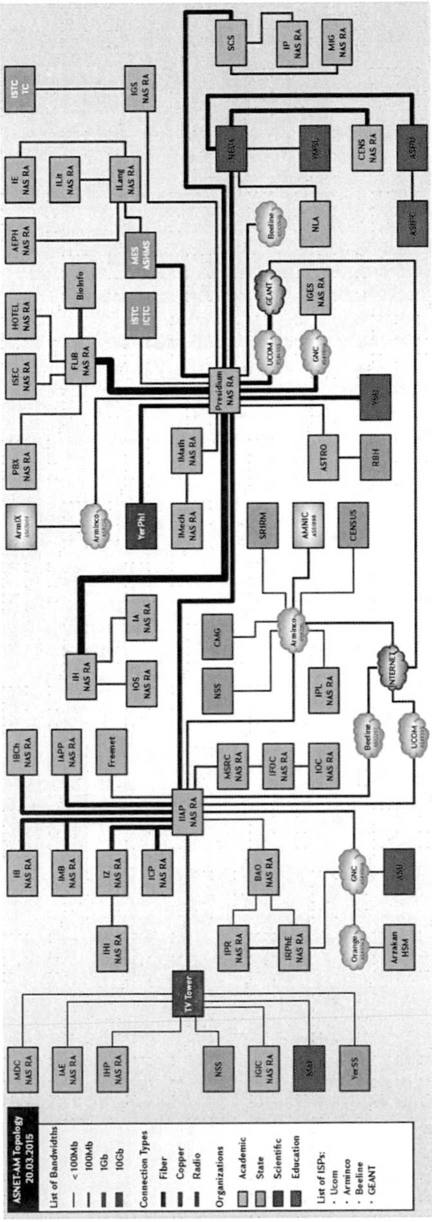

Since 1994, ASNET-AM has provided a high-quality infrastructure and services to the academic, research and educational community of Armenia by connecting more than 60 scientific research, academic, and cultural organizations. The ASNET-AM backbone consists of network communication nodes in 6 cities in Armenia, which are interconnected by fiber optics and wireless links (see fig. 1). A few key sites, such as the Presidium of the National Academy of Sciences and the IIAP, are interconnected at 10 Gb/s. ASNET-AM offering to the Armenian research and educational community access to the pan-European GEANT network.

Being a long-time Armenian academic network operator, ASNET-AM participates actively in developing regional networking infrastructures, such as a networking infrastructure in the Eastern Partnership (EaP) Region [3]. With connections to the pan-European GÉANT EaP network enables scientists and academics in the region to engage in global collaborative projects and bring the EaP countries closer to EU.

IIAP coordinates the ArmNGI, which is an Armenian national effort to establish nationwide computational resources [4]. Now the computational resources (about 500 cores) of Armenian Grid infrastructure distributed among our leading research (National Academy of Sciences, Yerevan Physics Institute) and academic (Yerevan State University, State Engineering University of Armenia) organizations are located in the cities of Yerevan and Ashtarak (see fig. 2).

Fig. 1: Topology of ASNET-AM

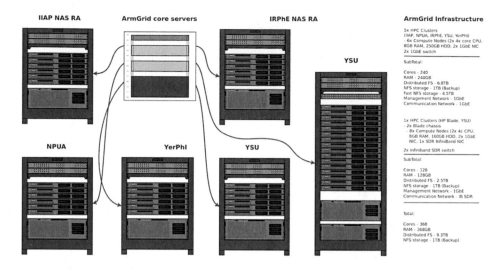

Fig. 2: Topology of ArmNGI infrastructure.

The move to a collaborative cloud computing in Armenian academic sector has already started. Experimental cloud infrastructures based on OpenStack platform have been deployed in Armenia and beyond in the region (see fig. 3).

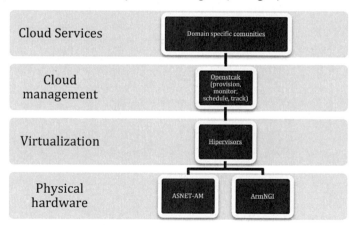

Fig. 3: Topology of collaborative computing infrastructure.

The topology presented above illustrates the four layers of the collaborative computing infrastructure. The bottom layer consists of all High-Performance computing resources in Armenia in term of computational resources, storages, and network facilities. Then we have also all virtual machines based on different Hypervisors, among these virtual resources there are also HPC clusters, storages. Next, we have the cloud management service, which is based on OpenStack, by which all these below mentioned resources are consolidated into one single platform and can be used by a single access. And finally, at the top, we have dedicated cloud services for several scientific

22

communities based on different tools and packages, which are proposed or suggested by these communities itself.

OpenStack is a free and open source cloud platform providing mainly two solutions: virtual machines with different resources based on dedicated images, and data storage facility. The platform takes into consideration that all HPC resources can also be attached or used by the system when the virtualization is supported. Several dedicated virtual environments have been developed enabling the scientists to spin up the virtual machine and have the necessary environment ready to be used, without a need to install anything manually. The cloud single sign-on dashboard has been implemented allowing users to get information about all the provided services, also register on the system. The platform is a complete solution for different scientific communities in Armenia, and also for the end-users. Each user is provided with a cloud storage, and an access to the OpenStack dashboard from which the user can run and use several virtual machines with different flavors range from tiny instances (1 vCPU and 1 GB RAM) to very large one (16 vCPU and 48 GB RAM).

Energy consumption is a primary concern for datacenters' management. Numerous datacenters are relying on virtualization, as it provides flexible resource management means such as VM checkpoint/ restart, migration and consolidation.

In nowadays cloud, memory is generally statically allocated to VMs and wasted if not used. Techniques (such as ballooning) were introduced for dynamically reclaiming memory from VMs, such that only the needed memory is provisioned to each VM. However, the challenge is to precisely monitor the needed memory, i.e., the working set of each VM. The main techniques in the Xen hypervisor have been implemented and defined different metrics to evaluate their efficiency [5]. Based on the evaluation results, a Badis system is proposed, which combines several of the existing solutions, using the right solution at the right time. An energy optimization methodology has been elaborated to explore, optimize, and report the energy consumption and $CO2$ emission of data, computing, and networking resources [6]. This method has been applied for ASNET-AM and ArmNGI resources and in a case study to demonstrate it and to illustrate its effects in example experiments.

3 Collaborative Cloud Services

The cloud services for various scientific and societal challenges have been developed.

The web-based weather data visualization and analytical platform for weather data in Armenia integrate the three existing infrastructures for observational data, numerical weather prediction, and satellite image processing [7]. The weather data used in the platform consists of near-surface atmospheric elements including air temperature, pressure, relative humidity, wind and precipitation. The visualization and analytical platform has been implemented for 2-m surface temperature. The platform gives Armenian State Hydrometeorological and Monitoring Service analytical capabilities to analyze the in-situ observations, model and satellite image data per station and region for a given period.

An integrated web-based interactive data platform for molecular dynamic simulations uses the datasets generated by different life science communities from Armenia [8]. The suggested platform, consisting of data repository and workflow management services, is vital for current and future scientific discoveries in the life science domain. We focus on interactive data visualization workflow service as a key to perform more in-depth analyzes of research data outputs, helping to understand the problems efficiently and to consolidate the data into one collective illustration platform. The functionalities of the integrated data platform are presented as an advanced integrated environment to capture, analyze, process and visualize the scientific data.

Nowadays quantum physics is crucial for several scientific applications, where it is no longer possible to neglect the environmental interaction, like dissipation and decoherence. In these cases, the quantum systems are usually treated as open systems and their time-evolution is described by a density matrix in frames of the master equation, instead of the Hilbert-space vector and the Schrodinger equation. The visualization of such quantum systems allows users to calculate and study the sensitivity of the parameters, like excitation photon numbers or photon number distribution functions or Wigner functions. A cloud service for numerical calculations and visualization of photonic dissipative systems has been developed, which enables numerical simulations and visualizations of a wide variety of Hamiltonians, including those with arbitrary time-dependences widely used in many physics applications [9]. The service allows creating graphics and charts for interacting complex systems and simulating their time evolution with many available time evolution drivers.

Earth Science community depends on the exploration, analysis and reprocessing of high volumes of data as well as the modeling and simulation of complex coupled systems on multiple scales. A new hydrological modeling service [10] based on the Soil and Water Assessment Tool model has been developed using high efficiency, resource sharing and low cost cloud computing resources. Such a Desktop as a Service approach allowing users to work from anywhere, and gives centralized desktop management and great performance.

Processing of high-resolution time series satellite images typically requires a large amount of computational resources and time. A cloud based scientific gateway has been developed for computing the Normalized Difference Vegetation Index time series data [11]. Based on a distributed workflow using the Web Processing Service standard, the gateway aims to be completely interoperable with other standardized tools. The availability of this gateway help researchers to acquire knowledge of land cover changes more efficiently over very large spatial and temporal extents, which is especially important in the context of Armenia for which timely decision-making is needed.

5 Conclusions

As a developing country the implementation of Cloud services is very important for two aspects, first, it provides useful capabilities for all scientists and researchers to use distributed computing resources in a very flexible and easy way. The second aspect is to have several dedicated services based on local storage facilities which enable the Armenian's communities to use these resources with a high economic gain, because the major parts are provided free of charge, or with very minimum prices. Gathering all these parts together enable the users to collaborate, share their data, use a web browser to use these resources from anywhere in the world, and to have their data saved and backup to prevent any future failover problems or data lose.

References

1. T. Hey, A. Trefethen, Cyberinfrastructure for e-Science, Science, 308 (5723), pp. 817-821, May 2005, DOI: 10.1126/science.1110410.
2. H. Astsatryan, V. Sahakyan, Yu. Shoukourian, P.-H. Cros, M. Dayde, J. Dongarra, Per Oster, Strengthening Compute and Data intensive Capacities of Armenia, IEEE Proceedings of 14th RoEduNet International Conference - Networking in Education and Research (NER'2015), Craiova, Romania, pp. 28-33, September 24-26 2015, DOI: 10.1109/RoEduNet.2015.7311823.
3. P. Bogatencov, M. Dombrougov, V. Galagan, V. Shkarupin, E. Martynov, H. Astsatryan, A. Aliyev, R. Kvatadze, A. Tuzikov, E-infrastructures and e-services in the Eastern Partnership Countries, IEEE Proceedings of the RoEduNet Conference 13th Edition: Networking in Education and Research Joint Event RENAM 8th Conference, DOI: 10.1109/RoEduNet-RENAM.2014.6955298, pp. 1-6, 2014.
4. H. Astsatryan, V. Sahakyan, Yu. Shoukourian, Recent Developments of e-Science Infrastructures in Armenia, Reports of National Academy of Sciences of Armenia, Volume 113, No 4, 2013, pp. 352-356, ISSN 0321-1339.
5. Vlad Nitu, Aram Kocharyan, Hannas Yaya, Alain Tchana, Daniel Hagimont, and Hrachya Astsatryan, Working Set Size Estimation Techniques in Virtualized Environments: One Size Does not Fit All. Proc. ACM Meas. Anal. Comput. Syst. 2, 1, Article 19 (March 2018), 21 pages. https://doi.org/10.1145/3179422
6. H. Astsatryan, W. Narsisian, A. Kocharyan, G. da Costa, A. Hankel, A. Oleksiak, Energy Optimization Methodology for e-Infrastructure Providers, Willey Concurrency and Computation: Practice and Experience, 29 (10) February 2017 doi: 10.1002/cpe.4073.
7. H. Astsatryan, W. Narsisian, E. Gyulgyulyan, A. Poghosyan, Y. Mamaskhalisov, P. Wittenburg, An Integrated Web-based Interactive Data Platform for Molecular Dynamics Simulations, Scalable Computing: Practice and Experience, 19:2, pp. 79-86, 2018.
8. H. Astsatryan, H. Grogoryan, E. Gyulgyulyan, A. Hakobyan, A. Kocharyan, W. Narsisian, V. Sahakyan, Yu. Shoukourian, A. Mkoyan, R. Abrahamyan, Z. Petrosyan, J. Aligon, Weather Data Visualization and Analytical Platform, Scalable Computing: Practice and Experience, 19:2, pp. 149-156, 2018.
9. Hayk Grigoryan, Hrachya Astsatryan, Tigran Gevorgyan, Vahe Manukyan, Cloud Service for Numerical Calculations and Visualizations of Photonic Dissipative Systems, Journal Cybernetics and Information Technologies, 2017, Volume 17, No 5, ISSN 1311-9702, pp. 89-100, DOI: 10.1515/cait-2017-0058.
10. H. Astsatryan, W. Narsisian, Sh. Asmaryan, SWAT Hydrological Model as a DaaS Cloud Service, Springer Earth Science Informatics, 9(3), pp. 401-407, March 2016, DOI: 10.1007/s12145-016-0254-6.
11. H. Astsatryan, A. Hayrapetyan, W. Narsisian, Sh. Asmaryan, V. Muradyan, Y. Guigoz, G. Giuliani, N. Ray, An Interoperable Cloud-based Scientific Gateway for NDVI Time Series Analysis, Elsevier Computer Standards & Interfaces, 2015, 31(40), pp. 79–84, doi: 10.1016/j.csi.2015.02.001.

A Batching Location Cloaking Algorithm for Location Privacy Protection

Guillermo Tobar, Patricio Galdames, Claudio Gutiérrez-Soto,
and Pedro Rodríguez-Moreno

Departamento de Sistemas de Información, Universidad del Bío-Bío
Ave Collao 1202, Casilla 5-C, Concepción, Chile
http://dsi.face.ubiobio.cl
gtobar@alumnos.ubiobio.cl,{pgaldames,cogutier,prodrigu}@ubiobio.cl

Abstract. Many reporters have highlighted that Location-Based Services (LBS) have opened several questions concerning privacy. When a client releases her location to a LBS, she could put herself in danger. To mitigate this issue, researchers have proposed several location cloaking techniques. However, these solutions have several drawbacks. Most of them are based on an anonymizer and they do not address the scalability issues faced by the server when a high demand for location privacy protection is requested. Also, they do not consider the potential negative impact on the LBS when posteriori processing of many location-cloaked queries (LCQ). This paper considers the problems of efficient construction of location cloaking areas when a trusted anonymizer needs to provide location privacy protection for heterogeneous LBS clients and to limit the cost of processing many LCQs at the LBS. Our key goal is to build shared cloaking regions for LBS users located nearby each other and having similar privacy concerns. We propose several batching approaches for building proper cloaking regions. Throughout extensive simulations, we will show our approach can balance both the anonymizer workload and LBS workload.

Keywords: Location cloaking · k-anonymity · location privacy · batch processing.

1 Introduction

Many reporters have announced the fast growing of the Location-Based Services (LBS) market in the US and worldwide [4, 20]. A LBS is a Geographic Information Systems connected to the Internet whose main goal is to track the location of their users within a wireless network. When this service is needed, These users report their whereabouts by using their location-enabled mobile devices. Having received users' location, a LBS offer them real-time information on what these users might find relevant in their own immediate surroundings. For example, a user experiencing a health problem may submit its location as soon as possible to get promptly medical support. A tourist, arriving in the first time to a city, may need to find the closest taxi to get her to her destination.

However, when LBS users release their locations, they could endanger the integrity of their privacy. According to Beresford et al. [2], location privacy corresponds to the ability to prevent external entities from learning about our whereabouts in some period of time. An attacker, listening a users location, could determine the user's identity and could decide to track it to any place it goes. Moreover, the same LBS providers may not be trustworthy in keeping user data in confidential and may release this information to unknown third parties. These issues have motivated a series of research on location cloaking techniques.

The key idea is to reduce location resolution to achieve a desired level of protection. When requesting a LBS, users report a cloaking region instead of their exact position. A cloaking region needs to contain a user's current position and encloses other locations in where the user can also be. Most of the proposed techniques ([9, 8, 16, 3, 22–24, 21, 13, 26], etc.) are based on an anonymizer which builds a cloaking region containing the locations of at least K users currently moving in the service area. Other techniques [6, 12, 15, 18, 17, 14] assume the same users, collaborating with other peers, compute their own cloaking regions. Also, a few articles have proposed a hybrid approach, in which an anonymizer and users collaborate to create cloaking regions [11, 19, 10].

Most of these proposed techniques support anonymous uses of LBS ([9, 16, 3, 22, 8]). An adversary will not know the identity of the user located at each location even if she manages to identify all these users by matching the cloaking region with public information available in white and yellow pages. In contrast, the techniques in ([23, 24, 17]) ensure that each cloaking region contains locations that have been visited by at least K different users. Since these users visit a region at different times, it prevents an adversary from identifying the user who was inside of this region at the moment the LBS service was requested. Thus, the user's location privacy is protected from the time dimension.

Reducing location resolution mitigates privacy risks, but introduces more workload on the LBS server and the anonymizer. First at the LBS server, a precise location is more convenient since the query result is only computed with respect to a specific position. However, when a user location is cloaked, i.e., the user's real location is mixed with other possible locations; the LBS server needs to compute the response also for these additional locations as well. We will refer a query in which its location has been cloaked as a location-cloaked query (LCQ). In a system with many users, the processing of LCQs can be overwhelming to the LBS server and can overwhelm it. This is especially problematic when the server must deal with large cloaking regions, which happens when users request a high level of protection (for example, a large value for K).

Second, the performance associated with the anonymizer can also be problematic. Building an optimal cloaking region for each user, can become an overwhelming task, especially when the anonymizer is dealing with a high number of cloaking region requests. Thus, a response cloaking region request may be quite delayed which is undesirable when supporting real time applications. A solution for this issue may be to build the smallest number of cloaking regions that satisfy the privacy concerns of every client. However, this approach can end up returning large and non-optimal cloaking regions compromising the performance at the LBS. Therefore, an approach that balances the LBS and anonymizer workloads is needed.

This paper considers the problem of the efficient building of a set of cloaking regions (CRs) for many users having heterogeneous location privacy concerns. Our idea is to build CRs in a large-scale system if the anonymizer has processing resources available. In such a real-time processing model, a CR request is computed upon its request arrival without any latency when the anonymizer is under load. But when the anonymizer is overloaded, the incoming CR requests are queued. Queued CR requests are batch processed as soon as the anonymizer has processing resources available. Our research focuses on addressing the scalability dilemma between the anonymizer and the LBS.

This paper makes the following contributions. We propose a batching algorithm for efficient building of CRs demanding location privacy requirements. Our algorithm addresses the problem of improving scalability at the anonymizer without largely compromising the LBS workload. To our knowledge, this problem has not been addressed properly. Intuitively, every CR pending request is processed one by one in the order of first-in-first-out (FIFO). This approach ensures the fairness in CR processing, but does not leverage the fact that users may share a CR if they are located nearby and share similar privacy requirements. Combining these observations, our system can improve the anonymizer performance without increasing excessively the LBS workload. To measure the effectiveness of our approaches, we simulate different scenarios where users have similar and different location privacy concerns and they are disseminated in different places of the service area. We measure the anonymizer workload and latency in term of the average number of computed CRs and we assume the LBS workload is estimated as a function of the average size of a cloaking region.

The remainder of this paper is organized as follows. We provide a system overview in Section 2 and present our scalable location privacy algorithms in Section 3. The performances of all proposed techniques are evaluated in Section 4. and then conclude this paper in Section 5.

2 System Overview

Fig. 1. Traditional architecture of a LBS   **Fig. 2.** Partitioning of the network area

Without loss of generality, we assume a single and trustworthy anonymity server is used to manage all users. In Fig. 1 shows the architecture traditionally used in our context. Here, each user u submits a protection request to the anonymizer including its current and real location represented as a 2D point (X_u, Y_u) and its location based query. This query could be either a range query [5], a K-Nearest Neighbor query [12] or other type of location-based queries [1, 13]. Then, the anonymizer computes a cloaking region for u based on its demands of its location privacy requirement. Usually this requirement is defined in term of a K-anonymity value (for example, [9]) or an entropy parameter (for example, [24]). In this work, we assume a K value denoted as K_u is released by user u. Thus, our anonymizer builds a cloaking region for u containing at least K_u different locations. Then the anonymizer submits a transformed query to the LBS, denoted as a location cloaked query. This query is defined like the original query but the exact location of user u is replaced by a cloaking region (CR).

We assume our system receives a set of requests for location privacy protection. To efficiently process each request, the entire network area is partitioned into a set of $n \times n$ cells with equal size (As shown in Fig. 2). Since users report their current locations in each request, the server can estimate a request probability, that is, how likely a request can be submitted from a given cell. Formally, we define this probability similarly as proposed by Niu et al. [18].

$$q_i = \frac{\text{Number of CR requests originated from cell i}}{\text{Total number of requests originated from the network area}} \quad (1)$$

Where $\sum_{i=1}^{n^2} q_i = 1$ for all $i = 1, 2, ..., n^2$. Then we define how we determine the quality of a chosen CR. Suppose a given CR is set as $\{c_1, c_2, c_3, ..., c_K\}$. Then the entropy (H) of this cloaking region is defined as:

$$H(CR) = -\sum_{j=1}^{K} p_j \cdot \log_2(p_j) \quad (2)$$

Where p_j represents the normalized request probability of cell c_j. This probability is computed as $p_j = \frac{q_j}{\sum_{l=1}^{K} q_l}$ where $l = 1, 2, .., K$. The higher the entropy of a CR is, the better the location privacy protection is.

3 Our Batching Location Cloaking Technique

We define the following notation to describe our location cloaking technique.

- Let C be, the ordered set of all cells ($c_i, i = 1, 2, ..., n^2$) in which the network area N is partitioned. This set C is sorted according to each cells request probability (See Equation 1).
- Given a user u, we say c_u is the current cell containing us exact location.

- Let $S(r)$ be a subset of C, which consists of those r neighbor cells (c_j) in C whose request probability is greater or equals to c u s probability and those r cells whose request probability is smaller. Thus, the set $S(r)$ contains $2r + 1$ distinct cells.
- Let K_u , is the degree of anonymity demanded by a user u.
- U_{batch} : Set of users demanding location privacy protection at some time t.
- $U(K)$: Set of users having a location privacy requirement equals to K.

Our solution is divided in two stages. First, we run a state of the art cloaking technique, called DLS [18] as an Algorithm 1, to find a cloaking region for a selected user u. Then, Algorithm 2 is executed and, it applies a filtering criterion to check if other users having similar location privacy requirements may also use this computed cloaking region. In this work, we assume users sporadically engage in LBSs. Later, we will discuss the case for continuous LBS.

Algorithm 1 basically tries to choose $K - 1$ cells that are also highly probable to contain the real location of user u. This is achieved by choosing cells whose entropy is like the entropy of the current cell for user u. This process is repeated m times and the procedure outputs the set CR having the largest entropy. This process is carried out to prevent the adversary (LBS) from concluding the exact location of a target user (its current cell, since it can be one of K alternatives) and eventually conclude its identity. Although, we use DLS to build a cloaking region, we can choose and run any desirable location cloaking technique.

The values of Δ and m in these algorithms, are system parameters that will determine the computational cost of finding an acceptable cloaking region. For example, the greater the value of m is the higher is the cost (latency) of finding a cloaking region. Besides, Δ sets how many times given CR is tested to check if it satisfies the location privacy requirements of other users.

Algorithm 1: [18], it computes a cloaking region for a given user u

---

Data: set C,user u, m
Result: A Cloaking Region (CR_u) for user u
1 CR $\leftarrow \emptyset$;
2 Find subset $S(K_u)$ of C;
3 i $\leftarrow 0$;
4 **for** $i < m$ **do**
5 $\quad$ O $\leftarrow \{c_u\}$;
6 $\quad$ Choose randomly $K - 1$ distinct cells from subset $S(K_u) \setminus \{c_u\}$;
7 $\quad$ Add each cell into set O;
8 $\quad$ **if** $(CR==\emptyset$ or $H(O) > H(CR))$ **then**
9 $\quad\quad$ | CR $\leftarrow$ O;
10 $\quad$ **end**
11 $\quad$ i $\leftarrow$ i+1;
12 **end**
13 Return CR;

Algorithm 2 is the main procedure and is run by our anonymizer. Given a set of users demanding location privacy protection, its goal is to find a cloaking region for each user as soon as possible. Each CR must satisfy its corresponding users location privacy requirement (K). The idea is to first build a cloaking region for the user demanding the highest location privacy protection. Then one of the following criteria is chosen to check if a computed CR can be shared or adjusted for other users.

1. **Filtering Criterium 1 (FC1)**: A given CR_u is only shared with other users having a location privacy requirement (K) such that $K_u - \Delta < K \leq K_u$. (Then $0 \leq \Delta \leq K_u$)
2. **Filtering Criterium 2 (FC2)**: Apply FC1. If v is another user sharing CR_u and K_v is smaller than K_u then K cells are chosen randomly from CR u to become vs cloaking region.
3. **Filtering Criterium 3 (FC3)**: Apply FC1. If v is another user sharing CR_u and K_v is smaller than K_u then K cells having the highest entropy are chosen from CR u to become vs cloaking region.
4. **Filtering Criterium 4 (FC4)**: Apply FC1. If v is another user sharing CR_u and K_v is smaller than K_u then CR_v is set as CR_u . Here user v gets more privacy protection than required.

Algorithm 2: A set of cloaking regions for users in U_{batch} is computed in batch

---

Data: set U_{batch}, Δ
Result: A set of CRs for each user in U_{batch}
1 $K_{max} \leftarrow$ Find the largest K from all users in U_{batch};
2 $K \leftarrow K_{max}$;
3 **do**
4   Choose any user u in $U(K)$;
5   Find set $S(K)$;
6     $CR_u \leftarrow$ **Algorithm1**(U, K_u, K_{max});
7     $A(CR_u) \leftarrow$ Set of users in U whose current cell is in CR_u and its location privacy requirement is equals or smaller than K_u;
8   **for** *each user v in* $A(CR_u)$ **do**
9         $CR_v \leftarrow$ by applying a chosen $FC_i(\Delta)$ (i:1,2,3 or 4) on CR_u;
10   **end**
11     $U_{batch} \leftarrow U_{batch} \setminus A(CR_u)$;
12     $K \leftarrow$ Find the largest K from all pending users in U_{batch};
13 **while** $U_{batch} \neq \emptyset$;

---

4 Empirical Evaluation

We will evaluate the performance of our proposed techniques using simulation. Four performance metrics are used, including:

- **Computational cost**: We want to measure the average total amount of work (complexity time) incurred on building a set of cloaking regions.

- **Size of a cloaking region**: The average number of cells conforming a cloaking region. This size can be equals or higher than the degree of location privacy protection (K) demanded by a user.
- **Number of cloaking regions built**: we want to measure the number of CR built by the anonymizer. The minimum value is one, since only CR can be built to protect all users at one. The maximum value corresponds to the number of users deployed in the network area, since for each of them a CR can specifically be built.
- **Entropy a cloaking region**: We can apply formula 2 to compute the entropy of CR and to obtain the average entropy of the computed CRs. With this metric we want to evaluate the quality of the location privacy protection offered by a CR. The higher the entropy the better the quality is.

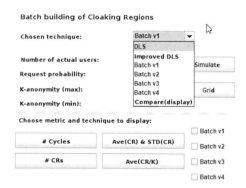

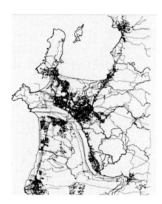

Fig. 3. Java interface to configure our simulator

Fig. 4. Layout of the city (Concepcion,Chile) in which simulations were performed.

We developed a Java based simulation, as shown in Fig. 3, in which you can set the location cloaking technique and the network area. As a network area, we consider a medium-size city as shown in Fig. 4. We generate a network domain of 1515. We disseminate a fixed number of users in this area between $[1, 60]$. The distribution of users is done according of the density of roads, i.e., the more roads an area has, the higher is the likelihood a user is deployed there. We then generate a number of requests for cloaking regions. The value of K ranges from 5 to 15. We are mainly interested in comparing how the anonymizer performance is impacted and the quality of the computed cloaking regions when we run independently the four variants of our techniques (denoted as FC1, FC2, FC3 and FC4) against an state-of-the-art cloaking technique as DLS [18] running at the anonymizer. We set $\Delta = 0$ for FC1, and $\Delta = K_u$ when we apply either FC2, FC3 or FC4.

In Fig. 5, we measure the complexity cost of all technique. We observe DLS shows the highest cost since each cloaking region is computed independently.

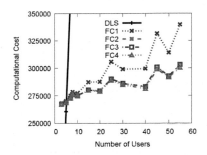
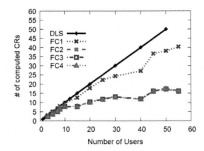

Fig. 5. Computational cost vs Number of users

Fig. 6. Number of computed CR vs Number of users

On the contrary our approaches are more scalable. Specifically, FC1 shows the largest cost among all variants since it computes a cloaking region for every user except those requesting the same location privacy protection (K) and having their current cells in the same cloaking region.

In Fig. 6, we measure the number of computed cloaking regions, which at most correspond to the number of users. As we expected DLS computes as much cloaking regions as needed. However, in our approaches since the cloaking regions are computed in batch, some users may share cloaking regions and therefore the anonymizer computes a smaller amount of CRs. Specifically, FC2, FC3 and FC4 receive the smallest values since they want to set a given CR to as many users as much as possible.

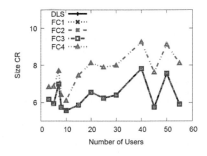
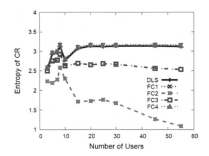

Fig. 7. Average Size Cloaking Regions (CR) vs Number of users

Fig. 8. Entropy of a Cloaking Region (CR) vs Number of users.

In Fig. 7, we observe the average size of a cloaking region. As we expected FC4 achieves the largest values since it can assign to a user an over-sized cloaking region.

In Fig. 8, we observe the quality (entropy) of the computed cloaking region. We observe DLS and FC4 shows the greatest values. Specifically, FC4 shows more uncertainty in a users location for each CR and therefore it has a higher entropy than the others variant. FC2 shows the worst results since a cloaking region is mostly chosen at random for most of the users.

5 Conclusion

This paper introduced a batching algorithm to build cloaking regions for large number of users having diverse location privacy requirements. Our proposed technique tries to balance computational cost at the anonymizer and the Location-based Service. Our technique takes advantage of building efficiently cloaking regions of users having similar location privacy requirements and located nearby.

From the results, our techniques offer cost-effective solutions at the anonymizer to build location privacy protections. Our variant FC3 shows a good balance between quality of a cloaking region, its size (which measures the impact at the LBS) and its computational cost at the anonymizer. Moreover, the LBS can take advantage of the high degree of overlapping among the cloaking regions, and therefore from their corresponding LCQs as well. This fact can make the posteriori LCQ processing at the LBS more efficient as was suggested by Galdames et al [7].

Our results are preliminary yet promising. We are planning to test more diverse scenarios. We want to find optimal values for some system parameters such as m and Δ. In addition, we would like to build efficiently cloaking regions that also satisfy other location requirements like location safety [25]. Finally, our cloaking technique is able to provide privacy protection for sporadic LBS. We plan to address the problem of location privacy for continuous LBS in the future. In this context, users periodically demand location privacy protection and the cloaking area builder wants to protect a user mainly from an inference attack.

Acknowledgements

This paper was supported in parts by the Universidad del Bío-Bío, under grant DIUBB GI 150115/EF and grant DIUBB 184615 1/L.

References

1. Benetis, R., Jensen, S., Karciauskas, G., Saltenis, S.: Nearest and reverse nearest neighbor queries for moving objects. The VLDB Journal **15**(3), 229–249 (2006)
2. Beresford, A.R., Stajano, F.: Location privacy in pervasive computing. IEEE Pervasive Computing **2**(1), 46–55 (Jan 2003)
3. Cheng, R., Zhang, Y., Bertino, E., Prabhakar, S.: Preserving user location privacy in mobile data management infrastructures. In: Proceedings of the 6th International Conference on Privacy Enhancing Technologies. pp. 393–412. PET'06 (2006)
4. Chin, N.J.P.: Critical Success Factors of Location-based Services. Master's thesis, University of Nebraska-Lincoln, Lincoln, Nebraska, USA (2012)

5. Chon, H.D., Agrawal, D., Abbadi, A.E.: Range and kNN Query Processing for Moving Objects in Grid Model. Mobile Networks and Applications **8**(4), 401–412 (2003)
6. Chow, C.Y., Mokbel, M., Liu, X.: A peer-to-peer spatial cloaking algorithm for anonymous location-based service. In: Proc. of ACM Int'l Siymposium on Advances in Geographic Information Systems (GIS'06). pp. 171–178. Arlington,VA,USA (November 10 - 11 2006)
7. Galdames, P., Cai, Y.: Efficient processing of location-cloaked queries. In: 2012 Proceedings IEEE INFOCOM. pp. 2480–2488 (March 2012)
8. Gedik, B., Liu, L.: Protecting location privacy with personalized k-anonymity: Architecture and algorithms. IEEE Transactions on Mobile Computing **7**(1), 1–18 (Jan 2008)
9. Gruteser, M., Grunwald, D.: Anonymous usage of location-based services through spatial and temporal cloaking. In: Proceedings of the 1st International Conference on Mobile Systems, Applications and Services. pp. 31–42. MobiSys '03 (2003)
10. Gupta, R., Rao, U.P.: A hybrid location privacy solution for mobile lbs. Mobile Information Systems (2017)
11. Koo, S.G.M., Lee, C.S.G., Kannan, K.: A genetic-algorithm-based neighbor-selection strategy for hybrid peer-to-peer networks. In: Proceedings. 13th International Conference on Computer Communications and Networks (IEEE Cat. No.04EX969). pp. 469–474 (Oct 2004)
12. Ku, W.S., Zimmermann, R., Wan, C.W., Wang, H.: MAPLE: A Mobile Scalable P2P Nearest Neighbor Query Model for Location-based Services. In: Proc. of the 22nd Int'l Conf. on Data Engineering, (ICDE'06). pp. 182–222. Atlanta (2006)
13. Lahe, A.D., Kulkarni, P.: Location privacy preserving using semi-ttp server for lbs users. In: 2017 2nd IEEE International Conference on Recent Trends in Electronics, Information Communication Technology (RTEICT). pp. 605–610 (May 2017)
14. Li, X., Miao, M., Liu, H., Ma, J., Li, K.C.: An incentive mechanism for k-anonymity in lbs privacy protection based on credit mechanism. Soft Computing **21**(14), 3907–3917 (Jul 2017)
15. Liu, F., Hua, K., , Do, T.: A p2p technique for continuous knearest-neighbor query in road networks. In: Proc. of the 17th International Conference on Database and Expert Systems Applications (DEXA'07). pp. 264–276. Krakow, Poland (September 04 - 08 2007)
16. Mokbel, M., Chow, C., Aref, W.: The new casper: Query processing for location services without compromising privacy. In: Proc. of ACM Int'l Conf. on Very Large Databases (VLDB'06). pp. 763–774. Seoul, Korea (September 12-15 2006)
17. Niu, B., Gao, S., Li, F., Li, H., Lu, Z.: Protection of location privacy in continuous lbss against adversaries with background information. In: 2016 International Conference on Computing, Networking and Communications (ICNC). pp. 1–6 (Feb 2016)
18. Niu, B., Li, Q., Zhu, X., Cao, G., Li, H.: Achieving k-anonymity in privacy-aware location-based services. In: IEEE INFOCOM 2014 - IEEE Conference on Computer Communications. pp. 754–762 (April 2014)
19. Nosouhi, M.R., Pham, V.V.H., Yu, S., Xiang, Y., Warren, M.: A hybrid location privacy protection scheme in big data environment. In: GLOBECOM 2017 - 2017 IEEE Global Communications Conference. pp. 1–6 (Dec 2017)
20. Rais, Z.: The Future of Location Based Marketing. Web page at https://www.entrepreneur.com/article/273856 (April 2016)
21. Xie, Q., Wang, L.: Privacy-preserving location-based service scheme for mobile sensing data. MDPI Sensors **16**(12), 1993 (Dec 2016)

22. Xu, T., Cai, Y.: Location anonymity in continuous location-based services. In: Proceedings of the 15th Annual ACM International Symposium on Advances in Geographic Information Systems. pp. 39:1–39:8. GIS '07 (2007)
23. Xu, T., Cai, Y.: Exploring historical location data for anonymity preservation in location-based services. In: IEEE INFOCOM 2008 - The 27th Conference on Computer Communications (April 2008)
24. Xu, T., Cai, Y.: Feeling-based location privacy protection in location-based services. In: Proc. of ACM Int'l Conf. on Computer and Communications Security (CCS'09). pp. 348–357. Chicago, IL, USA (September 12-15 2009)
25. T. Xu and Y. Cai: Location cloaking for safety protection of ad hoc networks. In: Proc. of IEEE Int'l Conf. on Computer Communications (INFOCOM'09). pp. 1944–1952. Rio de Janeiro, Brazil (April 19-25 2009)
26. Zhang, H., Wu, C., Chen, Z., Liu, Z., Zhu, Y.: A novel on-line spatial-temporal k-anonymity method for location privacy protection from sequence rules-based inference attacks. PloS One **12**(8) (Aug 2017)

Reconfigurable Hardware and Adaptive Software for the Internet of Things: How Runtime Flexibility Changes Embedded Systems

Gregor Schiele

University of Duisburg-Essen, Bismarckstrasse 90, 47057 Duisburg
gregor.schiele@uni-due.de
http://www.uni-due.de/es/

Abstract. When embedded systems are connected to the Internet of Things, they must face new challenges that require them to move beyond static systems to dynamic systems that can be changed flexibly at runtime. To do so, we believe that a platform combining adaptive (system) software and reconfigurable hardware is needed. In this short paper we present our current approach towards such a platform and discuss its use for lightweight authentication and on-device machine learning.

Keywords: Internet of Things · Embedded System · Runtime Flexibility.

1 Introduction

Over the years embedded systems have evolved from isolated electronic devices with fixed functionalities to Internet-connected cyber physical devices that are part of the so-called *Internet of Things* (IoT). The IoT is widely expected to transform fundamentally our homes (smart homes), cities (smart cities), agriculture (smart farming) and businesses (Industry 4.0). However, making embedded systems part of the IoT poses a number of challenges that must be met to produce high quality solutions. In the following we first describe some of these challenges. We then propose a solution for them, namely runtime adaptation and its support by adaptive software as well as reconfigurable hardware. We present our experimental platform for this and demonstrate its use in two example scenarios – lightweight authentication and on-device machine learning. Then we conclude the paper with an outlook on current and future work.

2 Challenges of the IoT

The IoT interconnects billions of embedded devices into a world-wide network, similarly to the "classical" Internet. Much work has been done on how to integrate such low-power and often battery powered devices into the Internet and many new communication technologies and often Cloud-based data collection systems have been developed [1][6][2]. However, we argue that embedded systems in the IoT face more challenges than 'just' connecting them to the Internet. In the following we briefly discuss some of the most important of these challenges on future embedded systems.

Evolving Security Threads: Security has always been a central requirement for embedded devices. It is the basis for privacy as well as for safety. However, traditionally, embedded systems have often been deployed in relatively closed environments that are difficult to attack. In contrast to this, embedded systems in the IoT are exposed to the open Internet and to continuously evolving security attacks from all over the world. To keep a device secure, we need to update it continuously to counter new attacks and security holes. This makes it impossible to provide a finished system that will stay secure for long.

Evolving Applications: Just like threads in the IoT change over time, so do applications. While embedded systems traditionally have been developed with a fixed set of functions in mind, this becomes much harder for the IoT. Individual devices are no longer operating in isolation to provide their services. Instead. they become part of a dynamic set of distributed applications that are deployed and make use of changing sets of devices, e.g. by selecting sensors nearby a mobile user. Therefore, embedded systems must be able to handle fluctuating and often unforeseeable workloads. They must be able to become part of new applications that have not existed at the time of their deployment and must provide new functions for them.

High workload peaks: At the same time, new approaches like deep machine learning and voice and image recognition put increased workload on embedded devices, often resulting in short periods of very high workload peaks that can overwhelm small embedded MCUs. Since many systems are battery powered, they cannot just include a more powerful MCU that will be idle most of the time. A common solution for this is to offload such workload peaks to a remote server, e.g. in the Cloud. However, this induces high latencies and potential privacy as well as reliability risks, in case the remote server is attacked.

3   The Case for Runtime Flexibility

As discussed, embedded systems in the IoT face much more dynamic and unforeseen execution contexts. To react to these, they can no longer be static, i.e. be developed once, then deployed and not changed anymore. They must become flexible systems that can change and adapt their behaviour after being deployed. Such flexibility is often achieved by developing more and more functionality in software and deploying software updates regularly, e.g. using over-the-air updating protocols. In addition, using approaches originating from pervasive and organic computing [7], embedded systems can adapt their behaviour at runtime e.g. by offloading functions to the Cloud or by switching between different software components that are available locally or on nearby devices.

This software-based runtime flexibility however can lead to poor overall system performance due to slow software execution on embedded MCUs, overhead for communication and coordination between devices, and increased system complexity due to the need for distributed algorithms. Therefore, we argue that embedded systems cannot rely on software-based runtime flexibility with adaptive software alone but should also include support for runtime flexibility in hardware by using reconfigurable hardware.

4 The Elastic Node

To enable research on the usage of hardware-based runtime flexibility in the IoT, we are developing an experimental hardware system that combines two heterogeneous cores: (i) a low-power embedded micro-controller (namely an Atmel ATMega64 MCU) and (ii) a reconfigurable field programmable gate array (namely a Xilinx Spartan 6 LX9 FPGA). We call this platform the *Elastic Node* (see Figure 1).

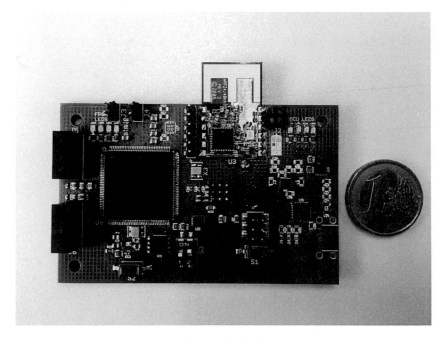

Fig. 1. Elastic Node Hardware

The components were chosen to achieve high energy efficiency in combination with the ability to handle short workload peaks. The device also includes an

IEEE 802.15.4 module to communicate wirelessly. The Elastic Node can operate in two active modes (as well as a low-power sleep mode). In the normal mode, only the MCU is active while the FPGA is deactivated. The MCU can handle normal workload and e.g. reading sensor measurements and performing basic data filtering tasks. If a high workload peak is detected, the FPGA can be activated and programmed with different hardware configurations that enable it to simulate different types of hardware efficiently. This way, at one time it can e.g. implement a special chip for machine learning. At a later time, the FPGA can be switched to a different configuration, this time implementing e.g. an encryption chip. New configurations can be downloaded wirelessly. This allows the Elastic Node to evolve over time and provide suitable hardware support for changing workloads.

In addition to our Elastic Node hardware, we are developing an adaptive system software that allows application developers to use the different cores on the device more easily [4]. The system software provides a function-call based abstraction API that allows to offload peak workloads to the FPGA by calling special hardware functions in a C application executed on the MCU. Once a hardware function is called, the system software automatically starts and reconfigures the FPGA to the best hardware configuration, transmits all necessary data parameters, starts the calculations, receives results from the FPGA and returns them to the MCU software.

So far we have demonstrated the potential of our Elastic Node for two different application cases, (i) lightweight authentication and (ii) on device machine learning. In the first case, we use the FPGA to implement a so-called physically unclonable function (PUF). This PUF can be used to create a kind of electronic fingerprint for an embedded device that allows to authenticate the device securely at a remote server without using heavyweight encryption. By switching between different PUF implementations and placements on the FPGA, we are able to increase the security of the resulting solution [3]. In the second case, we implement an artificial neural network (ANN) on the FPGA that can be used for deep learning applications. Deep learning is used in a multitude of current scenarios, e.g. for object recognition and artificial intelligence. Our approach allows us to execute such applications locally on the embedded device instead of offloading them to a remote Cloud. This can lead to lower energy consumption and reduce the resulting latency of the system by several orders of magnitude [5].

5 Conclusion

In this short paper we have presented our approach to experiment with runtime flexibility for embedded systems in the IoT. Such flexibility combines two layers: first, adaptive (system) software that provides an abstract execution environment to ease the development of adaptive applications. Second, reconfigurable hardware allows to provide different hardware architectures that are optimised for different kinds of workloads and can be switched at runtime. This provides far more efficient solutions than purely software-based systems. We have successfully demonstrated the benefits of such an approach in different application scenarios. However, our work has just begun. For one, it is currently not clear how the availability of reconfigurable hardware may influence the implementation of system software and networking stacks, including memory management and task scheduling. In addition, we continue to develop our Elastic Node platform further, e.g. to increase the data exchange rate between MCU and FPGA, and to reduce the size and energy consumption of the hardware. Finally, we are currently examining additional application cases for the Elastic Node, e.g. image and video processing.

References

1. Adelantado, F., Vilajosana, X., Tuset-Peiro, P., Martinez, B., Melia-Segui, J., Watteyne, T.: Understanding the limits of lorawan. IEEE Communications Magazine **55**(9), 34–40 (2017). https://doi.org/10.1109/MCOM.2017.1600613
2. Al-Fuqaha, A., Guizani, M., Mohammadi, M., Aledhari, M., Ayyash, M.: Internet of things: A survey on enabling technologies, protocols, and applications. IEEE Communications Surveys Tutorials **17**(4), 2347–2376 (Fourthquarter 2015). https://doi.org/10.1109/COMST.2015.2444095
3. Babaei, A., Schiele, G.: Spatial reconfigurable physical unclonable functions for the internet of things. In: International Conference on Security, Privacy and Anonymity in Computation, Communication and Storage (SpaCCS 2017) (December 2017)
4. Burger, A., Cichiwskyj, C., Schiele, G.: Elastic nodes for the internet of things: A middleware-based approach. In: 2017 IEEE International Conference on Autonomic Computing (ICAC). pp. 73–74 (July 2017)
5. Burger, A., Schiele, G.: Deep learning on an elastic node for the internet of things. In: (demo) IEEE International Conference on Pervasive Computing and Communications (PerCom 2017) (March 2018)
6. Erbati, M.M., Schiele, G., Batke, G.: Analysis of lorawan technology in an outdoor and an indoor scenario in duisburg-germany. In: 2018 IEEE 3rd International Conference on Computer and Communication Systems (ICCCS 2018) (April 2018)
7. Krupitzer, C., Roth, F.M., VanSyckel, S., Schiele, G., Becker, C.: A survey on engineering approaches for self-adaptive systems. Pervasive Mob. Comput. **17**(PB), 184–206 (Feb 2015). https://doi.org/10.1016/j.pmcj.2014.09.009, http://dx.doi.org/10.1016/j.pmcj.2014.09.009

A Survey of Resource Positioning Strategies

Daniel Moreno[1], Sergio F. Ochoa[2], Nelson Baloian[2]

[1] Department of Computer Science, Universidad de Talca, Chile
danmoreno@utalca.cl
[2] Department of Computer Science, Universidad de Chile, Chile
{sochoa, nbaloian}@dcc.uchile.cl

Abstract: The advances in wireless communication have enabled the spread of the mobile computing paradigm, in which resource positioning plays a key role. Positioning is the process of determining the position of a resource in a given environment. This survey describes the main positioning techniques and the methods used to address the positioning problem, as well as determining their overall performance in outdoor scenarios based on a proposed set of metrics. Through a set of comparison tables on the performance of the positioning methods, this paper helps designers of mobile applications to choose suitable techniques to support the services these systems provide.

1 Introduction

In the last few years, there has been a growing interest in context-aware systems, particularly in those providing location-aware or location-based information services (positioning). These services are accessible through mobile devices by means of communication networks, and allow resources to determine their positions [1]. Promising applications include vehicle navigation, fraud detection, resource management, crowdsourcing and automated billing [2].

In order to meet the needs of users and offer adaptive and convenient personal services, positioning systems provide users with ubiquitous location information, in places such as their homes, offices and also at the street. Different approaches have been proposed to solve the positioning problem; each of them addresses positioning based on the scenario (context) where the positioning systems is deployed [3], e.g., GPS for outdoors and fingerprinting or proximity for indoor environments.

Depending on the application to be supported or service to be provided, different types of positioning information could be required by the system. According to Hightower et al. [3], the main types of positioning are physical, symbolic, absolute and relative. These categories must also consider the indoor and outdoor positioning.

In this work, we explain the different techniques used to estimate the position of users and devices (resources), and also offer a comparison of their performance in outdoor environments. This comparison helps designers of mobile applications to decide which techniques can be used to support a certain computing scenario.

Next section introduces the notion of positioning, as well as current location techniques and their most commonly implemented methods. Section 3 describes the set of metrics that will be used to measure the performance of the techniques. Section 4 presents the comparison tables and a discussion on the performance of the positioning methods. Section 5 reviews the related work, and Section 6 shows the conclusions and future work.

2 Resource Positioning

The *position* of a resource is a representation of its location in a given environment; and *positioning* is the process of determining that position. Such a process can be roughly divided in two categories: *outdoor* and *indoor*. In outdoor environments, the GPS (Global Positioning System) is currently the most widely used. It offers maximum coverage for positioning with relatively little effort [4]. However, its performance is limited on indoor environments, mainly due to obstructed line-of-sight (LOS) transmission between receivers and satellites, which severely affect GPS' accuracy.

On the other hand, indoor environments tend to be more complex [5] due to the presence of several types of obstacles, which carry about issues with signal readings, and thus to a higher error on the positioning estimations. In addition, transitioning between indoor and outdoor positioning strategies on the run (i.e., from using fingerprinting while inside a building, to using GPS while outside) is still an open issue. Given the inherent differences of these scenarios, there is no single solution, and rather the users must switch between indoor and outdoor strategies on demand. This issue and possible solutions will be further discussed in future work.

Depending on the positioning requirements and limitations of the user applications, different types of positioning information could be required. According to Hightower et al. [3], the main types of positioning are *physical*, *symbolic*, *absolute*, and *relative*. Physical positioning is expressed in the form of coordinates, which identify a point on a multi-dimensional map (i.e., 2-D or 3-D). Symbolic positioning expresses a location in a natural-language way, such as "in the office". Absolute positioning uses a shared reference grid for all located objects. Relative positioning depends on its own frame of reference, and its information is usually based on the proximity to known reference points or base stations [6].

The following subsections provide a summarized review of the most widely used strategies for positioning. In general, most methods attempt to measure one or more signals, and then process these measurements in order to estimate the position of a resource. Based on the information measured and how the position estimation is performed, we can classify positioning techniques in four groups: (1) *angulation* and *lateration*, (2) *proximity*, (3) *fingerprinting*, and (4) *image scene analysis*. Angulation, lateration, fingerprinting, and radio scene analysis can provide absolute, relative and proximity position information, while proximity only provides proximity information. Next the article describes each of them.

2.1 Angulation and Lateration

Angulation and lateration use the geometric properties of triangles and a set of reference points with known locations to estimate the position of a resource. The accuracy of this positioning approach improves when more reference points are used for the estimation process. An advantage of this method is that it involves a small setup effort in order to start calculating the resources location [3].

The *lateration*, also known as *range measurement*, estimates the position of a resource measuring its distance to at least three reference points with known geographical coordinates. Using the direction or length of the vectors drawn between the location to be estimated and the reference points, the absolute position of the target can be calculated [7]. Five methods are commonly used to estimate positions using lateration: *time of arrival* [8], *time difference of arrival* [8], *round-trip time of flight* [9], *received signal strength* [10], and *signal attenuation* [11]. Note that GPS is a special case of lateration.

The *angulation*, or *direction of arrival*, calculates the position of a device by computing the angles relative to two or more reference points with known geographical coordinates. Using the angle of the vectors drawn between the target's location and the reference points, it calculates the absolute position of the desired resource [7]. The most well-known method used for angulation is the *angle of arrival* [12].

2.2   Proximity

Proximity positioning usually relies upon a dense grid of detectors, each with a well-known position. When a mobile device is detected by a single antenna, it is considered to be collocated with it. When more than one station detects the mobile target, it is considered to be collocated with the one that receives the strongest signal [13], or at the intersection of both stations. The accuracy of proximity positioning systems depends on which detection technology is used, and on the number of reference points deployed in the physical environment. The greater the density of reference points, the higher the accuracy.

This method is relatively simple to implement over different types of physical media, although an important setup effort is required on early deployment stages. Positioning systems using *infrared radiation* (IR) and *radio frequency identification* (RFID) are often based on this method. Five methods have been considered for proximity positioning: *Cell ID* [14], *radio frequency identification* [15], the *closest neighbor algorithm* [16], and the *least square algorithm* [16].

2.3   Fingerprinting

This technique, also known as *radio scene analysis*, calculates the position of resources in a bounded physical space, by comparing the current measurements of a given set of signals with pre-measured data related to particular locations. Typically, it involves two phases: an offline training phase and an online estimation phase. During the offline phase, samples of location related data (e.g., Wi-Fi received signals strength) are collected for the whole physical space considered for the estimation process. Then, during the online stage, the currently observed signal strengths of a resource are used in conjunction with the previously collected data to figure out an estimated position for the target resource.

Fingerprinting can be performed by using pattern recognition based methods and probabilistic methods. The main idea is to use sets of received signal strengths (RSSI) from several access points, which is used during the training phase to assemble a "directory" of positions based on perceived RSSIs, and then during the positioning phase, a device uses its perceived set of RSSI to determine its position.

2.4 Image Scene Analysis

This technique analyzes images received from one or more capturing points (e.g., cameras) to attempt identifying one or more target resources [17]. Real-time analysis of images or video is feasible when a small number of objects are present; otherwise, it is more efficient to combine this technique with fingerprinting or proximity techniques. Using vision analysis involves an important effort during the setup phase, because they rely heavily on monitoring equipment.

Vision-based positioning systems can be greatly influenced by interference sources, such as weather, light, motion, etc. Although a variety of algorithms can overcome most of these difficulties, a solution must work fast enough to make the system responsive to the occupants of a certain area. The *Simultaneous Localization and Mapping* (SLAM) technique tries to address these problems considering a mobile resource (usually a robot) that navigate an unknown environment. While navigating the robot seeks to acquire a map of its environment, and at the same time it wishes to localize itself using its map [18]. The use of SLAM can be motivated by two different needs: (1) detailed environment models or (2) an accurate sense of a mobile robot's location. Although SLAM serves both purposes, we will focus only on the positioning part.

3 Metrics for the Measurement of Positioning Strategies

The performance of positioning techniques cannot be measured only using accuracy; a number of metrics must be defined in order to perform an accurate benchmark. For our classification, we have settled on the following metrics: *accuracy*, *precision*, *scalability*, *complexity*, *deployment cost*, and *robustness*. Usually, positioning systems offer a tradeoff between these metrics, such as sacrificing accuracy to lower complexity, and so on. These tradeoffs depend entirely on the application requirements of the system.

Since authors use different ranges and metrics to measure their own results, we have established a simple interval-based qualitative measuring scale for our evaluation: *Low*, *medium*, and *high* scores, which is based on the maximum and minimum values observed for each metric in the authors' work. If the exact values are not available, estimations are made based on the performance of similar methods. This scale will be addressed in depth in future work. Next we describe the metrics we have considered for our comparison.

Accuracy, also known as *location error*, is the most important requirement of positioning systems. The mean distance error, which is the average Euclidean distance between the estimated location and the true location, is usually adopted as the accuracy metric. The higher its accuracy, the better the system; however, there is often need for a tradeoff between accuracy and other characteristics.

Precision considers *how consistently a positioning technique works*. In other words, it reveals the variation in the performance of a positioning technique over many trials [19],[20]. Accuracy only considers the value of mean distance errors, while precision measures cumulative probability functions of the distance error.

The scalability of a positioning system is determined based *how it performs when the positioning scope changes*. Positioning systems may need to scale on two axes: geography and density. Geographic scaling implies covering different volumes of areas without important performance issues. Density scaling requires that the performance is not affected by a great number of simultaneous estimation requests.

The complexity of a positioning system can be attributed to *hardware, software, and operation factors*. If the computations of a positioning algorithm are performed on a centralized server, with powerful processing capability and sufficient power supply, the calculations could be considered trivial. However, if the computations are performed on a mobile unit, the complexity of the positioning methods becomes more evident, since most mobile units lack powerful processing units and long battery life.

The overall cost of a positioning system depends on many factors, such as *money, time, space, weight, and energy*. Energy is an important factor of a system, for it determines how long it can remain active. The time factor is related to installation and maintenance (see deployment cost). Mobile units may have tight space and weight constraints, as is the case with mobile devices. In some instances, we can consider *sunk costs*, which reduce the overall cost of a positioning system by taking advantage of existing infrastructure.

The deployment cost of the physical components of a positioning system is *highly dependent on the positioning technique and technologies that will be used* during the positioning process. This includes equipment installation, man or machine power, and the necessary training for the method to work. The effort required to put the system online should also be considered as a deployment cost.

Robustness measures a positioning system resistance or countermeasures to failure. A positioning system is expected to operate normally even when some signals are not available or bear values off the accepted range.

4   Performance of Positioning Methods on Outdoor Environments

The metrics introduced in the previous section were used to elaborate a comparison of the performance of the positioning methods reviewed in this survey. The rows of each table indicate the methods and the columns list the considered metrics. In order to allow a better visualization of the tables, the metrics have been abbreviated as follows: accuracy as *ACC*, precision as *PRE*, scalability as *SCA*, complexity as *COM*, overall cost as *OC*, deployment cost as *DC*, and robustness as *ROB*.

4.1 Angulation and Lateration

The methods considered are time of arrival (TOA), time differential of arrival (TDOA), roundtrip time of flight (RTOF), received signal strength, (RSS), received signal phase (RSP), GPS, and angle of arrival (AOA). The first three methods work under the same basic principle; thus, they all share common traits and display a similar performance. The same holds for the RSS and RSP methods, which work under similar assumptions. For the GPS performance, no hybrid-GPS methods have been taken into account.

The *TOA, TDOA* and *RTOF* methods have medium to high accuracy, with a 30m estimation error under favorable conditions [21], as well as reliable precision. TDOA and RTOF have better accuracy and precision than TOA, at the cost of increased complexity and the need for special equipment. This is due to the use of multiple signal measurements to estimate positions, though synchronization errors might still affect these measurements [20]. Moreover, a greater distance from the reference points induces additional error due to signal time delay [15], and an accurate synchronization between all participants is required to obtain meaningful results [22]. Only a small effort is needed to setup a system using these positioning methods [7].

RSP and *RSS* have diminished accuracy, mainly due to environmental effects that affect the signal measurements. These same effects also influence the precision negatively. For RSS, scalability becomes a major issue due to the size of the coverage area, since greater areas require more calculations, bigger position databases, and possibly additional equipment. The deployment cost remains low due to the possibility of reusing available infrastructure to deploy the system with minimum additional devices. As for robustness, although multipath and loss of signal are not as relevant on outdoor scenarios, environmental effects such as sunlight and fog tend to increase estimation errors.

The accuracy of *AOA* depends on the accuracy of the angle measurements [6], while its precision is consistent as long as the angle measurements are not affected by external factors. AOA also has a high calculation requirement due to the amount of operations needed to estimate distances and angles from reference points to target, which increases its complexity [19]. In addition, it requires expensive equipment and a setup and calibration phase [22], and the increased coverage area of outdoor environments require additional computational power.

The *GPS* has an accuracy error of up to 15m on the ground, with a precision of 95% any time of the day [21]. It also has low computational requirements, especially for mobile devices [23], and a cheap transceiver is all that is required to access GPS positioning. Scalability is not an issue, since this method is used worldwide at every hour of the day since its public release. Since GPS uses an array of satellites and a simple mobile transceiver unit, its deployment cost is inexpensive. Even so, this method's accuracy can be affected by environmental effects and atmospheric conditions [15]. A comparison of lateration and angulation methods is presented in Table 1.

Table 1. Performance of lateration and angulation methods in outdoor environments.

	ACC	PRE	SCA	COM	OC	DC	ROB
TOA	High	High	High	Medium	Medium	Low	Medium
TDOA	High	High	Medium	High	High	Low	High
RTOF	High	High	Medium	High	High	Low	Medium
RSP	Low	Low	Low	High	High	Low	Medium
RSS	Medium	Low	Low	High	High	Low	Medium
AOA	High	Medium	Low	High	High	Medium	Medium
GPS	High	High	High	Low	Low	Low	Medium

4.2 Proximity

For proximity, the methods considered are *cell-ID* (CID), *radio-frequency ID* (RFID), *closest neighbor* (CN), and *least square* (LS). Particularly, *CID* tends to have low accuracy due to how it works. Both its accuracy and precision are highly dependent on the size of the coverage area, which can range 200m to over 30Km [21]. However, this method supports a larger quantity of simultaneous requests than others with relatively little computational effort. It is also inexpensive and requires almost no deployment effort if there is an existing infrastructure.

RFID technology is not quite suitable for outdoors due to its small effective coverage area and large deployment cost. Therefore, it is frequently not used outdoors, except for parking lots, warehouses and the like. Its accuracy is low because of its limited range, although it has reliable precision, to an extent. To increase accuracy, more radio-frequency tags are required, increasing both the overall and deployment costs without substantial gain.

The accuracy of the *CN* method is akin to that observed for CID. It can only estimate the position of a resource at the exact position of its closest base station [16]. Although it has a good precision due to the iterative refining of the estimations, the size of the coverage area of outdoor scenarios renders this method's computing requirements almost unbearable for most computational equipment. Thus, powerful processing units are required. Despite, its overall cost remains low, although an important effort must be made during the setup and training of this method.

The accuracy of *LS* method is low due to the increased size of the coverage area. Since LS is an iterative process, small errors at early iterations adversely affect the final estimations. Its precision remains the same, though it cannot support too many targets due to the intense computational effort required to apply the minimizing function [24]. This method also requires an important effort during setup stages.

Table 2. Performance of proximity positioning methods in outdoor environments.

	ACC	PRE	SCA	COM	OC	DC	ROB
CID	Low	Low	High	Low	Low	Low	High
RFID	Low	High	Low	Low	Medium	High	Low
CN	Low	Medium	Low	High	Low	High	Low
LS	Low	Medium	Low	High	Low	High	Medium

4.3   Fingerprinting

Given the nature of fingerprinting, it is seldom used for outdoor positioning, due to scalability and complexity issues. For this reason, it has not been considered for comparison in this work, given that the overall score for complexity, deployment cost, and overall cost would have rendered the strategy unusable due to the size of the environment. A complete comparison of the performance of this technique for indoor and outdoor environments is part of the future work.

4.4   Vision Analysis

Although vision analysis can be applied to outdoor scenarios, its maximum effective coverage area is not large enough to compete with other methods. In addition, most SLAM-based proposals address navigation and mobility of robots, as well as resource tracking, both of which use coverage and ranges too small to be compared with other outdoor techniques. As with fingerprinting, a complete comparison will be provided in future work.

5   Related Work

Gu et al. [15] presents a set of indoor positioning systems, categorized based on how the position of a resource is estimated. For each system, they address their advantages, disadvantages, and limitations. Then, they provide an evaluation of single and hybrid methods' performance based on several metrics: security and privacy, cost, performance, robustness, complexity, user preference, availability, and limitations. Finally, they state hybrid systems improve the quality of positioning services, and then describe some of the current location sensing technologies and positioning projects in development at the time.

In their work, Ruiz-López et al. [19] provide a survey of various positioning techniques and technologies, showing their advantages and disadvantages based on what they call *functional requirements* (essentially, metrics). They believe the environment must be taken into account before deciding which strategy to use, and that positioning services should be based on interoperable components, allowing combining different techniques and the technologies that support them in order to build hybrid systems.

Liu et al. [6] elaborated an extensive survey on indoor positioning techniques and systems. They discuss three positioning techniques and some of the positioning methods used to implement them, describing several tradeoffs based on a performance measurement criteria. Then, they offer a review of positioning systems and solutions based on which technology is used by their authors (i.e., GPS-based, RFID-based or cellular-based). This taxonomy is condensed into a set of tables, showing the technology used, the algorithms, and the performance of each addressed solution.

Zeimpekis et al. [25] present an overview of positioning techniques, categorized based on where the positioning process is carried out (self-positioning or remote positioning). They follow with a discussion of potential mobile applications and services that would benefit from the use of positioning techniques. They also elaborate a taxonomy of indoor and outdoor positioning services, classifying them as Business-to-Consumer, and Business-to-Business. Finally, they discuss limitations and research challenges on mobile positioning techniques for indoor and outdoor environments.

The work of Kanaan et al. [16] presents a comparison of various geo-location algorithms for indoor scenarios. After describing these algorithms, they define *Channel Models* as the contextual conditions that introduce different amounts of errors to the measurements; these channel conditions are Line-of-Sight, Obstructed LOS and mix of them. A set of comparison tables for the reviewed algorithms for each channel condition is presented, with an evaluation of the performance of these algorithms in relation to the size of the indoor area over which a user is to be located.

Hightower et al. [3] provides a taxonomy for an easier evaluation of positioning systems. They define a set of metrics to evaluate their taxonomy (localized location computation capability, accuracy, precision, scale, recognition, cost, and limitations). These metrics are used to survey research and commercial positioning technologies. Finally, they establish that future work should focus on lowering cost, reducing deployment cost, improving scalability, and creating flexible systems more than on improving accuracy or precision.

The paper of Madigan et al. [26] presents an approach that allows the positioning estimation of multiple wireless clients based on a Bayesian hierarchical model. Although it works only on indoor scenarios with available wireless networks, its results are similar to those of other methods. The innovation of the method presented by Madigan is the introduction of a fully adaptive zero profiling approach to location estimation that can track multiple targets simultaneously. The approach allows incorporating specific types of prior knowledge to improve the positioning process and results.

6   Conclusions and Future Work

Positioning is an open field, full of research opportunities. The appearance of new technologies and scientific breakthroughs combined with the availability of wireless networks and mobile devices, allows for different practical applications of positioning services. This is especially true for mobile devices, particularly smartphones. Advertising companies have begun using the position of users to offer tailored services, and social networks allow users to publish location-associated content on the web. The growth in demand of positioning services, as well as the appearance of new technologies, makes positioning an area full of research opportunities.

This paper offers a survey of current positioning indoor and outdoor techniques and methods, and is intended to serve as a quick guide for researchers and software developers on common positioning techniques. A detailed description of most well-known methods of positioning is offered, classified based on the technique they use to estimate positions.

Using evaluation criteria based on proposed metrics, the performance of the reviewed methods on outdoor environments is presented. The comparison offered in Section 5 shows that every method has limitations, so tradeoffs must be established.

We believe that this comparison could allow developers to determine the best positioning technique for a given scenario, or at least the most suitable, given the conditions. Moreover, the comparison could help developers choose which techniques to combine into a single positioning system.

Future work includes an extension of this work, which provides a detailed outdoor performance comparison, as well as an indoor comparison for each reviewed positioning method. In addition, we could include a discussion on current research on new or hybrid positioning methods and how they could allow overcoming present limitations. Another area of interest would be the integration of indoor and outdoor scenarios, allowing for a single positioning system to track a target both indoors and outdoors using different positioning methods, depending on which are available.

7   References

1. Marmasse, N. ComMotion: a context-aware communication system. Proc. of the ACM CHI'99 extended abstracts on Human Factors in Computing Systems, pp. 320-321, Pittsburgh, Pennsylvania, (1999)
2. Mayorga, C.L.F., Della-Rosa, F., Wardana, S.A., Simone, G., Raynal, M.C.N., Figueiras, J., Frattasi, S. Cooperative positioning techniques for mobile localization in 4G cellular networks. IEEE International Conference on Pervasive Services, pp.39-44, (2007)
3. Hightower, J., Borriello, G. Location systems for ubiquitous computing. IEEE Computer, Vol. 34(8), pp. 57-66, (2001)
4. Hofmann-Wellenhof, B., Lichtenegger, H., Collins, J. Global Positioning System: Theory and Practice. Springer Press, Wien, Austria, (1993)
5. Ladd, A.M., Bekris, K.E., Rudys, A.P., Wallach, D.S., Kavraki, L.E. On the feasibility of using wireless ethernet for indoor localization. IEEE Transactions on Robotics and Automation, Vol.20(3), pp. 555-559, (2004)
6. Liu, H., Darabi, H., Banerjee, P., Liu, J. Survey of Wireless Indoor Positioning Techniques and Systems. Part C: Applications and Reviews, IEEE Transactions on Systems, Man, and Cybernetics, Vol. 37(6), pp. 1067-1080, (2007)
7. Vera, R., Ochoa, S.F., Aldunate, R.G. EDIPS: an Easy to Deploy Indoor Positioning System to support loosely coupled mobile work. Personal and Ubiquitous Computing, Vol. 15(4), pp. 365-376, (2011)
8. Fang, B.T. Simple solutions for hyperbolic and related position fixes. IEEE Transactions on Aerospace and Electronic Systems, Vol.26(5), pp. 748-753, (1990)
9. Günther, A., Hoene, C. Measuring round trip times to determine the distance between WLAN nodes. Proc. of the 4th IFIP-TC6 Int. Conf. on Networking Technologies, Services, and Protocols; Performance of Computer and Communication Networks; Mobile and Wireless Communication Systems, pp. 768-779, Waterloo, Canada, (2005)
10. Povalac, A., Šebesta, J. Phase of arrival ranging method for UHF RFID tags using instantaneous frequency measurement. Proc. of IEEE ICECom'10, pp. 1-4, (2010)
11. Ji, X.; Zha, H. Sensor positioning in wireless ad-hoc sensor networks using multidimensional scaling. Proc. of the 23th Annual Joint Conference of the IEEE Computer and Communications Societies (INFOCOM'04), Vol. 4, pp. 2652-2661, (2004)
12. Chen, J.C., Wang, Y.C., Maa, C.S., Chen, J.T. Network-side mobile position location using factor graphs, IEEE Transactions on Wireless Communications, Vol. 5(10), pp. 2696-2704, (2006)

13. Bravo, J., Hervás, R., Sánchez, I., Chavira, G., Nava, S. Visualization services in a conference context: an approach by RFID technology. Journal of Universal Computer Science, Vol. 12(3), pp. 270-283, (2006)
14. Trevisani, E., Vitaletti, A. Cell-ID location technique, limits and benefits: an experimental study. Proc. of the 6th IEEE Workshop on Mobile Computing Systems and Applications (WMCSA'04), pp. 51-60, (2004).
15. Gu, Y., Lo, A., Niemegeers, I. A survey of indoor positioning systems for wireless personal networks. IEEE Communications Surveys & Tutorials, Vol. 11(1), pp. 13-32, (2009)
16. Kanaan, M.; Pahlavan, K. A comparison of wireless geolocation algorithms in the indoor environment. Proc. of the IEEE Wireless Communications and Networking Conference WCNC'04, Vol. 1, pp. 177-182, (2004)
17. Brumitt, B., Meyers, B., Krumm, J., Kern, A., Shafer, S. Easyliving: Technologies for intelligent environments. Handheld and ubiquitous computing, Springer Press, pp. 97-119, (2000)
18. Montemerlo, M., Thrun, S., Koller, D., Wegbreit, B. FastSLAM: a factored solution to the simultaneous localization and mapping problem. Proc. of the 18th National Conference on Artificial intelligence, pp. 593-598, (2002)
19. Ruiz-López, T., Garrido, J., Benghazi, K., Chung, L. A survey on indoor positioning systems: foreseeing a quality design. Distributed Computing and Artificial Intelligence, pp. 373-380, (2010)
20. Vossiek, M., Wiebking, L., Gulden, P., Wieghardt, J., Hoffmann, C., Heide, P. Wireless local positioning. IEEE Microwave Magazine, Vol. 4(4), pp. 77-86, (2003)
21. Mountain, D., Raper, J. Positioning techniques for location-based services (LBS): characteristics and limitations of proposed solutions. Aslib proceedings, Vol. 53(10), pp. 404-412, (2001)
22. Cheng, X., Thaeler, A., Xue, G., Chen D. TPS: a time-based positioning scheme for outdoor wireless sensor networks. Proc. of the 23th Annual Joint Conference of the IEEE Computer and Communications Societies (INFOCOM'04), Vol. 4, pp. 2685- 2696, (2004)
23. Van-Diggelen, F., Abraham, C. Indoor GPS technology. CTIA Wireless-Agenda 2001, Dallas, (2001)
24. Cong, L., Zhuang, W. Hybrid TDOA/AOA mobile user location for wideband CDMA cellular systems. IEEE Transactions on Wireless Communications, Vol. 1(3), pp. 439-447, (2002)
25. Zeimpekis, V., Giaglis, G.M., Lekakos, G. A taxonomy of indoor and outdoor positioning techniques for mobile location services. ACM SIGecom Exchanges, Vol. 3(4), pp. 19-27, (2002)
26. Madigan, D., Elnahrawy, E., Martin, R.P., Ju, W.H., Krishnan, P. Bayesian Indoor Positioning Systems. Proceedings of the 24th Annual Joint Conference of the IEEE Computer and Communications Societies (INFOCOM'05), Vol. 2, pp. 1217-1227, (2005)

Scientific Paper Recommendations
More Than Just a Single Task

Laura Pilz

Peakwork AG, Rheinallee 9, 40549 Düsseldorf, Germany
laura.pilz@peakwork.com

Abstract. The last decade was marked by the development of an abundance of recommender systems for scientific papers. But nearly all of these systems treat the recommendation of scientific papers as a single task without differentiating between different use cases. Accordingly, requirements for desired recommendations are not specified. This paper identifies and discusses problems of paper recommender systems and addresses them by describing several metrics. With these metrics, different recommendation tasks can be clearly defined and differentiated.

Keywords: Recommender Systems · Scientific Paper Recommender Systems

1 Introduction

Today, more than 200 scientific papers exist that address the task of recommending scientific papers [1]. Yet the research is still in its early stages. Beel et al. identified several problems in the existing works. For example, algorithms and systems are hard to compare to one another as implementations are often unknown and no gold standard dataset exists. Moreover, the used evaluations are often flawed as well [2].

But a problem not addressed in the above mentioned literature surveys is that many of the existing papers concern the problem of *scientific paper recommendation* – without specifying what purpose the recommendations should serve. Yet I argue that *recommending scientific papers* is not a single task but a conglomerate of related ones. And trying to devise an algorithm that shines at every one of them is a futile attempt, as findings by Torres et al. indicate [7].

2 Related Work

Few scientific papers on paper recommender systems indicate the existence of different recommendation tasks. In a study by Torres et al. [7] users were presented with different recommended papers and were asked to characterize each paper as *novel, introductory, survey / overview, authoritative, specialized,* or a combination of these. The papers characterized by the users had been generated by various algorithms. As a result of this study it was shown that different algorithms produced recommendations that were characterized differently.

In studies by McNee et al. [3] [4] users were also asked to assign the recommended papers attributes.

In a few other papers different recommendation tasks are addressed more specifically. In [4] study participants selected one of four recommendation tasks at the beginning of a study for which recommendations were then generated and evaluated. Unfortunately, the results of the compared algorithms are not reported separately but are combined for all tasks. This implies the aim of devising an allrounder algorithm that excels at any recommendation task. In another study [8] participants were also asked to select one of four recommendation tasks.

Many other papers seem to be unaware that recommending scientific papers is not a single task. When describing the task their system should accomplish one can often find generic phrases such as "help[ing] users sort through the abundance of available research and find papers of interest" [7, p. 228]. What exactly *papers of interest* are is not specified.

From personal experience I believe that these shortcomings are often based on a lack of experience in the specific research area. In the first study I conducted on paper recommender systems I also overlooked the necessity to differentiate between different recommendation tasks [6]. Similarly, the majority of the authors of scientific papers on scientific paper recommender systems only wrote one paper on the topic [1].

3 Definition of Tasks with Metrics

Given that the wording *recommending scientific papers* encompasses multiple tasks, tools are needed with which these tasks can be defined. For this I propose the use of metrics.

Using a set of metrics, tasks could be specified with the aid of user studies. Moreover, if the characteristics of recommender algorithms were measured with the same metrics, it would make the comparison of different algorithms much easier and more reliable.

Note that two kinds of metrics should be distinguished: Those that describe the characteristics of a single paper and those that describe the characteristics of a set of papers.

3.1 Examples of Tasks

Depending on the purpose for which the recommended papers shall be used, different tasks can be distinguished. In the following all recipients of the recommended papers are scientists. The following list contains examples for what purposes recommended papers can be used.

- Aquiring a coarse overview of a scientific field / topic, e.g. when beginning to conduct research in an area
  - Recommended papers should cover different aspects of the field

- The whole set of recommendations is of importance
- Answering a specific question
  - Recommended papers can be similar, contain redundant information
  - A single good recommendation can be sufficient
- Finding a paper that backs up a claim, e.g. to use as a citation in a paper
  - Recommended papers can be similar, contain redundant information
  - Well known, often cited papers are to be preferred
  - A single good recommendation can be sufficient
- Brainstorming to find new research ideas
  - The recommended papers should be diverse, e.g. in their topics
  - It might be beneficial to recommend newly published papers
- Staying up to date on a specific topic
  - The newest papers should be preferred

3.2 Existing Metrics

In [5] I defined metrics that measure the following three criteria:

- *Diversity* of a set of papers
- *Coverage* of a set of papers
- *Prototypicality* of a single paper

Diversity The diversity of a set of scientific papers denotes whether the papers cover the same topic or not. The more the covered topics differ, the more diverse the papers are.

Coverage Given a scientific topic T and a set of subtopics S that together make up topic T. The *coverage* of a set of papers P with regard to topic T is proportional to the extent by which the subtopics S are addressed by papers in P. Note that this notion of coverage differs from the definition often used in evaluating recommender systems.

The notions of coverage and diversity are related, but not two sides of the same coin: Coverage is defined in relation to a specific topic, whereas diversity is not limited to a single topic. Although most often a set of papers with a high coverage will also be diverse, this is not necessarily the case. For example, a set of papers can have a high coverage and yet a low diversity if each paper alone has a high coverage of a certain topic and every paper covers the same subtopics.

Prototypicality The *prototypicality* of a single research paper denotes in how far it is a representative of a specific research line. For example, the first paper written by a group of authors on a topic is no representative as no other research by the same authors on this topic exists yet. However, a later paper can be representative of a succession of papers if it is the intellectual descendant of the previous papers and summarizes previous findings.

3.3 Further Metrics

However, not every possible task can be adequately characterized with metrics that measure the above given three criteria. Further criteria, and therefore other metrics, are needed. In the following ideas for further criteria and ideas to measure them are presented.

Novelty The *novelty* of a single scientific paper denotes in how far the paper contains new ideas. While it is hard to detect a masterstroke, ideas may also be novel for the target audience. Thus, ideas or theories taken from other research fields to a new realm may also be considered novel. The latter might be measured by examining the interdisciplinarity of the citation graph of the paper in question. In graph theory a cut vertex is a vertex that when deleted increases the number of components in the graph. In the context of a citation network, such a vertex would connect two or more components – research areas – and would thus form the interdisciplinary junction between them. This is illustrated in Fig. 1.

Such a metric could be used to measure the novelty of a single paper p. Note that it would need to use the undirected citation network up to the point in time at which the paper p was published. Later papers must not be considered, because if p started an interdisciplinary exchange, the two research communities might be connected via other papers published after p.

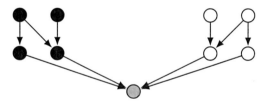

Fig. 1. The vertices in this graph represent papers. The edges denote the *is cited by* relation. The gray vertex is a cut vertex, because if it were deleted the graph would disintegrate into two weakly connected components – the white and the black vertices.

Comprehensibility Another characteristic worth investigating is the comprehensibility of scientific papers. For example, this could be used to tailor recommended papers to a target group, e.g. Bachelor students, professors from the same field or researchers from another discipline. A metric could make use of the distance of the cited papers in the citation graph to determine the level of detail of the topic covered by a specific paper. For example, a paper that provides an overview can be expected to cite papers that are several citations away from one another. In contrast, a research paper on a very specific topic might cite papers that are also directly linked via citations among another. This is illustrated in Fig. 2.

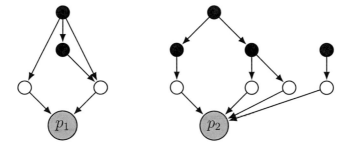

Fig. 2. The vertices in this graph represent papers. The edges denote the *is cited by* relation. The papers cited by paper p_1 – the white vertices on the left – are more directly connected among themselves than the papers cited by paper p_2 – the white vertices on the right.

4 Conclusion

In order to maximize the advantage of metrics for the field of scientific paper recommender systems, three main research goals need to be met.

1. Further metrics have to be defined and evaluated in user studies to verify that they measure the intended criteria.
2. Recommendation tasks have to be defined with metrics with the aid of user studies.
3. Existing algorithms have to be characterized by a common set of metrics in order to be comparable.

With these three steps, several shortcomings the community is suffering from today might be overcome: The incomparability of recommendation algorithms and the focus on accuracy as the sole used measure in evaluations, as described in [1].

References

1. Beel, J., Gipp, B., Langer, S., Breitinger, C.: Research-paper recommender systems: a literature survey. International Journal on Digital Libraries pp. 1–34 (2015)
2. Beel, J., Langer, S., Genzmehr, M., Gipp, B., Breitinger, C., Nürnberger, A.: Research paper recommender system evaluation: a quantitative literature survey. In: Proceedings of the International Workshop on Reproducibility and Replication in Recommender Systems Evaluation. pp. 15–22. ACM (2013)
3. McNee, S.M., Albert, I., Cosley, D., Gopalkrishnan, P., Lam, S.K., Rashid, A.M., Konstan, J.A., Riedl, J.: On the recommending of citations for research papers. In: Proceedings of the 2002 ACM conference on Computer supported cooperative work. pp. 116–125. ACM (2002)
4. McNee, S.M., Kapoor, N., Konstan, J.A.: Don't look stupid: avoiding pitfalls when recommending research papers. In: Proceedings of the 2006 20th anniversary conference on Computer supported cooperative work. pp. 171–180. ACM (2006)

5. Steinert, L.: Beyond Similarity and Accuracy - A New Take on Automating Scientific Paper Recommendations. Verlag Dr. Hut (2017)
6. Steinert, L., Chounta, I., Hoppe, H.U.: Where to begin? Using network analytics for the recommendation of scientific papers. In: Collaboration and Technology - 21st International Conference, CRIWG 2015, Yerevan, Armenia, September 22-25, 2015, Proceedings. pp. 124–139 (2015)
7. Torres, R., McNee, S.M., Abel, M., Konstan, J.A., Riedl, J.: Enhancing digital libraries with techlens+. In: Proceedings of the 4th ACM/IEEE-CS joint conference on Digital libraries. pp. 228–236. ACM (2004)
8. Woodruff, A., Gossweiler, R., Pitkow, J., Chi, E.H., Card, S.K.: Enhancing a digital book with a reading recommender. In: Proceedings of the SIGCHI conference on Human Factors in Computing Systems. pp. 153–160. ACM (2000)

Toward Reliable Visual Analytics

Benjamin Weyers

RWTH Aachen University and JARA-HPC, Aachen, Germany

weyers@vr.rwth-aachen.de

Abstract. Since visual analytics software underlies the same restrictions and conditions as every interactive system, this software has to consider usability, user experience and requirements issued by the human in the loop. Additionally, visualization itself needs to address such aspects as visual integrity, thus the visualization should represent the data exclusively and support the users without misleading them. In this work, we present a conceptual framework to define and measure reliability of visual analytics. By means of an example, we present the potential and use of the framework. Future work will address the use of formal models of user interfaces as well as further refinement of the framework.

Keywords: Reliability · Visual analytics · Interactive data analysis · Visualization · Quality criteria · Empirical estimation

1   Introduction

Visual analytics aims at "…visually represent[ing] information, allowing the human to directly interact with it, to gain insight, to draw conclusions, and to ultimately make better decisions" [1, p. 9]. Thus, visual analytics addresses three major topics. First, the visual representation of information or data is considered, which is investigated and developed in the broad research area of visualization [2]. Second, interactivity is a crucial element, which might address the visualization directly, as in case of adapting the camera position in a 3D visualization or the filtering of the data, for example to filter out certain data points in the visualized data set and make them invisible, or operation on a higher abstraction layer such as in case of multi-view application if the user needs to configure or setup a more complex visualization environment. Both, visual representation and interactivity should lead to the third major topic which is the user's interpretation of the presented data, which is a research area addressing cognitive psychology and perception [14].

Visual analytics tools can be interpreted as an interactive computing system, which has the specific characteristic that in the implemented control loop, the human user is involved. Don Norman describes this human-in-the-loop paradigm by his human action cycle [3]. A crucial part in Norman's work is his discussion of the *gulf of execution* and *the gulf of evaluation* (as shown in Figure 1). Both gulfs characterize a potential gap between the users' mental model (including their mental state and their knowledge) and the interactive system used in context of the users' task. The user needs to understand the current system state as well as the available set of operations implemented in the system's internal functional core, which is presented by the user interface to the users.

For example, the users might have a certain goal in mind but their mental model of the system's state might be wrong because the interpretation of the perceived system values presented on the user interface is wrong or incomplete (*gulf of evaluation*). Another example might be that the user wants the system to execute a certain operation but unfortunately presses a wrong button (*gulf of execution*).

If this is mapped back to visual analytics applications, the gulf of evaluation becomes very critical as this results in a wrong interoperation and thus an error-prone model of the visualized data. Considering that visual analytics is meant to support the user "...to gain insight, to draw conclusions, and to ultimately make better decisions" [1, p. 9] (see above), the gulf of evaluation may prohibit or even corrupt the interpretation of the visualization. In the worst case, the visualization breaks visual integrity as has been characterized by Tufte [4] with the so called *lie factor*. The lie factor relates the effect present in the data to the size of the graphical element representing it. For instance, consider two data points with the values 1 and 2 in the data set, which might be represented by squares with 1 and 2 cm edge length, respectively. This results in a lie factor of 4 as the value is represented with an area of 4 cm^2 (thus 4 times the size of the 1 cm^2) compared to the present effect of 2-1=1. Beyond the lie factor, visual integrity should also address the mapping of data to more complex spatial geometries and structures. This asks for a throughout extension of Tufte's definition of visual integrity, which we plan to investigate in future work.

To control the system and to apply any kind of operation influencing the visualization, all rules of usability and user experience need to be applied to prevent or minimize the gulf of execution. Thus, if these basic rules are not followed, visual analytics software tools might get unusable, generate unhelpful or even wrong results, which contradict with the original goal of these tools of supporting the scientific process.

Considering the full scientific process [5], the requirements for visual analytics tools get even stronger and harder to handle as visual analytics is only one element in a much bigger iterative process (see Figure 1) which includes various types of data producers (such as simulator) or data providers (as data sets), complex data processing pipelines, as well as the need for producing a scientific publication. Especially the latter is often neglected although scientific fields which are strongly driven by data sciences do not only ask for reproducible data, simulations and data analysis processes, which is often addressed by provenance tracking and metadata, but for reproducible visualizations and figures as these represent scientific evidence in various publications [6].

The general problem of reproducibility of results gained from visual analytics has been identified in the visualization community as can be seen from various existing works that consider provenance tracking for visual analytics processes [7, 8]. However, these solutions focus on tracking the analysis process and making it reproducible in the sense of a replay. They either depend on a strong embedding into a software framework [8] or rely on a reliable implementation of tracking code in the visual analytics application [7]. None of these approaches consider methods and tools enabling any type of validation of such applications as developed in the field of engineering of interactive systems, specifically those that use formal methods [9]. Beside validation or verification, formal methods also support the design, development and adaption of interactive systems. Because we are convinced that these methods are equally applicable to visual analytics applications, this work introduces the concept of *reliable visual analytics*. It specifies a conceptual framework that characterizes the general challenge of unreliability of visual analytics application if the user in the loop and the type of visualization method are considered. Therefore, Section 2 gives a detailed introduction into this conceptual framework, where Section 3 presents an example of an immersive visualization tool. This example shows how the measures defined in context of the framework are mapped to a specific application. The example is followed by a short discussion of our observations. We conclude the paper with a short summary and a discussion of future steps (Section 4).

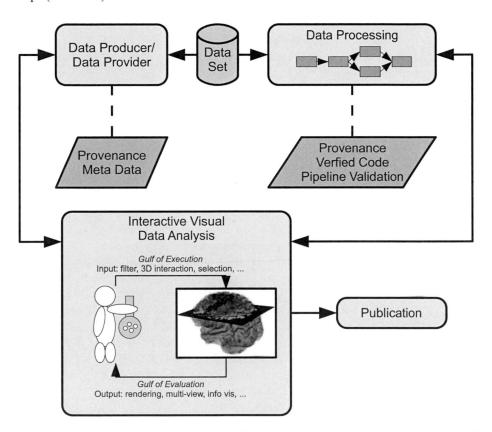

Fig. 1. Scientific and data driven process including data sources and providers, the application of data processing methods as well as interactive visual data analytics tools. The final outcome should be a publication including the obtained results.

2 Reliable Visual Analysis

The general goal of the reliable visual analysis framework is to offer a set of quality criteria (QC) that can be instantiated by an empirical estimation gathered in, for instance, a collaborative work in which users (of various levels of experience) rate the subjective reliability of the inspected visual analytics application. Additionally, formal descriptions and models of the application's entities add an objective layer to the empirical reliability analysis since such models can be used to validate the system against requirements. Thus, *reliability* in this work can be defined as *the degree of accuracy of the user's mental model representing the visualized data*. Beyond the aspect of *visual integrity* as defined by Tufte (see above), reliability considers the *user interface* as well as the *interactive analysis process* implemented by this user interface. This is crucial for visual analytics as it defines the potential *exploration space* (defined as set of all possible interactive analysis processes) implemented by the user interface and thus by the set of operations offered by the visual analytics application and its dialog model. All three reliability dimensions, *visual integrity* (VI), *user interface* (UI), and *interactive analysis process* (IP), are embedded into the context of the user's task, experience, goals and organizational context in which the analysis takes place. This embedding is done by gathering of subjective estimations of the QCs mapped to the dimensions during using the tool solving a representative analysis problem in the working context and organization. Thus, by empirically estimating representative QCs along the three dimensions of reliable visual analytics, the outcome will be an estimation of the reliability of the visual analysis tool under consideration.

Considering the previous discussion, we identified the following three QCs as a first step towards a complete set of criteria. The semantics of the QCs depend on their interpretation in the context of each individual reliability dimension. Their characterizations directly lead to the measures described further below.

- **Accuracy (AC)** may be defined as *the potential of error prevention the visual analytics system offers*. Depending on the reliability dimensions, *accuracy* may address correctness of the user's interpretation (in case of VI), usability of the user interface considering the analysis task (in case of UI), or robustness if it comes to the execution of operation sequences such that the visual analytics system offers all necessary operations when needed such that interaction errors are prevented (in case of IP).
- **Adequacy (AD)**: may be defined as *the level of suitability of the visual analytics system for the general analysis question*. Depending on the reliability dimensions, *adequacy* may address the quality of the mapping of data to their visual representation (in case of VI) or the suitability of provided operations (e.g. in number) of the user interface considering the user's task (in case of UI and EF).
- **Efficiency (EF)**: may be defined as *the performance the visual analytics systems enables for the general analysis question*. Depending on the reliability dimensions, *efficiency* may address how easy the visualization can be read (in case of VI), how simple to use the user interface (in case of UI), and fast an analysis workflow can be executed using the visual analytics system (in case of IP).

This mapping of QCs to the three reliability dimensions result in a matrix shown in Figure 2, where each combination of reliability dimension and quality criteria is mapped to a set of specific *measures*. These have to be determined with the previously outlined empirical approach for a given visual analytics application. In the following, we present more details on the various measures. Therefore, we use the outlined abbreviations in Figure 2, such that for [RD|QC]M, RD is the reliability dimension, QC the quality criteria and M the addressed measure.

- **[VI|AC]Correctness**: This measure addresses the degree of correctness of the visual representation of values in the considered data set, a constraint for visual integrity. For instance, representing the value 4 with a visual representation for 5 would render to low correctness. Nevertheless, correctness may also be defined in a way that uncertainty in the data is mapped to a visual representation in such a way that the user is able to correctly interpret this uncertainty in context of the data point and the whole data set.
- **[VI|AC]Mapping**: This measure represents the reciprocal of Tufte's lie factor and thus is the sufficient condition for visual integrity.
- **[VI|AD]Mapping**: This measure is similar to that of [VI|AC]Mapping but with a stronger focus on the addressed task the user wants to solve.
- **[VI|AD]Layout**: This measure quantifies how adequate the design of a visualization is for a given task.
- **[VI|EF]Readability**: This measure is the reciprocal of visual clutter, which occurs if the visualization is overloaded such as in case of very complex graphs rendered in limited screen space.
- **[VI|EF]Layout**: This measure also takes the task into account, because the visualization itself should be structured such that the relevant content for a certain task is easily recognizable.
- **[UI|AC]Readability**: This measure quantifies how easy the user interface is to perceive or "read".
- **[UI|AC]Intuitiveness**: This measure quantifies the level of the intuitiveness of the user interface, which for instance represents how easy it is to identify the right operation/widget for a specific sub-task the user wants to execute.
- **[UI|AC]Ergonomics**: Depending on the user's task, this measure quantifies how good the user interface design is with respect to, for instance, reachability of widgets or operations. Additionally, ergonomics refers to the quality of the types of input and output devices used, for example, how heavy a hand-held input device is or how intrusive a display is (e.g., the weight of a head mounted display).
- **[UI|AD]Perceivability**: This measure represents a quantification of how simple it is to find a certain widget or element the user is looking for depending on the task.
- **[UI|AD]Usability**: This measure addresses the fulfillment of ISO 9241-11 on usability with a focus on addressing a certain task.
- **[UI|EF]Usability**: This measure addresses the fulfillment of ISO 9241-11 on usability with a focus on efficiency of completing a certain task.
- **[UI|EF]UserExperience**: This measure addresses the fulfillment of user experience requirements and measures.
- **[IP|AC]Intuitiveness**: The measure is equivalent to [UI|AC]Intuitiveness but addressing the analysis process.
- **[IP|AC]Learnability**: The measure is equivalent to [UI|AC]Learnability but addressing the analysis process.

- **[IP|AC]Robustness**: This measure is addressing the aspect of how robust the tool is regarding wrong user input etc. For instance, if the user changes the camera position wrongly, the tool should enable to the user to undo this change.
- **[IP|AD]Complexity**: The potential interaction sequences should as complex as required to the needs of the user's task and the user's experience. A too high complexity might lead to frustration and errors, a too low complexity may lead to a lower level of concentration which might lead to missing operations such that the task cannot be finished.
- **[IP|AD]Structure**: Similar to complexity, this measure addresses the overall structure of the interaction space defined by the tool's interaction process/dialog.
- **[IP|AD]Mapping**: This measure addresses in how far the mapping of the user's task to operation sequence is adequate for that specific task.
- **[IP|EF]Sequence Length**: This measure describes the needed number of operations to finish a given task. A specific measure could be the number of mouse clicks needed or the number and complexity (measured, e.g., in time) of gestures.
- **[IP|EF]Usability**: The measure is equivalent to [UI|AC] but addressing the analysis process.
- **[IP|EF]UserExperience**: The measure is equivalent to [UI|AC] but addressing the analysis process.

Quality Criteria ⟍ Reliability	Accuracy [AC]	Adequacy [AD]	Efficiency [EF]
Visual Integrity [VI]	- Correctness - Mapping	- Mapping - Design	- Readability - Layout
User Interface [UI]	- Readability - Intuitiveness - Ergonomics	- Perceivability - Usability	- Usability - UX
Interaction Process/ Dialog [IP]	- Intuitiveness - Learnability - Robustness	- Complexity - Structure - Mapping	- Seq. Length - Usability - UX

Fig. 2. Measure matrix to characterize reliable visual analytics by means of three reliability dimensions and by means of quality criteria of a visual analytics application.

This set of measures is a first draft and might be extended and refined in future work. In the next section, we present a first example that illustrate how these measures may be applied to a specific visual analytics tool.

3 Example and Discussion

Immersive data analysis is a field of research in the context of visual analytics and interactive visualization that focuses on the use of virtual reality hardware and methods to allow researchers to visually inspect data using *stereoscopic rendering*, *head tracking* and *multi-modal spatial interaction*. In neuroscience, various types of spatial data is collected and gets analyzed. Major research subject is the brain, which is a very complex three dimensional structure. Thus, the working hypothesis is that immersive analytics helps the visual inspection and analysis of this type of data, either gathered by experiments or simulations. Various examples exist which use VR as interface for visual analysis of neuroscientific data, such as VisNEST [10] or BrainX³ [11]. Taking VisNEST as an example, VisNEST's major visualization component provides a geometric rendering of the macaque monkey's brain including individual geometries for the brain areas of the monkey's visual cortex. The visualized data originates from a NEST [12] simulation of a model of the visual cortex [13] and represents the activity of the neurons in a dedicated area as times series in the resolution of the simulation's time steps.

Based on VisNEST, we will specify the relevant aspects of this visualization according to some measures as outlined in the matrix presented in Figure 2. Suppose the user wants to start or stop the animation to inspect the activity in the brain areas in more detail. In an efficient user interface ([UI|EF]), a widget might be part of the virtual environment such as a 3D slider. However, if it is too small (resulting in low [UI|AC]Readability & [UI|AC]Ergonomic) it will be hard to use, such that [UI|EF]Usability will be low. Another example might be that the used colors for representing the activity of a brain area are not well perceived, for instance due to color blindness issues of the user. This would lead to low [VI|AD]Mapping as well as [VI|EF]Readability. A final example is the function to interactively reposition the various area geometries, allowing the user to look into the structure. If the tool would not offer a reset function such that all area's position get reset to the original position, the visualization might get cluttered, which leads to lower [VI|EF]Layout and [VI|EF]Readability values.

All these examples show potential steps to influence the visual reliability of the presented visualization. What is currently missing is a specific quantification, which is led to future work. Additionally, we plan to investigate in more detail how formal methods of modeling user interfaces might help and to compute a quantification of the various measures not only during usage but also during design time.

4   Summary

This work presents ongoing research on the development of a conceptual framework for the characterization of reliability of visual analytics. We presented a general overview of the problem domain and identified the potential error-prone mental representations a user gathers during an interactive and visual analysis of a data set. Due to this problem, we defined the term of reliability in visual analytics and characterized it by means of three major dimensions: visual integrity, user interface, and the interaction process. Additional dimensions, quality criteria and measures will be developed and investigated in future work. By means of three major quality criteria, we presented a set of measures that can be used either in the empirical analysis including the user or by defining analysis methods for formal models describing the user interface, the task, the user, or the possible dialog. Finally, we presented an example of an immersive visualization application of computational neuroscience. With this example, we highlighted some aspects of the tool and show how the measures might be used to estimate the reliability of this specific tool.

As previously outlined, our future work will focus on further investigation of the presented measures and on the empirical study design to gather data. Additionally, we will further investigate how formal methods of interaction can be facilitated and generate data for the measures. Finally, we will formalize the presented framework to enable comparability of visual analytics methods to a certain degree and to enable tool support as far as possible.

References

1. Keim, D. A., Mansmann, F., Schneidewind, J., & Ziegler, H. (2006). Challenges in visual data analysis. In Information Visualization, 2006. IV 2006. Tenth International Conference on (pp. 9-16). IEEE.
2. Kirk, A. (2016). Data visualisation: a handbook for data driven design. Sage.
3. Norman, D. (1988). The Design of Everyday Things, 1988 New York, Doubleday/Currency Ed. ISBN 0-465-06709-3
4. Tufte, E. (1991). The Visual Display of Quantitative Information, Second Edition, Graphics Press, USA, 1991, p. 57 – 69.
5. Senk, J., Yegenoglu, A., Amblet, O., Brukau, Y., Davison, A., Lester, D.R., Lührs, A., Quaglio, P., Rostami, V., Rowley, A., Schuller, B., Stokes, A.B., van Albada, S.J., Zielasko, D., Diesmann, M., Weyers, B., Denker, M., Grün, S. (2016). A Collaborative Simulation-Analysis Workflow for Computational Neuroscience Using HPC. In Jülich Aachen Research Alliance (JARA) High-Performance Computing Symposium (pp. 243-256). Springer, Cham.
6. Senk, J., Carde, C., Hagen, E., Kuhlen, T. W., Diesmann, M., & Weyers, B. (2018). VIOLA-A multi-purpose and web-based visualization tool for neuronal-network simulation output. arXiv preprint arXiv:1803.10205.
7. Hänel, C., Khatami, M., Kuhlen, T. W., & Weyers, B. (2016). Towards Multiuser Provenance Tracking of Visual Analysis Workflows over Multiple Applications. In Proc. of EG EuroVis Workshop on Reproducibility, Verification, and Validation in Visualization.

8. Silva, C. T., Freire, J., & Callahan, S. P. (2007). Provenance for visualizations: Reproducibility and beyond. Computing in Science & Engineering, 9(5).

9. Weyers, B., Bowen, J., Dix, A., & Palanque, P. (Eds.). (2017). The handbook of formal methods in human-computer interaction. Springer International Publishing.

10. Nowke, C., Schmidt, M., van Albada, S. J., Eppler, J. M., Bakker, R., Diesmann, M., Hentschel, B. & Kuhlen, T. (2013). VisNEST—Interactive analysis of neural activity data. In Biological Data Visualization (BioVis), 2013 IEEE Symposium on (pp. 65-72). IEEE.

11. Betella, A., Cetnarski, R., Zucca, R., Arsiwalla, X. D., Martinez, E., Omedas, P., Mura, A. & Verschure, P. F. (2014). BrainX³: embodied exploration of neural data. In Proceedings of the 2014 Virtual Reality International Conference (p. 37). ACM.

12. Gewaltig, M. O., & Diesmann, M. (2007). Nest (neural simulation tool). Scholarpedia, 2(4), 1430.

13. Schmidt, M., Bakker, R., Diesmann, M., & van Albada, S. J. (2015). Construction of a multi-scale spiking model of macaque visual cortex. ArXiv e-prints.

14. Spence, R. (2001). Information visualization (Vol. 1). New York: Addison-Wesley.

Towards Human-Centered Paradigms in Verification and Validation Assessment

Ekaterina Auer[1], Wolfram Luther[2]

[1] Department of Electrical Engineering, University of Applied Sciences Wismar
ekaterina.auer@hs-wismar.de
[2] Computer Science and Applied Cognitive Science, University of Duisburg-Essen
wolfram.luther@uni-due.de

Abstract. In this paper, we aim at widening the focus of the scientific computations community from one of reliable numerical algorithms and efficient implementations using standardized arithmetic to a broad user-centered system modeling approach and validation design. A four-tier verification and validation (V&V) management procedure proposed in [1] makes a first step in this direction. It does not only define requirements for classification of systems and processes as a result of precise assessment procedures, but also addresses user support with the help of appropriate recommending techniques and user interaction via adequate human machine interfaces. Modern applications generate huge amounts of heterogeneous input and output data and usually exhibit high complexity. Dealing with these challenges requires novel visual and collaborative approaches to interpret the results, which has to be accounted for in the general V&V procedure. We propose to use reliable visual analytics (VA) as a solution to this task. This analysis needs to go along with an assessment of (meta-)data and code quality, with a choice of adequate data types, with selection of methods to propagate and bound uncertainty and, lastly, with formally rigorous validation efforts. Collaborative outcome analytics done by various stakeholders with multiple expertise should be a precondition for system model evaluation, problem solving and corresponding follow-up actions. We illustrate the general ideas with the help of use cases implementing relevant parts of the proposed enhanced V&V assessment[1].

Keywords: Verification and validation assessment · accurate modeling and simulation systems · reliable collaborative visual analytics · data quality assessment

1 Introduction

Employment of ambient intelligence (AmI) can be advantageous for both application designers and their users. For example, ambient assisted living (AAL) systems with AmI support people in their surroundings based on information gathered and used for inference by corresponding devices or their networks. Nowadays, such environments deal with a wide spectrum of tasks, for instance, those at peoples' homes, from the

---

[1]   Cf. publications and projects SCG: http://www.scg.inf.uni-due.de/

areas of elderly care or general healthcare, pertaining to commerce and business, to museums and other leisure activities as well as to group decision-making [2]. Apart from the obvious societal concerns about privacy loss, a number of technical difficulties must be overcome before such systems can fulfill all the various requirements and are really appreciated by the relevant stakeholders of the process to be enhanced by AmI. Among these difficulties are the challenges posed by huge amounts of gathered heterogeneous data or by the necessity to develop adequate sensor networks and new communication protocols for smart grids. Moreover, novel concepts are needed for collaborative human computer interaction based on new task (meta-)models for post-WIMP (windows, icons, menus, pointer) devices, for solving appropriate user awareness, security and privacy issues or for providing satisfactory user experience. Smart city applications and smart environments together with the Internet of Things and reliable cloud computing technologies supporting mobile users in all areas of daily life must guarantee excellent performance, high data integrity, privacy, network security and accuracy in the outcome of algorithms, especially if human health is threatened.

To fulfill these requirements, it is essential that a modern verification and validation assessment includes appropriate user interaction and recommending services based on adaptive criteria. In 2009, the authors proposed a four-tier numerical V&V taxonomy refined in [1] that demarcated a first step in this direction. The lowest class in this taxonomy requires only the use of a standardized floating or fixed point arithmetic and detailed documentation of the results. The remaining higher classes take into account the fidelity of the model translation into a programming language, the degree to which uncertainty is quantified and propagated throughout the system, the availability of reliable error bounds for algorithms or the use of tools with result verification for (parts of) the whole system. Here, the term validation concerns the process of determining the degree to which a computer-based model is an accurate representation of the real world and is appropriate for its purpose. It can be carried out using special metrics that help to establish the similarity degree to real life or to compare reconstructed objects and their behavior with the real world instances. Verification is necessary to ensure that the implementation of the developed model of a system or a process and its result are correct. The major difference of the approach advocated in [1] to usual V&V methodologies is at this verification level. It is suggested to perform result verification for the appropriately prepared (parts) of a system or a process directly using methods such as interval analysis in cases where complete code verification or finding formal theoretical proofs is too difficult. Important factors for this analysis are, among others, the type of processed data, (inter-)action logic and hardware architecture.

In Figure 1, the traditional modeling and simulation cycle in engineering [3] is shown along with the accompanying V&V activities and uncertainty management. Additionally, we demonstrate where in this cycle features based on human-centered paradigms need to be introduced in order to deal with the challenges mentioned at the beginning of this section. One such additional feature concerns so-called visual analytics (VA): Huge amounts of heterogeneous input/output data and high system complexity of modern AmI applications require developing new data quality solutions to collect, prepare and organize input data complemented by visual and collaborative analytics (VA) to interpret the results.

Advanced data and visual analytics for sense-making in big data environments mainly rely on quality assessment, on awareness of data provenance and characteristics as well as on safety, security and privacy assurance. For example, Cai and Zhu [4] describe a dynamic assessment process based on a two-layer big data quality standard.

At the first level, there are five important assessment dimensions: availability, usability, reliability, relevance, and presentation quality. Reliability consists at the second level of accuracy, integrity, consistency, completeness and auditability. The last term means that it is possible for auditors to evaluate accuracy and integrity of data fairly. Another example is the publication by Blytt [5], in which the author emphasizes the frequently referred three Vs (volume, velocity, variety) as the biggest barrier to sense-making of big data. Veracity, validity, volatility and value are mentioned as further assessment factors and the big data value chain is highlighted as comprising data discovery, integration and exploitation. Moreover, advantages and challenges of VA methods are described, which is important not only in the context of big data, but also of system evaluation. Finally, "interaction in the context of VA" and "the need for collaborative analysis" are emphasized. In [6], VA is described as combining automated analysis techniques with interactive visualizations for an effective understanding, reasoning and decision-making on the basis of a very large and complex data set.

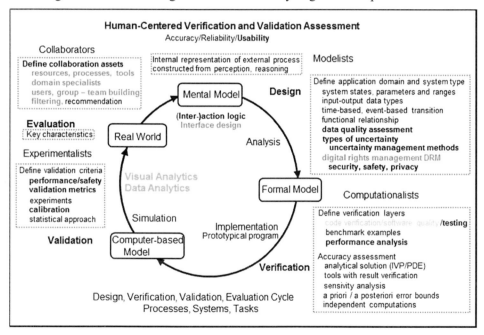

Fig. 1. Validation & Verification Assessment - common old and new assessed features of the presented three uses cases in section 3. Data quality, uncertainty management, performance/ safety validation, calibration, and interaction design are written in bold, special features in different shades of grey.

A further essential enhancement of the cycle in Figure 1 is the option of collaborative outcome analytics done by various stakeholders with multiple expertise to cover the topics of system evaluation, effective data mining and problem solving as well as to organize follow-up actions. An example of using collaborative VA is given in [7]. Here, a complete VA system and a collaborative touch-table application is designed and evaluated for solving real-world tasks with two integrated components: a single-user desktop and an extended system suitable for a collaborative environment.

Although VA methods can be employed efficiently for a variety of applications, some of them are sensitive w.r.t. their safety or reliability. For example, accurate understanding of complex health data is necessary to make informed decisions about treatment of critically ill patients. For this reason, *reliable* VA methods should be introduced in decision-making sessions of various stakeholders. Only few publications explicitly address reliable VA, the main topics of discussion being data conversion to standard formats for visualization on various devices, accurate understanding of outcome using reliable mapping algorithms and standardized procedures to automatically select, analyze, refine and combine visual data. This makes developing clear guidelines for ensuring the reliability of VA an important research direction. Prior to application of reliable VA techniques, it is necessary to assess (meta-)data and code quality, to take into account and propagate uncertainty and to validate the system with formal rigor.

Evaluation of a computer-based system model (cf. Figure 1) aims at computing key indicators and parameters which characterize it w.r.t. existing standards and rules, requirements, and individual needs. Such evaluation can be considered from the vantage points of stakeholders, designers, software engineers, the general public and researchers involved in the development and use of the model. In [8] and [9], an example of how such an evaluation can be conducted in health sciences is given. In [8], the quality of evaluation activities is assessed using the following four groups of standards: utility, feasibility, propriety and accuracy. In [9], it is shown how group analytics can be used to evaluate VA problem-solving and to support multi-stakeholder decision-making sessions in the context of child injury prevention. Here, typical questions concern group building, filtering visual data w.r.t. space, access time or relevance, collecting stakeholders' utterances, fusing and reporting. Collected data include stakeholders' observations, audio and video recordings, questionnaires, and follow-up interviews. The group analytics sessions are analyzed using the joint action theory protocol analysis and pair analytics methods [10] that prove the emergence of 'common ground', i.e., mutual, common, or joint knowledge, beliefs and assumptions among stakeholders. This is a precondition to collaboratively solving problems using VA.

In this paper, we emphasize the need for a semi-formal description of AmI systems and for clearly formulated requirements about privacy and security in AAL or healthcare applications. In general, this concerns all recommendations made by AI systems that directly affect human quality of life. We illustrate the theoretical concepts with the help of several use cases. For example, we show how to open the way for V&V, uncertainty quantification and sensitivity analysis in traffic simulation systems [11]. Further, we demonstrate how to enhance V&V assessment with the reasoning capabilities of VA through interactive visual interfaces, adding a dimension of collaboration to creation and evaluation of AmI systems. Visual layout and mapping features of reliable VA are defined with the help of a taxonomy for uncertain data visualization [12, 13, 14, 15]. Finally, we describe how involving people in collaborative and crowd-sourcing activities can transform museums into participatory spaces [16, 17].

As a typical cross-section research area which integrates knowledge from data sciences, computer graphics and cognitive science, VA fosters constructive process model validation, revision and improvement. Moreover, it supports semi-automatic data processing and result evaluation combining human-machine intelligence in interaction and collaboration. Several of these aspects are described in the next section.

2 Visual Analytics - Visualization and Interaction Techniques

The main advantage of the emerging area of VA is the ability to engage in the analytical process the whole of human perceptual and cognitive capabilities and augment them by advanced computations [6]. The key steps of the VA process include data representation and transformation, visual layout and mapping, model-based analysis, and interaction techniques [18].

Uncertainty modeling and visualization play a crucial role in ensuring the reliability and trustworthiness of the analytical process. Variables, parameters and descriptors can exhibit aleatory and epistemic uncertainty. Epistemic uncertainty is due to the lack of knowledge and can appear in various forms. Missing or non-reliable data and wrong or non-representative meta-data impact the process, its model and its visual representation. A consequence might be a negative influence on form, appearance and properties of data as well as on interaction or manipulation skills of the involved people. Compared to epistemic one, the term aleatory uncertainty refers to the random variability of the modeled objects or artefacts, of the occurrence of events, of the failure of system components or to the statistical distribution of model descriptors. It is shown in [19] that a combination of interval calculus and evidence theory can be an alternative to classical probability theory in VA. Rebner et al. [20] use the interval p-box approach to model epistemic uncertainty with intervals and aleatory uncertainty with discrete interval distributions. The approach combines interval arithmetic (IA) and stochastic models to compute guaranteed enclosures for a union of focal sets with interval-valued mass distributions. In this way, separate experts' opinions can be jointly represented and input uncertainty can be propagated through the system, which bounds the prediction uncertainty. The obtained bounds are then interpreted using upper and lower inverse cumulative distribution functions.

An important issue in the data representation and mapping process is a user-controlled selection of data types. To define a formal system model with its variables, we use ordered pairs of tuples for *input-output data* $((d_{i1},\ldots, d_{ik}), (d_{o1},\ldots, d_{oj}))$ and the corresponding *meta-data descriptors* $((m_{i1},\ldots, m_{ir}), (m_{o1},\ldots, m_{os}))$ to characterize the process and its outcome. A (nested) transfer function F or algorithm A, a probability distribution function (PDF) D and its parameters might be defined by a heterogeneous binary relation R: $(\mathbf{x}_i, \mathbf{y}_o)$, $\mathbf{x}_i \in \mathbf{d}_i$ resp. $\mathbf{m}_i$, $\mathbf{y}_o \in \mathbf{d}_o$ resp. $\mathbf{m}_o$, a dynamic process P or a system S and represent them using standard data types. The allowed data types and functions are Boolean or alphanumeric, numeric (e.g., integer, floating point IEEE 754/2008 or IEEE 1788/2015 interval numbers, operations and functions)[2]. The dimension of the model can be reduced by selecting few d_j or by defining a projection that restricts certain variables or parameters to a bounded interval, a set or a single value of a variable. Moreover, data dimensionality can be decreased by employing low variance or high correlation filters or principal component analysis [13]. Com-

---

2   IEEE Standard for IA: http://standards.ieee.org/findstds/standard/1788-2015.html

plexity can be reduced by selecting the respective ranges and values automatically, for example, by evaluating interval expressions and functions which might lead to overestimation of the bounds, or by employing a user–computer dialogue which makes it possible to supply tighter handcrafted bounds. These principles are illustrated in the next section and in the references given therein.

To visualize scientific or information ensemble data, Brodlie et al. [14] introduce the E notation which uses a subscript to indicate the number of independent variables or parameters and a superscript to indicate the type of dependent variables. Thus, E_1^S represents a model of a scalar function of one variable, and E_1^{kS} is used for k scalar functions. kE^S denotes multi-field scalar data, and E^V vector data. The letter E could be interpreted as 'exact' when applied to exact data. For uncertain data, the letter E is replaced with U. Uncertainty is visualized as a geometric form, such as a bar, a rectangle or a thick surface, a truncated upper and lower PDF or interval mean and the standard deviation of a PDF. Additionally, color maps, glyphs or isosurfaces with color U_{xyz}^S can be used. Glyphs are symbols to signify data through parameters such as location, size, shape, orientation, and color. Varying contour color or thickness and surface opacity, often augmented with uncertainty annotations, illustrate regions of uncertainty across the spatial domain.

A modern system architecture and an appropriate task model enable users to choose the devices and interaction styles that are best suited for their current task or collaboration style. Whereas WIMP interfaces utilizing mouse and keyboard-based interaction on screens are well suited for presenting text and 2D content, post-WIMP interfaces introduce new interaction paradigms for users to navigate, manipulate and interact with objects within a 3D virtual reality environment. This is done using 3D devices to navigate and select objects and to grab or grasp and manipulate items using an elastic arm and a virtual hand. Interaction styles are related to application scenarios including virtual and augmented reality, ubiquitous and context-aware computing and computer-supported cooperative learning or work. Extended post-WIMP task models have to include profiles depending on the application type (i.e., collaborative VA or highly interactive systems like CAVE [12]), adequacy of interaction elements, flexibility in partitioning the task among multiple actors as well as multimodal fault-tolerant and error-avoiding dialogues with forward and backward error recovery to deal with uncertainty issues.

3 Use Cases

In recent years, both authors and their collaborators have contributed software tools and frameworks in various application areas, e. g., reliable analysis of (bio-)mechanical systems, solid oxide fuel cell systems, steel technologies [21], reliable computer graphics and image processing, virtual museums and laboratories as well as microscopic traffic modeling [23]. Further works introduced a framework for development, assessment and interoperable use of verified techniques with applications in distance computation, global optimization, and comparison systematics, a human autonomy assessment system as well as uncertainty quantification via verified stochastic methods in geographic information system (GIS) applications. Moreover, a hardware and software architecture to assess and visualize important risk parameters and environment entities under uncertainty was described in [12] with the aim to process, format and present relevant everyday threats from several risk classes that appear in specific contexts with typical parameters in a virtual house of risk. The layered architecture approach provided risk data and meta-data in a virtual reality environment allowing for appropriate 2D and 3D visualization and various interaction styles, cooperation and co-creation of new content, and an individualizable degree of immersion into situations where threats typically happened.

A crucial issue is to select modeling and implementation languages carefully, since it can be seen that our use cases require different types of models, e. g., algebraic models, automata, dynamic system models described by ordinary and/or partial differential equations, deterministic and/or stochastic models. One example for a human-centered modeling and assessment would be to use a reference nets approach for modeling and reconfiguring user interfaces and their (inter)action logic as shown in [24]. It is described in [24] how two student groups working collaboratively and on their own constructed their roles in a standardized cryptographic protocol step by step. The system automatically generated a colored Petri net which was matched against the existing protocol logic and supported by the robust implementation framework Renew (http://www.renew.de/), a Java-based multi-formalism editor and simulator providing a flexible modeling approach.

These examples constitute relevant parts of a new human-centered V&V assessment including not only code and result verification, uncertainty management, validation and evaluation assessment, but also tailored user interaction, recommender techniques and reliable VA. In the following subsections, we will highlight three use cases which address relevant parts of an enhanced V&V assessment.

3.1 Microscopic Traffic Modeling and Simulation System (MTMSS)

In this subsection, we use the example of an MTMSS to illustrate code verification and model validation from the modeling and simulation cycle in Figure 1. Brügmann et al. [11] describe an approach to modeling microscopic traffic simulations by using executable formal semantics. The model comprises a specification of a simulation engine for implementation providing sequential or parallel operation with automatic domain decomposition. It illustrates code verification options for implementations of the specified simulation, supports formal and numerical solution verification for the simulation and all subject-specific models for vehicles, detector and tuning element models, traffic lights and is based on the fully functional real-world online traffic information system OLSIMv4 which is the updated version of the NRW traffic information platform (cf. Figure 2). Additionally, it provides a data model for arbitrary road traffic networks in highway and urban environments. Integrating the topological data model into the database allows for automated verification of the data integrity.

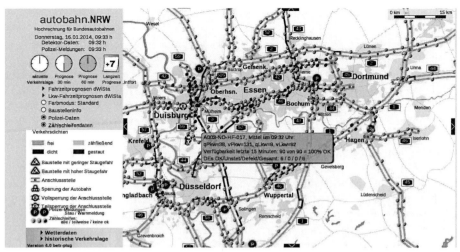

Fig.2. Restricted access area of the NRW traffic information platform

Due to its simplicity, expressive power and the opportunity to realize executable code, the declarative programming language Maude [22] was used to form and initialize the components for the highway network of North Rhine-Westphalia (Germany). A usability evaluation showed that the travel-time presentation of the web front end might serve for the refinement of the traffic information. As a result, users can choose origins and destinations of their trips now and get the total travel time not only for individual route segments, but also for each of the chosen routes.

The Maude system executed the simulation model to reproduce the well-known fundamental diagrams of the Nagel-Schreckenberg microscopic traffic model (velocity/flow to density). A numerical solution for a single lane scenario with periodic boundary conditions was presented together with considerations about the numerical solution verification; travel-time and performance validation were carried out and enabled the author to identify drawbacks of the concurrent ML implementation of OLSIMv4. With the conceptual design of the paper and Brügmann's thesis [23] presenting the verified specification in much more detail, a future implementation needs less calibration effort, that is, future V&V activities are facilitated. Although there is an archive providing simulation results of the last years, VA topics are not addressed.

The advantage of first refining and verifying the process models over implementing directly and refining subsequently is quite evident. If we keep in mind that a configuration file written in the OLSIM track data format (OTDF) has more than 100 000 lines of code, configuration errors can become quite common so that run time exceptions might occur. By contrast, the MAUDE approach allows users to implement simulation models such as the presented ones in a few thousand code lines. A direct implementation and an inline system refinement dealing with optimization details are mostly difficult, error-prone, and not easy to change. Moreover, the expected necessity to change the code bears the risk of reducing the code quality, as stated in [23, p.198]. Insights gained from the presented verification activities will allow for almost automatic reimplementation of a new OLSIM version.

3.2 Analysis of Steel Samples SILENOS©

In this subsection, we illustrate how to visualize big data influenced by uncertainty, an aspect pertaining to data quality assessment, uncertainty management performance analysis, and VA from the cycle in Figure 1. The inclusion processing framework, IPFViewer, has been designed by the first author of [15], [21] in cooperation with a large German steel production facility to analyze data collected about nonmetallic inclusions and other defects in steel samples using the steel inclusion level evaluation by numerical optical system SILENOS©[3]. The tool can analyze the ensemble data set in various ways, for example, perform outlier detection to identify samples and defects that differ from others by position, size, type and number. It can carry out trend analysis to study the influence of different process parameters on the steel samples and their meta-data and variance analysis to examine natural fluctuations within the samples and desired variations that result from process parameters.

After the three-dimensional shape of inclusions and other defects is reconstructed, the nonmetallic inclusions are classified in two steps. First, globular defects, crack-like defects and artifacts near the border of the sample volume are classified with the help of a support vector machine and 1462 defects from the database. The goal is to find the optimal descriptor and parameter set for obtaining the best possible correct classification rate. Second, the model is refined by splitting the class of globular defects into pores (gas bubbles) and nonmetallic inclusions having a nearly spherical form. If a further chemical analysis is desired, it is possible to ask the system for a map with interesting inclusions. These can be processed individually using a laser-induced breakdown spectroscopy system (LIBS). This step allows the engineers to analyze the spatial distribution of inclusions and defects in general, classify them according to their three-dimensional shape and visualize the items using real-time rendering methods.

Based on a new data and visualization model for the analysis of hierarchical ensemble data sets, IPFViewer utilizes multiple view techniques, data grouping and aggregation, data mining, and reference data visualization. Due to the immense size of the ensemble data set, which can contain up to a hundred thousand steel samples and ten billion defects, the main requirement was to present the relevant data in a way that enables the users to perform the evaluation quickly without having to deal with unnecessary details. When necessary, IPFViewer relies on new incremental, approximate analysis techniques to ensure the responsiveness of the application while sufficient precision is guaranteed for queries with fast response times [21].

Uncertainty visualization is used to analyze variations in the data: Small natural fluctuations from the production process can be visualized, as can larger variances due to variation in the process parameters (e.g., temperature in the smelting furnace). The design allows workers at the steel production facility to quickly and interactively analyze data with millions of data rows. The tool has a standardized and customizable reporting functionality and can be used with ensemble data sets generated using other application tools as well. IPFViewer employs a new data tree and visualization model for hierarchical ensemble data sets with operations for interactive tree manipulation: tree traversal, reference data selection, automatic percentile selection and ensemble

---

[3]   SILENOS is patent-protected by Hüttenwerke Krupp Mannesmann GmbH

member aggregation. Samples are sorted according to process parameters and filtered to include or exclude certain steel grades. The resulting data tree is visualized as a huge grid in a scrollable area. Each grid cell incorporates a multiple view system with such standard visualization techniques as scatter plots, bar charts and trend graphs.

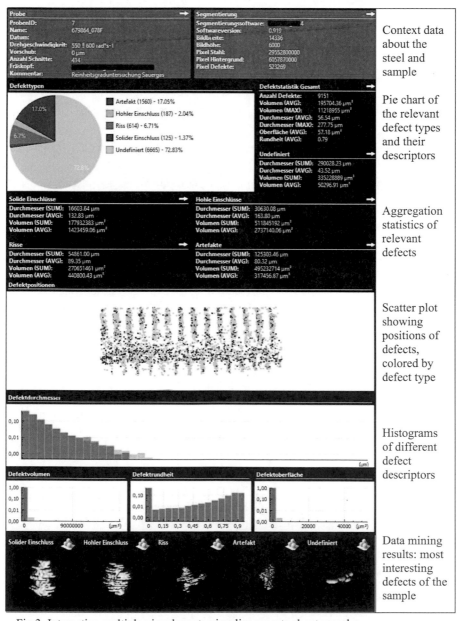

Context data about the steel and sample

Pie chart of the relevant defect types and their descriptors

Aggregation statistics of relevant defects

Scatter plot showing positions of defects, colored by defect type

Histograms of different defect descriptors

Data mining results: most interesting defects of the sample

Fig.3. Interactive multiple view layouts visualize reports about samples

In Figure 3, one of sample reports is shown. Each report provides a great deal of relevant data in one screen. If users want to see more details, they can click on a view and get a full screen representation of details with additional settings. At the bottom of the report, the largest defects and their descriptors found through data mining are shown. Steel experts examine the histogram about defect diameter and the largest found defects to evaluate a sample quickly without having to analyze each defect manually. They can also scroll through all the samples and compare them, create and save various layouts that visualize different aspects of the data in order to confirm or refute hypotheses. The development of two subsequent IPFViewer versions involved a dozen university researchers and employees of the industrial partner; an expert survey concerning usability, performance and visualization concepts is ongoing work.

3.3 Virtual Museums and Labs

In this subsection, we illustrate the aspect of collaborative design, creation, protection using watermarking and interface design from the modeling and simulation cycle in Figure 1. Moreover, we describe the new ViMCOX standard and software testing. Finally, there is an evaluation of visitors' usability issues and co-curation activities.

In [17], Biella et al. give an overview on crowdsourcing and co-curation practices in virtual museums. They present a concept that focuses on content development and enhancement realized by participatory practices and crowdsourcing, especially for Web-based museums and virtual science centers. Engaged nonprofessionals, software engineers, and field specialists support curators through co-curation on a common online platform in selecting and creating digital 2D or 3D exhibits, exhibitions, room design, object allocation using the virtual museum and cultural object exchange format (ViMCOX). Software engineers employ the multipurpose system ViMEDEAS that allows dynamic generation and publication of arbitrary room designs and generates virtual museum environments in line with given parameters and meta-data designs specified in the VM modeling language ViMCOX. Volunteers contribute or enhance digital 2D/3D exhibits and its meta-data, propose and disseminate tours on the museum's platform, including navigation in the 3D environment to predefined or individually specified viewpoints, and interact with exhibits. ViMCOX is based on international lightweight information describing objects (LIDO) v1.0 meta-data standard, provides the semantic structure of exhibitions and complete museums and includes new features, such as room and outdoor design, interactions with artwork, path planning and dissemination as well as DRM. Case studies are devoted to restoring lost or damaged artwork by the German-Jewish sculptor Leopold Fleischhacker, high-quality 3D shapes and Armenian cross stones. The Virtual Leopold Fleischhacker Museum (LFM) consists primarily of annotated photographs and reconstructed tombstones and hosts about 200 pictorial exhibits in 13 rooms; 3D assets include plants, pillars, glass vitrines, benches and information tableaux. Twenty-nine tombstones were reconstructed via the crowd technology using photographs, Blender and X3D export and carefully placed outside in a virtual Jewish cemetery. Several masks were reconstructed together with one greatly enlarged seal presented in the entrance hall.

The paper also reports on various evaluation activities: Prior to the start of the project, a preliminary questionnaire was developed within a knowledge-based evaluation setting. Divided into five parts, it helped to identify goals for all the parties involved and gather relevant information about the collections, digitization, meta-data techniques and interoperability standards to be used in the field. After realization of a prototypical LFM, a further knowledge- and rule-based evaluation dealt with software stability in accordance with either the ISO/IEC 9126 or the ISO/IEC/IEEE 29119 norm, failure-free system operation over a specified time, stress tests for fluent navigation and display, and confirmation of complete and correct realization of the curator's content specifications. Another survey designed as an interview with targeted questions provided two use cases including free and guided navigation through the exhibition rooms and outdoor area exhibition.

The usability concept, co-curation contributions by the crowd and support by curators and software engineers were examined and evaluated during an exhibition of Fleischhacker's estate at the Düsseldorf Memorial to the Victims of Persecution from November 10, 2015, to January 27, 2016. In the new Julo-Levin hall, four terminals were installed with four different versions of the LFM. In addition to the version with gamepad, QR-codes and overhead projection, on the left side of the room, there was a kiosk with touch screen, track ball and reduced keyboard to support point-and-click operations and protect the browser and operating system against manipulation, allowing free exploration and guided tours through the exposition. Additionally, two modern all-in-one screens on the other side of the room ran Windows 8.1 in kiosk mode configured for assigned access to selected apps in full screen mode. To navigate, users employed familiar touch screen gestures such as tapping, pressing, sliding, swiping and rotating. Seven video tours were available, in addition to the version already used on the kiosk system [16, 17].

4   Conclusions

This paper introduces human-centered paradigms into a formal V&V assessment within a workflow for designing, modeling, and implementing various real life processes and AmI environments. We showed that numerical result verification is only one of the important issues. Big data quality assessment, accurate task and process modeling, user interaction and reliable visual analytics should also be carried out. We described toolboxes supporting reliable VA for visualizing steel artifacts, virtual museums and GIS applications. V&V assessment and evaluation of these systems was conducted from various vantage points concerning design, code or numerical result verification, software testing, recommendation and usability.

References

1. Auer, E.: Result verification and uncertainty management in engineering applications. Habilitation thesis, University of Duisburg-Essen, Dr. Hut (2014)

2. Sadri, F.: Ambient Intelligence: A Survey. ACM Computing Surveys 43 (4) Article 36. Publication date: October 2011

3. Schlesinger, S. et al., Terminology for Model Credibility. Simulation, 32 (1979) 103-104

4. Cai, L., Zhu, Y.: The Challenges of Data Quality and Data Quality Assessment in the Big Data Era. Data Science Journal, 14 (2) (2015) 1-10

5. Blytt, M.: Big Challenges for Visual Analytics - Assisting Sensemaking of Big Data with Visual Analytics. NTNU (2013) 13p

6. Keim, D., Andrienko, G., Fekete, J.-D., Görg, C., Kohlhammer, J. and Melançon, G.: Visual Analytics: Definition, Process, and Challenges. In Information Visualization, A. Kerren et al. eds., Berlin, Springer (2008) 154-175

7. Jeong, D. H., Ji, S.-Y., Suma, E. A., Yu, B., and Chang, R.: Designing a collaborative visual analytics system to support users' continuous analytical processes, Human-centric Computing and Information Sciences, 5 (5) (2015), Springer DOI 10.1186/s13673-015-0023-4

8. Framework for Program Evaluation in Public Health, MMWR Recommendations and Reports, September 17, 1999 / 48(RR11) 1-40
https://www.cdc.gov/mmwr/preview/mmwrhtml/rr4811a1.htm

9. Al-Hajj, S., Fisher, B., Smith, J., and Pike, I.: Collaborative Visual Analytics: A Health Analytics Approach to Injury Prevention. Int. J. Environ. Res. Public Health, 14 (2017) 1056

10. Arias-Hernandez, R., Kaastra, L. T.: Joint Action Theory and Pair Analytics: In-vivo Studies of Cognition and Social Interaction in Collaborative Visual Analytics. Proc. 33rd Annual Conf. of the Cognitive Science Society, Boston, MA, USA (2011) 3244–3249

11. Brügmann, J., Schreckenberg, M., and Luther, W.: A verifiable simulation model for real-world microscopic traffic simulations, Simulation Modelling Practice and Theory 48C (Nov. 2014) 58–92

12. Weyers, B., Luther, W.: Risk Communication and Perception in Low- and High-Immersion Virtual Environments. APSSRA6, 28-30 May 2016, Shanghai, China, H.W. Huang, J. Li, J., Zhang & J.B. Chen (editors) (2016)

13. Potter, K., Rosen, P., and Johnson, C. R.: From Quantification to Visualization: A taxonomy of uncertainty visualization approaches. IFIP Advances in Information and Communication Technology, 377 (2012) 226-249

14. Brodlie, K., Allendes Osorio, R., and Lopes, A.: A Review of Uncertainty in Data Visualization: Expanding the Frontiers of Visual Analytics and Visualization. Springer, London (2012) 81-109

15. Thurau, M., Buck, Chr., and Luther, W.: IPFViewer: Incremental, approximate analysis of steel samples. Proceedings of SIGRAD (2014), Linköping University Electronic Press (2014) 1-8

16. Sacher, D.: A generative approach to virtual museums using a new metadata format. A curators', visitors' and software engineers' perspective. PhD thesis, University of Duisburg-Essen. Logos, Berlin (2017) ISBN 978-3-8325-4627-4

17. Biella, D., Pilz, T., Sacher, D., Weyers, B., Luther, W., Baloian, N., and Schreck, T.: Crowdsourcing and Co-curation in Virtual Museums: A Practice-driven Approach. Journal of Universal Computer Science, 22 (10) (2016) 1277–1297

18. Sun, G. D., Wu, Y. C., Liang, R. H., Liu, S. X.: A survey of visual analytics techniques and applications: State-of-the-art research and future challenges. Journal of Computer Science and Technology, 28 (5) (2013) 852–867

19. Zio, E., Pedroni, N.: Literature review of methods for representing uncertainty. No.2013-03 des Cahiers de la Sécurité Industrielle, Toulouse (2013) http://www.FonCSI.org/fr/

20. Rebner, G., Sacher, D., Weyers, B., Luther, W.: Verified stochastic methods in geographic information system applications with uncertainty. Structural Safety, 52 (2015) 244-259

21. Thurau, M., Buck, Chr., Luther, W.: IPFViewer: A Visual Analysis System for Hierarchical Ensemble Data. Proc. 5th Int. Conf. IVAPP-VISIGRAPP Lisbon, Scitepress (2014) 259-266

22. The Maude System: http://maude.cs.illinois.edu/w/index.php?title=The_Maude_System

23. Brügmann, J.: Modelling and implementation of a microscopic traffic simulation system. PhD thesis, University of Duisburg-Essen. Logos Edition Berlin (2015) ISBN 978-3-8325-4133-0

24. Weyers, B., Luther, W., and Baloian, N.: Cooperative Reconfiguration of user interface models for learning cryptographic protocols. International Journal of Information Technology & Decision Making, 11 (6) (2012) 1127-1154

25. Buck, Chr.: Computerbasierte Modellierung und Analyse der Gestalt und Verteilung von Partikeln zur Optimierung des Reinheitsgrades von Stahlwerkstoffen – Konzeption und Implementierung eines Rahmenwerks (in German). PhD thesis, University of Duisburg-Essen (2016), http://duepublico.uni-duisburg-essen.de/servlets/DocumentServlet?id=42570

Preliminary Assessment of Public Transportation Routes Using Free Available Cloud Services and Belief Routes

Nelson Baloian[1], Jonathan Frez[2], José Pino[1], Gustavo Zurita[3], Arthur Dolmajian[4]

[1]Department of Computer Science, Universidad de Chile, Santiago, Chile
{nbaloian,jpino}@dcc.uchile.cl
[2]Universidad Diego Portales, Santiago, Chile
jonathan.frez@mail.udp.cl
[3]Management Control and Information Systems Department, Universidad de Chile
gzurita@fen.uchile.cl
[4]College of Engineering, American University of Armenia, Yerevan, Armenia

Abstract. When planning a route for a bus it is necessary to estimate the demand of the people for this service as well as the time a bus will take from one stop to the other. This may require considerable amount of time and resources. Nevertheless, the results might not be accurate enough since conditions change day by day. In this paper we explore the use of existing crowdsourcing data (like Waze and OpenStreetMap) and cloud services (like Google Maps) to support a transportation network decision making process. The goal is to test the hypothesis whether it is possible to make a forecasting which provides useful information using data which can be obtained from freely available public information. This would serve to make a preliminary study for decision makers for example, when evaluating the implementation of a new bus line, more specifically, the Origin-Destination (OD) evaluation, based on the Dempster-Shafer theory about plausibility.

Keywords: Dempster-Shafer theory · transportation networks · smart cities.

1 Introduction

When planning and evaluating the usefulness of a new bus line, it is necessary to estimate at least f the demand for that route, which could be represented by the number of passengers that would like to take the bus at a certain stop; and the traveling time of the bus between all two consecutives stops of the route. Since the route does not exist yet, it is difficult to estimate with high certainty the demand that the service will have. Studies may be conducted based on data about population living along the route and facilities, services and amenities near it, but this requires data gathering which might not be very simple to perform (Chen et al. 2014). The traveling time is something which is predictable with some certainty since the existing traffic is likely not to change too much with the introduction of a single new bus line. Nevertheless, it requires some work which will require some tasks to be performed.

It would be very useful if we could do at least some preliminary evaluation of the new planned route without having to spend too much time and/or money in the process, in order to decide the feasibility of a new route at an early stage, The research question that inspired the work presented here is whether we can use the data freely available "in the cloud" to accomplish tasks to what is known as a "smart city" and would require in many cases an enormous effort in time and money for gathering the required data. As an example, in this work we use services provided by Google Maps, OpenStreetMap (Haklay et al. 2008) and Waze (Silva et al. 2013) to download and use data to feed a Spatial Decision Support System for transportation network planning, specifically for estimating the demand and congestion along a planned route of a bus line of the public transportation system, what is commonly known as the Origin-Destination (OD) route evaluation. For this purpose, we use an approach based on the Dempster-Shafer theory (DST) (Shafer, 1976). This theory allows to model decisions based on uncertain and incomplete data, by studying the extent a hypothesis can be supported by data.

We focus on spatial DSS using belief functions (Frez et al, 2014), in particular Dempster-Shafer theory. DST proposes to use sets of hypotheses regarding a variable (e.g. the temperatures at a location are between t1 and t2) associated with a probability of being correct. Using belief functions we can provide a "hypotheses support value" called belief. The belief can be assigned to a certain geographical area satisfying a hypotheses set.

2   The Origin-Destination (OD) Route Problem

As we stated in the first section, we would like to find out the possibility of making a preliminary evaluation with data obtained exclusively from free sources on the web, specifically from OpenStreetMap and Waze. For this purpose, we propose to use "Belief Maps" (Frez et al., 2014), which are Suitability Maps (Hopkins, 1977) built with incomplete data, based mostly on beliefs rather than facts. Suitability maps are used to determine the appropriateness of a given area for a particular use. This process is called suitability analysis and its fundamental principle "is that each aspect of the landscape has intrinsic characteristics that are to some degree either suitable or unsuitable for the activities being planned. Suitability is determined through systematic, multi-factor analysis of the different aspect of the terrain" (Murphy, 2005). In a Belief Map we formally identify a set of hypotheses that may reinforce or weaken the plausibility and certainty about the occurrence of a certain fact, which will be used when computing the suitability of a certain location or area. Various hypotheses can be combined with different weights to compute what in DST is called the "accumulated mass" that supports a belief. Based on similar principles as Belief Maps we now introduce the concept of Belief Route, which will be used to estimate the numbers of possible passengers that would like to use a public transportation bus serving that route in its various sections. Each section is delimited by two contiguous bus stops. A Belief Route is composed of 3 basic elements: 1) The origin and destination points; 2) The polyline connecting these two points which describes the route followed by the bus in order to travel from origin to destination. 3) A set of hypotheses specifying a possible transportation demand of an OD. Besides estimating the possible demand for the route, in some planning scenarios it is important to estimate the traffic congestion along the whole route in order to evaluate if the traveling time between stops as well as from the origin to the destination is both predictable and it takes reasonable time. Using Belief Route and Belief Congestion Route maps, the decision maker can compare various paths and evaluate their ability to satisfy the transportation requirement of the population along the route.

Given the polyline representing the route and the hypotheses set, the first step for computing the Belief Route is to divide the area in 150x150 meters disjunct rectangles. Then we compute the mass for each rectangle the route goes through according to the set of hypotheses used as rules to predict the chance of finding people wanting to use the transportation service. To each hypothesis we assign a weight that will determine the amount of mass that will be assigned to the rectangle where the hypothesis holds.

After this step, the initial configuration for the predictor is complete and all masses are correctly distributed, the next step is to combine the mass in order to compute the belief for each rectangle. At this point, it is assumed that the mass of each rectangle is independent of the other rectangles and there is a spatial decay for the mass contribution to neighbor cells; this decay is estimated with a normal cumulative distribution function (CFD). As seen in the following equation:

$$mass(d) = \begin{cases} 1 & if \ d = 0 \ (inside) \\ 1 - \frac{1}{2}(1 + erf(\frac{d-\mu}{\sigma\sqrt{2}})) & if \ d > 0 \ (outside) \end{cases}$$

In the equation μ and σ are the average and standard deviation distances of the normal CDF to be used. When a cell is affected by more than one hypothesis, the Dempster Rule is used to combine and compute the conjunction mass through their basic probability assignments. See equation below:

$$m_{1,2}(\Phi) = 0$$
$$m_{1,2}(A) = \frac{1}{1-K} \sum_{A=B\cap C \neq \Phi} m_1(B)m_2(C) \quad K = \sum_{B\cap C=\Phi} m_1(B)m_2(C)$$

K is only used for normalization purposes. The result of this process is a belief map, since the focus of the problem is the route; the next step is to find the subset of cells from the belief map that intersects with the route. The final result omits all other cells and only keeps those which represent a location of the route. Then we normalize the subset of cells in order to adjust the scale of belief to the new domain.

The Belief Congestion Routes are computed in a similar way than the Belief Route, with the difference that the only hypothesis is that each report about a traffic jam in Waze adds mass to the rectangle where it was geo-referenced by the reporter. According to the Waze information for both paths, route 1 has more belief of having congestions or traffic jams which implies less reliability.

3   Belief Route Evaluation

The most critical aspect for the success of the Belief Route and Belief Congestion Route is a correct estimation of the hypotheses which would generate the "mass" supporting the possibilities of the demand and congestion estimations along the planned route. In general, hypotheses used with DST should be stated by an expert who has the necessary knowledge. In this case, for calculating Belief routes we use the hypotheses that people will use public transportation near areas where shops and services are located. We now want to test if these hypotheses were a correct guess. The testing method is simple: we will use real data from the public transportation system; if the prediction generated by the hypotheses set "matches" the real data then we assume the hypotheses hold and the generated Belief Routes are valid. We used data about time and location where people start using each service from the Santiago integrated public transportation system called "Transantiago" (Fernández et al. 2008), which uses exclusively plastic cards with magnetic bands pre-loaded with money as payment method. In this way, the system registers the point where every passenger starts her/his trip. However, it does not register the point where it ends. Data were obtained from the Chilean Ministry of Transport.

For the test we selected an area with high transportation activity in the city of Santiago. This area was selected because it has various types of zones: residential, commercial, city hall and services, subway stations, and industrial areas. The locations of the zone types are briefly described in Figure 1. We will use the residential areas #1 and #2 as well as the industrial area to analyze the demand, since these are the areas where people start their trips according to the data.

Now we will compare this data against the prediction we obtain when computing the Belief route using DST and information we can get from the web. As we already said the tested hypotheses are 1) People require more transportation near shop areas; and 2) People require more transportation near amenity places.

In order to obtain a general overview of the transportation demand, we are not including the time dimension (different days, hours).

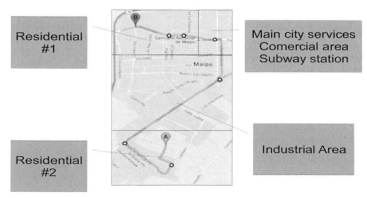

Fig. 1: Zone types of the analyzed area.

These hypotheses are tuned to comply with the categories used by OpenStreetMap for the type of objects it stores. Apart from streets, we can get information about facilities classified as amenities and shops located in a certain area. Amenities refer to commercial places offering services like cafés, bars, restaurants, schools, universities, libraries, etc., while shops are related to commercial places selling goods like bakeries, convenience stores, supermarkets, medical supplies, etc. Figures 2, 3 and 4 show the real demand vs. the predicted Belief route for the three selected areas.

Real Demand   **Predicted**

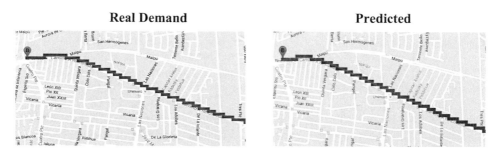

Fig. 2: real demand vs. predicted demand for residential area #1

For residential area #1 (Figure 2), we verify the prediction was quite accurate for this route section. The Belief Route predicts a high concentration of the demand at the center of the route section, which almost fully matches the real demand. It also predicts a medium demand concentration in almost all the rest of the route which also matches the real data. The only noticeable difference is that the Belief route predicts a medium-high demand at the end of this route section which is not backed by real data.

For the industrial area there is also a good matching between the real demand and the belief route: the real data shows a medium demand in almost all the route section except for the last part of the section, where a high demand is shown. The predicted Belief Route also shows a medium demand on almost the whole section except for the same high level demand at the end. The only difference is that the Belief route predicts low demand at the middle of the section (colored with light blue) which is not backed by real data (Figure 3).

Real Demand   **Predicted**

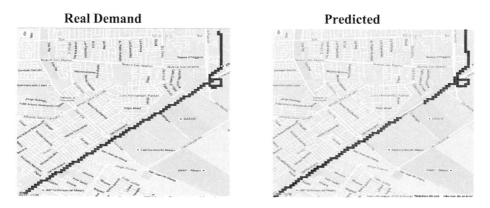

Fig. 3: real demand vs. predicted demand for industrial area

86

The prediction for the section going through the residential area #2 presents more differences than the other two areas (see Fig. 4), but it also shows many matches. The prediction shows a small sub-section with medium-high demand at the beginning of the section whereas the real data shows only medium demand. After that, both figures show a medium demand until the point where the route makes a 90° left turn, where both, the real demand and the belief route show a high demand. After the turning point there is a small section where the real data shows a medium-low demand whereas the Belief Route shows a medium demand followed by a sub-section where both figures show a medium-high demand. At the end of the section, the Belief route predicts some sections of low demand whereas the real data show medium-low level demand. The explanation may be as follows: the last part of the real route goes through an area with few shops and amenities but since it is the end of the route (or the beginning, depending on the direction people take the bus), it concentrates more customers coming from the nearby areas. This factor can be considered as an additional hypothesis in future analyses and may be incorporated to the set of hypotheses for obtaining a better prediction.

We can see that the Belief Route has a high level of matches with real data and where it does not fully match it, the differences are not large. In fact, the Belief Route does never predict a high demand when the real data shows a low demand and vice versa. The most difficult place to predict the real demand seems to be the residential area where there are few shops and/or amenities and correspond to the beginning or end of the route.

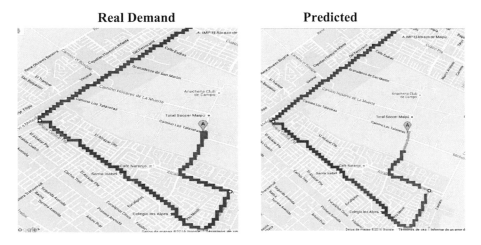

Fig. 4: real demand vs. predicted demand for residential area #2

4   Conclusions

In this work we present a method to use existing crowdsourced data to support a transportation network decision making process. The method uses the Dempster-

Shafer Theory to provide a framework to model transportation demand based on maps obtained from Google Maps, information about facilities located near the route from OpenStreetMap and information about the traffic from Waze. With this information the Belief Route and the Belief Congestion can be computed. The Belief Route predicts the possible demand along an OD route and the Belief Congestion Route predicts the congestion and thus the travel time for a bus on that route. This allows us to make a preliminary evaluation of the route without investing time and resources to perform all the necessary tasks to gather the necessary information for a comprehensive evaluation. Also an application which has all necessary functionalities to perform this preliminary evaluation is presented.

To test the validity of this approach we did an experiment with a real existing route: we compared the prediction of the demand obtained with the Belief Route against the data obtained from the Transportation Ministry about the number of passengers getting in the buses serving that route in each bus stop. The result obtained was that the computed Belief Route predicted the demand quite well. To test the usefulness of this approach, the Belief Route for a new route with the same origin and destination points but traveling through other streets was computed, finding out that this new route would have a greater demand, thus being more efficient with the transportation resources. The Belief Congestion Route could also be computed in order to check if the travel time would have been also acceptable. This latter analysis was not done for this paper.

5   References

1.   Chen, C., Zhang, D., Li, N., & Zhou, Z. H. 2014. B-Planner: Planning bidirectional night bus routes using large-scale taxi GPS traces. IEEE Transactions on Intelligent Transportation Systems, 15(4), 1451-146
2.   Fernández, R., Del Campo, M., & Swett, C. 2008. Data collection and calibration of passenger service time models for the Transantiago system. In European Transport Conference.
3.   Frez, J., Baloian, N., Zurita, G. and Pino, J.A., 2014. Dealing with Incomplete and Uncertain Context Data in Geographic Information Systems, IEEE Conference on Computer Supported Cooperative Work in Design (CSCWD), Hsinchu, Taiwan. 129-134.
4.   Haklay, M. and P. Weber, 2008. Openstreetmap: User-generated street maps. IEEE Pervasive Computing, 7(4): 12-18.
5.   Hopkins, L. D., 1977. Methods for Generating Land Suitability Maps: A Comparative Evaluation. Journal of the American Institute of Planners, 23(4), 386-400, 1977
6.   Murphy, M. D., 2005. Landscape architecture theory: an evolving body of thought. Waveland Press.
7.   Shafer, G., 1976. A mathematical theory of evidence (Vol. 1). Princeton: Princeton University Press.
8.   Silva, T.H., et al., 2013.Traffic Condition Is More Than Colored Lines on a Map: Characterization of Waze Alerts, in Social Informatics. Springer. p. 309-318.

Data Science in e-Health: Two Examples from Japan

Nelson Baloian[1], José A. Pino[1], Sergio Peñafiel[1], Jorge Quiteros[1],
Alvaro Riquelme[1], Horacio Sanson[2]

[1] Department of Computer Science, Universidad de Chile, Santiago, Chile.
{nbaloian,spenafie,jpino,jquitero}@dcc.uchile.cl
[2] Allm Inc. Tokyo, Japan.
horacio@allm.net

Abstract. Data Science is increasingly being applied in the realm of healthcare with encouraging results. This paper exemplifies two experiences in which Data Science can be applied in Medicine using different approaches. The first example uses Bayesian networks for recommending medical exams to be applied on patients arriving at an emergency unit of a hospital in order to have a more accurate diagnosis using patient symptoms as inputs. The second example uses a combination of machine learning and expert systems based on the Dempster-Shafer plausibility theory for predicting the risk of a patient of having a stroke in the near future given the clinical and the history of regular medical.

Keywords: Machine Learning · Data Science · Automatic Diagnose · Expert Systems · Health Risk Prediction.

1   Introduction

The number of studies on Data Science applied to healthcare has increased dramatically in the last decade, [1]. We have identified several explanations for this fact, which can be classified as related to advancements in computer science and others related to the medical realm. From the viewpoint of computer science, we can identify a solid development in algorithms and tools implementing them and the application of data analysis to almost any domain. On the other hand, there is the huge availability of medical-related data which makes the application of these techniques possible. There are several approaches to Data Science in Medicine which range from applying a pure statistical data mining approach to finding relationships among the available data and the expert system approach in which the expert's knowledge is modelled and coded into an application and the data is used to calibrate it. Of course, there are hybrid approaches on the whole spectrum.

This paper exemplifies two cases that have been applied in Japan by the Research and Development laboratory of the Allm Inc. Company. These cases were examined as part of several research grants provided by the Japanese government in order to boost the use of available health related data. The goal was to increase the efficiency of decision making in two scenarios: first, is the emergency unit of a hospital in which data analysis is used to develop and recommend a personal treatment plan including for incoming patients and to determine the appropriate tests and exams given the vital signs and symptoms of the patients. The second case concerns predicting the risk of a person to have a stroke in the near future given the information available of her/his past medical exams.

2 Bayesian Networks for Recommending Medical Exams in a Hospital's Urgency Unit

2.1 Problem Description, Requirements and Available Data

The Japanese public health system has two similar insurance programs that cover around 70% of nearly every medical procedure. In places like the emergency room of a hospital, medical procedures are tied to strict time and personnel constraints. Practitioners under pressure sometimes order unnecessary exams, increasing the cost of healthcare for the system and even exposing patients to secondary effects [2]. A software tool based on Artificial Intelligence could be of great help in suggesting to practitioners diagnostic exams based on a patients' data, symptoms and vital signs, as long as these recommendations are made in a fast and accurately way.

In cases where the access to good quality medical data is not possible, Bayesian networks appear as one of the most commonly used approaches for these kind of problems: Quick Medical Reference's significant adaptation to BNs (QMR- DT) [1] appeared only a few years after Bayesian networks were first introduced and are still used today [3]. Although many systems use Bayesian networks for medical diagnosis, not many focus on exam recommendation. The work presented here has its focus on suggesting useful exams based on pre-test probabilities.

A Bayesian network is a probabilistic graphical model representing a set of random variables (nodes) and their conditional dependencies (arcs) via a directed acyclic graph. Bayesian networks allow for efficient answering of queries related to arbitrary conditional probabilities involving the variables, such as the probability of a disease given a set of findings. A finding is defined as a symptom, a sign, or a laboratory image or any kind of exam result, that can move probabilities closer or away from a diagnosis. They usually have two associated numerical values: sensitivity, defined as the likelihood of a person who is ill to have a positive test result (true positive), and specificity, defined as likelihood of a healthy person having a negative test result (true negative) [4]. These sensitivity and specificity concepts are widely studied in the field of evidence based medicine and can be most of the time directly used with Bayesian network.

2.2 Methodology

Web Bayesian network models: Two different models of Bayesian networks were implemented. The first one is a typical BN2O network [5], a 2-layers network where diseases act independently in the form of a Leaky Noisy-OR [6]. This type of model does not use sensitivity and specificity values directly; it uses link probabilities and leak probabilities which can be estimated from sensitivity and specificity values [7].

Exact inference with a BN2O size is intractable, but sampling methods like Likelihood Weighting and Gibbs Sampling can be used. Although these methods converge to a precise solution, they can still take very long time if the required sample size is large.

The second model is much simpler: an array of independent Bayesian rules, where findings connect only to one disease at a time. In this model, sensitivity and specificity values can be directly used. Upon calculating a probability score for each disease, a ranking is elaborated. This method is not as precise as the first one, but allows for a much faster exact inference.

Database and Knowledge Base: Diseases were established using the Human Symptoms-Disease Network (HSDN) [8]. Data includes more than a hundred thousand symptoms-disease relationships for about 4000 diseases and around 350 symptoms and built from lexical co-occurrence of MeSH vocabulary terms [9] within medical literature.

After some filtering of diseases and symptoms, these links were translated into nodes and arcs for the network. The HSDN links included a TF-IDF score that was considered a general measure of symptom-disease medical relevance and therefore mapped to sensitivity and specificity values for the symptoms [10].

Prior probabilities for diseases were mapped from frequency values of medical emergency records (from Tsuyama Chuo Hospital in Okayama, Japan), using their ICD-10 medical codes and the Unified Medical Language System (UMLS) [11] and other sources.

Exam results and other findings were extracted from three different finding-disease web databases ([12], [13] and [14]). These databases were built by members of the medical community to organize such data resulting from medical studies making it available to anyone. Data included sensitivity and specificity values as well as the corresponding diagnosis. These findings were also mapped using the UMLS and later cleaned to finally obtain a big network of diseases and their related medical findings (symptoms, exams and others).

Exam Recommendation: The findings obtained from internet consist of signs, physical examinations, image and laboratory exam names (sometimes with results) and symptoms. Symptoms were tagged as so, thus they could be merged with the HSDN symptoms we already had and not appear as exam recommendations. Given that the goal is to recommend examinations, and that these can have different results for different diagnoses, these were manually post-processed to become exam and results where possible. Some exams (and diseases also) had gender or age constraints also integrated in the database.

With this preparation, the exam recommendation was made as follows: A patient's basic information along with a set of 5 or 6 present symptom names is used as input. A list of pre-test disease probabilities is calculated specifying one of the two models above. Based on this list, the non-symptom findings related to each disease are grouped together by examination name. This gives a list of exams which may help diagnose one or more of these diseases. The exams are then ranked based on the number of diseases they help to diagnose, and also according to how much is the probability change depending on its result.

2.3   Results

A preliminary test was developed with help of a medical expert. He assembled a list of 14 common and uncommon ER diagnoses, each one consisting of a set of up to six general symptoms, based on medical literature [15].

Figure 1 (left) shows, for each diagnosis, the proportion of correct differential diagnoses when using the simplified algorithm. Figure 1 (right) shows, for each diagnosis, the proportion of findings between the gold standard (the best available diagnostic test), other appropriate tests and other types of findings (like results from a physical exam) that could also be of use.

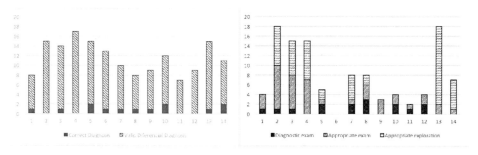

Fig. 1: Histograms showing (a) the proportion of correct and differential diagnoses and (b) the proportion of correct and appropriate exams, as well as non-exam appropriate findings (right).

Although the original list consists of about 4000 diseases, in most cases, specifying the presence of only a few symptoms leads to the correct diagnosis showing up as a candidate. The fact that there are also many other diseases that should not be discarded on a first inspection, shows that the processed HSDN symptom-disease links are rather significant.

As for the actual exam recommendation process, and given that it is based on the 20 pre-test most probable diseases, results show again that in most cases the diagnostic exams can be found in the final list. However, the results here are more disperse and are good for some diseases, like Laryngitis, but very poor for others, like Stroke. This fact probably occurs because the findings database we elaborated only has data for a fraction of the complete list.

We believe these results indicate that it is possible to build an exam recommendation tool which could potentially greatly improve the efficiency of the procedures of the ER even without the input of medical experts.

From a medical expert point of view, the results on the pre-test diagnoses show that the tool works quite well proposing differential diagnoses. Results on the proposed exams not only show the exam to be made but also the expected result on the exam. At this moment the system only pretends to suggest what exam should be made but in the future it could guide the practitioner to the most appropriate diagnosis using this results information.

3 Combining Machine Learning and Expert Systems' Approaches for Predicting Stroke Risk

3.1 Problem Description, Requirements and Available Data

Cardiovascular disease is the leading cause of deaths in the world. There were over 17.3 million deaths in 2013 and this number is expected to grow in the next years. Therefore, detecting the risk of developing this illness in early stages is recommended both for prevention and patients' treatment [16].

Records of patients' medical checkups have been collected in many countries. In the case of Japan, all active workers must have a medical checkup to monitor their health every year. The set of corresponding records are stored in large databases of health information which may be used to train classification or prediction models.

There are two basic approaches for designing predictive algorithms: the expert systems and the machine learning systems. The expert system encodes the experts' knowledge in some type of algorithm, such as if-then rules, Bayesian networks or association rules. Machine learning systems have algorithms which are applied directly on the massive data, searching for interrelations; examples include neural networks, decision trees, genetic algorithms, particle swarm optimization and multilinear regressions.

Both approaches have advantages and disadvantages. Expert systems need experts' work; they may be very busy or be unable to structure their knowledge, thus making it hard to code it into an algorithm. It may also be difficult to model some experts' uncertainties [17]. However, an advantage of expert systems is that they allow, to some degree, comprehending and checking why certain a prediction is made, which in the medical scenario is important, or even mandatory [18]. On the other hand, machine learning systems sometimes can help discover relationships and causalities that were not previously known by experts.

This chapter presents a classification model for the stroke risk prediction problem. The goal is to build a system that is accurate and with results which can be interpreted from a medical viewpoint; if this goal is achieved, the medical experts can participate in the classification process and can learn from it. The particular expert system approach we used is based on the Dempster-Shafer Theory of evidence [19]. The system was developed with an eclectic approach, in which the rules for the predictive algorithm developed under the expert system approach are inferred with machine learning techniques, which can be validated afterwards by the experts.

The proposed model is based on rules called hypotheses; each of these hypotheses has a mass assignment function and a condition to be applicable. The model fits the values of the mass assignment function according to the data using both statistical analysis and uncertainty measurement. After training, the model has a clear medical interpretation of the values obtained and its relation with the embedding of the patients in feature vectors.

The model developed was applied to a large data set of electronic medical records from the Tsuyoyama Hospital, Japan, which includes exam results and patient attributes. To evaluate the performance of the model, we also present results of some experiments comparing our method with some classic machine learning algorithms.

3.2   Methodology

The theoretical foundation for the methodology applied is the Dempster-Shafer Theory [19], which is a generalization of the Bayesian theory that does not require establishing prior probabilities to only single outcomes, it allows assigning "probabilities" to multiple outcomes measuring the degree of uncertainty of the process. Let X be the set of all states or events of a system. A mass assignment function m is a function satisfying:

$$m: 2^X \rightarrow [0, 1], \quad m(\emptyset)=0, \ \Sigma_{A \leq X} \ m(A)=1$$

The term $m(A)$ can be interpreted as the probability of getting exactly the outcome A, and not a subset of A.

The belief indicator is presented as the total evidence to support an outcome, and it is given by the following expression:

$$\text{Bel} (A) = \Sigma_{B \subseteq A} \ m(B)$$

The plausibility indicator is defined as the total amount of evidence that can support an outcome. This can be computed using a formula similar to the one for belief:

$$\text{Pl} (A) = \Sigma_{B \cap A \neq \emptyset} \ m(B)$$

It has been proved that belief and plausibility define lower and upper bounds for the real probability of the event [15], so then the following inequality is always true:

$$\text{Bel} (A) \leq \text{P} (A) \leq \text{Pl} (A)$$

The problem to be addressed can be described as, given a patient's historic medical information, which is the risk of he/she having a stroke? This problem can be reduced to one of discrete supervised learning, i.e., a classification problem. Under this approach the problem can be defined as follows: first, we consider two classes; the patient has a stroke or does not have it. The outcome of the algorithm is then the predicted class for each patient. However, this is not completely defined because outcome data is also time dependent; it is different for the classifier and for the further decision making process to have a stroke within the next year or in the next 10 years. To handle this in a convenient discrete manner, three future time intervals were established to evaluate the model: having a Stroke within one year, having a stroke within three years and finally, having a stroke within ten years. We believe the choice of these intervals suitably weighs the level of "emergency" of the patient's condition.

Embedding is the process of representing a study object as a feature vector. In this case, study objects are patients with their respective medical information. There are three data sources containing useful patient information that were used: patients' checkups, patients' attributes, and patients' disease history.

These data sources are not completely robust, since there are many missing values and in many cases joining the data sources for a patient is not possible. Therefore, we tried using three embedding structures for patients' information; from simple examination results to more complex feature vectors, as presented below. The first embedding takes into account the most recent result of each kind of exam a patient can have. In the Tsuyoyama data set there are 46 different types of exams, but not all patients have taken every exam so there are many missing values even in this simple representation. Most patients have less than 24 different exam results. The second embedding tested was to include, alongside the exam results, the patients' attributes. Now it is possible to obtain age and gender for all patients. The last embedding we tried is adding temporal information about the examinations and recent history. In this embedding, the gap in days between the evaluation time and the examination date of each type of exam is included, alongside the number of exams taken in the last year. The temporal information is used as a measurement of the relevance of each exam to the prediction.

Since the problem was defined as having two classes, the mapping to Dempster-Shafer theory requires a frame of discernment $X = \{$Stroke, No Stroke$\}$. Using this, a mass assignment function will operate from the power set of X, i.e.:

$$2^X = \{ \emptyset, \{\text{Stroke}\}, \{\text{No Stroke}\}, \{\text{Stroke, No Stroke}\}\}$$

For simplicity, let us call S the Stroke singleton, NS the No stroke singleton and E the Either group (which accounts for the uncertainty).

A rule is defined as a pair containing a predicate $p : X \to B$, which is a Boolean function to be evaluated using the feature vectors, and a mass assignment function m. A rule can be interpreted as the following: if p is true for a patient then it is known that m is applicable. Interpretability is straightforward from the mass assignment function because each component of the function of a rule can be interpreted as: S measures the certainty of having stroke, NS measures the certainty of not having stroke and E measures the uncertainty of both outcomes.

Rules can be established directly by experts or they can be inferred from data. For this work we developed a method to build rules considering certainty and uncertainty sources from data.

3.3 Results

A subset of the patients' data set was used. Patients with few different exam results (12 or lower) were not accounted. The evaluation date was set to July 2015 and consequently all data before this date was used to build the corresponding embedding for each patient. The data up to one year, after July 2015 (i.e. July 2016), was used to query the history and determine the class (Stroke, No Stroke). The resulting set was separated into two sets: a training set (70%) for the classifier to learn the rules and a testing set (30%) for performance evaluation. In addition to our model, three other machine learning methods were tested: Multilayer perceptron (MLP), Quadratic Discriminant Analysis (QDA) and Naive Bayes (GNB). All four methods used the same data set and embedding Model.

Each result is presented as a Receiver Operating Characteristic (ROC) curve and/or a Precision-Recall (PR) curve. These are two commonly used methods to evaluate performance in binary classification: the ROC curve corresponds to a chart that illustrates the rate of true positives to false positives when moving the acceptance threshold and the PR curve shows the performance of the classifier over certain class, showing the variation of the true positive rate with the total number of positive predictions when varying the acceptance threshold.

The first experiment consisted in using the proposed model with the first embedding, setting the number of bins for parsing the continuous data to 6. The result obtained can be visualized in the ROC curve of figure 2

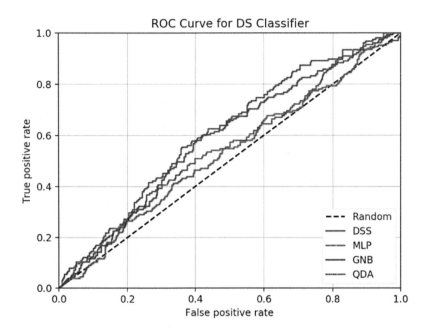

Fig. 2. ROC curve for stroke prediction using exam embedding.

The next experiment consisted of including the patients' attributes to feature vectors (embedding 2) obtaining the ROC curve shown in figure 3.
    The next experiment was performed only varying the number of bins for the continuous data, the same training and testing sets for each number of breaks were used. The result is shown in figure 4.
    The following experiment compared the strategies used to deal with missing values. Two of these strategies were tested: Mean imputation, which means to complete missing values with the mean value of each attribute, and skip missing values, which is the method used in the previous experiments. The result is presented in figure 5.

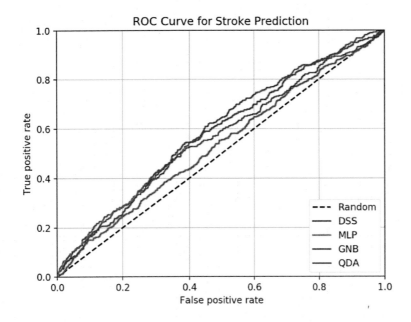

Fig. 3. ROC curve for stroke prediction using exam and attributes embedding.

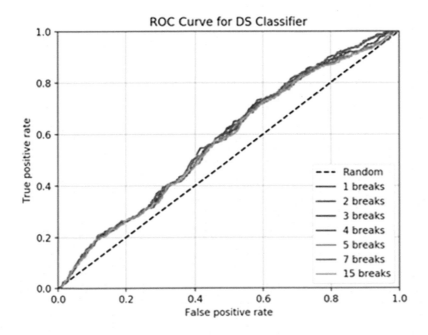

Fig. 4. ROC curve for stroke prediction varying the number of bins.

The final experiment included temporal information of the exams and the exam frequency using the third embedding. It uses 3 bins for continuous data and skips missing values. The results are shown in figure 6.

The results presented show that the proposed model performs better than the classic machine learning algorithms in most cases. Overall it achieved an accuracy of 60%.

Results of figure 2 show that even in non-complex embedding predicted, the proposed model performs well in accuracy. The addition of extra attributes to feature vectors shown in figures 3 and 6 helps to improve the accuracy of all methods, but the classic machine learning approaches tend to increase accuracy and approaches the ROC curve of the DS method. However, figure 6 shows that the proposed method performs better in the stroke class which is the interesting class to be predicted, and then it gives a better true positive rate than the others.

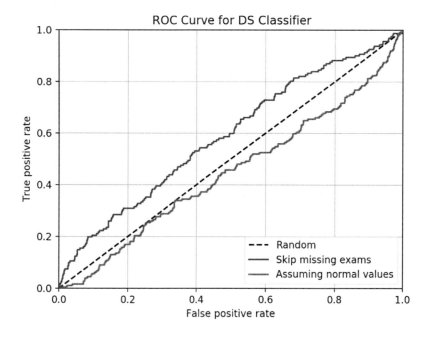

Fig. 5. ROC curve for stroke prediction using various strategies for missing values.

4   Conclusions

We have presented two examples of application of Data Science to e-Health. Both are from data from two hospitals in Japan. They show these approaches are applicable in terms of experimenter's effort, execution time and usability of the results. The cases have been abstracted from previous publications [10, 20].

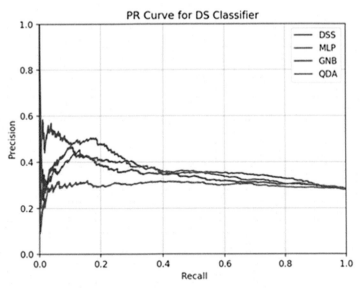

Fig. 6. PR curve for stroke class using exams, patients' attributes and temporal information.

Acknowledgments. Sergio Peñafiel was partially supported by Conicyt (Chile) scholarship N°22180506

References

1. Shwe, M.A., Middleton, B., Heckerman, D., Henrion, M., Horvitz, E., Lehmann, H., Cooper, G.: Probabilistic diagnosis using a reformulation of the internist- 1/qmr knowledge base. Methods of information in Medicine 30(4), 241–255 (1991).
2. Derlet, R.W., Richards, J.R.: Ten solutions for emergency department crowding. Western Journal of Emergency Medicine 9(1), 24 (2008).
3. Zagorecki, A., Orzechowski, P., Holownia, K.: A system for automated general medical diagnosis using bayesian networks. In: MedInfo. pp. 461–465 (2013).
4. Akobeng, A.K.: Understanding diagnostic tests 1: sensitivity, specificity and predictive values. Acta paediatrica 96(3), 338–341 (2007).
5. Henrion, M., Druzdzel, M.J.: Qualitative propagation and scenario-based explanation of probabilistic reasoning. arXiv preprint arXiv:1304.1082 (2013).
6. Srinivas, S.: A generalization of the noisy-or model. In: Uncertainty in Artificial Intelligence, 1993, pp. 208–215. Elsevier (1993).
7. Nikovski, D.: Constructing bayesian networks for medical diagnosis from incomplete and partially correct statistics. IEEE Transactions on Knowledge and Data Engineering 12(4), 509–516 (2000).
8. Zhou, X., Menche, J., Barabasi, A.L., Sharma, A.: Human symptoms–disease network. Nature communications 5, 4212 (2014).
9. Lipscomb, C.E.: Medical subject headings (mesh). Bulletin of the Medical Library Association 88(3), 265 (2000).

10. Quinteros, J., Baloian, N., Pino, J.A., Riquelme, A., Peñafiel, S., Sanson, H., Teoh, D.: Diagnostic test suggestion via bayesian network of non-expert assisted knowledge base. In: Advanced Communication Technology (ICACT), 2018 20th International Conference on. pp. 340–346. IEEE (2018).

11. Lindberg, D.A., Humphreys, B.L., McCray, A.T.: The unified medical language system. Methods of information in medicine 32(04), 281–291 (1993)

12. Browse databases and tools, https://www.essentialevidenceplus.com/content/eee

13. A database of sensitivity and specificity, http://getthediagnosis.org/

14. Jolis, T.W.: Sensitivity and specificity, http://www.sensitivityspecificity.com/.

15. Guzmán, L., Sánchez, F.J., Martín, M.F., Encinas, A.P., Arellano, I.J.P., Ruiz, J.L., Guzmán, C.M.J.L.: Diagnóstico diferencial en medicina interna. Elsevier, (2005).

16. Organization, W.H., et al.: Noncommunicable diseases country profiles 2014 (2014)).

17. Heckerman, David, Eric Horvitz, and Bharat N. Nathwani. "Toward normative expert systems part i." Methods of information in medicine 31 (2016)..

18. Bratko, I.: Machine learning: Between accuracy and interpretability. In: Learning, networks and statistics, pp. 163–177. Springer (1997).

19..Shafer, G.: Dempster's rule of combination. International Journal of Approximate Reasoning 79, 26–40 (2016) 22.

20. Peñafiel, S., Baloian, N., Pino, J.A., Quinteros, J., Riquelme, A., Sanson, H., Teoh, D.: Associating risks of getting strokes with data from health checkup records using Dempster-Shafer theory. In: Advanced Communication Technology (ICACT), 2018 20th International Conference on. pp. 239–246. IEEE (2018)

Chat Bot Improves the Motivation Toward Using a Self-Guided Mental Healthcare Course

Takeshi Kamita[1], Tatsuya Ito[1], Atsuko Matsumoto[2], Tsunetsugu Munakata[3] and Tomoo Inoue[4]

[1] Graduate School of Library, Information and Media Studies, University of Tsukuba, Tsukuba, Japan
s1730527@u.tsukuba.ac.jp / s1721654@s.tsukuba.ac.jp
[2] Graduate School of Comprehensive Human Science, University of Tsukuba, Tsukuba, Japan s1130368@u.tsukuba.ac.jp
[3] SDS Corporation, Icikawa, Japan munakata21@yahoo.co.jp
[4] Faculty of Library, Information and Media Science, University of Tsukuba, Tsukuba, Japan inoue@slis.tsukuba.ac.jp

Abstract. Mental healthcare has been in strong demand recently, and the number of experts such as counselors and medical doctors is not enough. Thus, both self-guided method of mental healthcare to promote employees' self-care efforts and a means to utilize the data of such employees' efforts to promote experts' more effective collaborative support are needed. A digital content of a self-guided mental healthcare course based on the counseling method SAT has been developed so far, but improving the user's motivation and convenience was an important issue. Use of a chat bot is proposed to solve the issue in this research. We built a chat bot course that is easier to use than the existing course, which improves the motivation of using the course.

Keywords: Mental Healthcare, Chat Bot, SAT method

1   Introduction

Research of online courses on mental health care has become active, as the importance of keeping good mental health has been widely recognized. Keeping employees' good mental health in companies has even been legislated recently in Japan. This resulted in sudden increase of the number of potential clients for mental counseling most of whom are not in sick, whereas the number of psychological experts or counselors to inspect does not. To cope with this issue, there is an increasing need for means to promote employees' self-care effort and to help the experts to manage and improve employees' mental health more effectively.

In order to realize such means, firstly, Nakanishi et al. [1] [2] started to have converted the SAT (Structured Association Technique) counseling method [3] into a digital content and developed a self-guided mental healthcare system with wearing a VR (Virtual Reality) Head Mounted Display (HMD), and eventually obtained good stress relief evaluation. The purpose of the system is not only to reduce stress but also to be aware of unaware automatic thinking and cognitive bias which are not normally easy to know by oneself without expert support. The accumulated date of such system will be also valuable for experts to support employees and improve the employees' mental health.

However, assuming that the course is utilized as mental health measures of companies, it shall be considered that employees who have various level of motivation in mental health efforts use it. In case of using the VR system, a dedicated HMD is installed in a common space of company such as a healthcare room or a relaxation room. Users have to move there whenever they use the tool, and the number of users at a time is naturally limited. If it is expected to be used on daily basis, this burden on users and the limitation are issues for convenience and practicality. Further, from the view point of usability, it is desirable to provide more simple and familiar operation to many users so as not to feel troublesome.

In this research, instead of using VR, we developed a self-guided mental healthcare course using a smartphone terminal popularized in general and a chat bot on the LINE[1] popularized as SNS platform in Japan. By using user's own familiar terminal, convenience and practicality will be improved. Also, by using the chat application, user will carry out the course more easily as if he/she is chatting with someone. Automatically guided course by chat bot will reduce user's troublesome operation by oneself and bring good effect of the user's motivation. We conducted a comparative evaluation experiment with an existing web course without a chat bot in order to investigate the chat bot effect on user's motivation to use the course.

2   Related Work

2.1   Use of a Smart Phone for Mental Healthcare

Mobile terminals are useful for mental health care because mobile terminals such as smartphones with remarkable popularity enable clients to obtain information on therapy freely and to promote active participation in care more than that [7]. In recent years, "Mood Mint" [9] was developed as a training tool to reduce anxiety and depression with reference to the Cognitive Bias Modification [8], which attracted attention as a counseling technique, mainly in the West. This application changes sensitivity to stresses by repeated training, but, does not bring the effect of stress reduction by one use. It provides incentive points of the token economy method [10] to keep the user's motivation for every use. Mindfulness-based stress reduction using meditation and mindfulness cognitive therapy is also active in research and psychology clinic in Europe and the United States [11] [12]. The "Headspace" [13] of the smartphone application is commercially available. This application provides courses for each purpose, such as coping with anxiety and dealing with depression and assists the progress of meditation. It is necessary to conduct while talking about a voice lecture 10 ~ 30 sessions 10-15 minutes once in one course, high motivation for users. In addition, the meditation method has a risk of increasing discomfort and pain [14], and it is considered that it should be handled carefully as a self-tool.

---

[1]"LINE" is a trademark of LINE CORPORATION.

2.2   Mental Healthcare Using a Chat Bot

Chat bot, a program that automatically talks through texts and voices has been developed since ELIZA [15] was developed in 1966.

In 2016, the development environment was opened as a messaging function of two social networking service platforms, Facebook[2] [16] and LINE [17], which enabled us to offer chat bots through SNS.

Chat bots in the field of mental health care have been developed to support interpersonal skills as a training component of a depression treatment program rather than therapy [18]. In addition, chat bots specialized to cope with stress problems have been also studied. Based on the Perceptual Control Theory, a self-help program MYLO in the form of a chat bot has been developed. In comparison with ELIZA on MLYO effectiveness, MYLO and ELIZA led to relief of pain, depression, anxiety and stress, MYLO was thought to be more useful for problem solving [19].

Besides that, an automatic conversational chat bot "Woebot" using Facebook messenger has been developed, based on Cognitive Behavior Therapy (CBT) which is a type of psychotherapy that encourages cognition and eases feelings [20]. As a result of an evaluation experiment using "Woebot" for college students, it was found that the subjects' depressive symptoms were significantly reduced. They commented that using "Woebot" was more receptive than traditional therapies. However, Woebot does not provide a program to carry out self-guided therapy, but programs of psychoeducation and training unique to CBT. It is necessary to continue training for a certain period of time before the achievement can be realized. That's why to maintain user's motivation is an important issue.

We aim to develop a self-guided mental healthcare course with using chat bot on a smartphone, in which user can carry out a self-therapy process and get an achievement to reduce or solve daily stresses for each use, and be promoted to continuously use.

3   SAT Method

3.1   Overview of SAT Method

SAT counseling method is a structured and interview form counseling method proposed by Munakata. The SAT method has a wide effective range such as a mental disorder (such as Depression, bipolar disorder, obsessive-compulsive disorder, personality disorder, schizophrenia, etc.) and various stress diseases. Unlike other conventional counseling methods focusing on the psychological aspects, the SAT method puts an importance on physicality and approaches mental problems from the bodily symptoms. Therefore, instead of working thought by linguistic stimulus, use visual stimulus from the presented image. It is possible to grasp unconscious true feelings and an essential desire in a short time because it can functionalize an association and a flash and intuition well.

---

[2]"Facebook" is a registered trademark of Facebook, Inc.

3.2 SAT Imagery Therapy using Light Image and Surrogate Face Representation

When a person who wants to have counseling recalls a stress scene, it is perceived as physical discomfort (such as Stomach shrinks, nervous, sweating hands, chest tightening). The SAT Imagery Therapy using Light image is a technique to change the discomfort to a good feeling and reduce the stress by the light image selected and perceived as a pleasant stimulus using it [5].

The SAT Imagery Therapy using Surrogate Face Representation is a technique for transforming the image for self to a good one by replacing the primitive landscape (for example scenery that many yells at around childhood) in the interpersonal relationship of the consultant with the image of surrogate face representation symbolizing pleasure. In psychology research, it is generally known that influence on self-esteem of a person is influenced by how the childcare attitude of a child career is positive or negative. By allowing the person to select an image of surrogate face representation with a sense of good feeling and recalling the image of the scene that makes a sense of security and providing a feeling of security, person perceives a sense that is safely protected, enhances self-esteem and encourages stress reduction.

4 Self-Guided Course Based on SAT Method

SAT counseling method does not need a client to tell his/her traumatic episodes or secrets and uses visual stimulation by images of light and positive face representation instead of nuanced linguistic expressions. Also, it is well structured which can be practiced in relatively short time in 5 to 10 minutes. But, in the light image method and representative face image method of the conventional SAT Imagery Therapy, the expert evokes client's association through hearing, counseling or presenting thumbnails on paper media without images (Fig. 1). In some cases, the image is not sufficiently evoked by merely looking at the image on the paper medium, and the counselor has a supplementary voice call or encourages eyes to close to arouse the image while seeing the

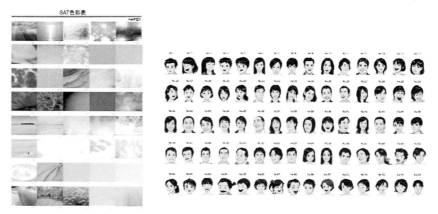

Fig.1. The list of images in printed form used in SAT method

reactions such as the words and expression Counselors play an important role in their progress. In this research, we created a chat bot course as a technique that can make self-progression even without counselor guidance support by converting SAT method to digital content and using chat bot.

4.1 Chat Bot Course

Based on the SAT method, the composition and procedures of the chat bot course are classified into three categories: (1) knowing their own mental condition (Assessment Part), (2) stress reduction (Solution Part), (3) knowledge and training to improve mental resistance (Learning Part). In this paper, we deal with assessment part and solution part.

4.1.1 Assessment Part

In the assessment part, we conducted a mental characteristic check test (Table 1) using the SAT six psychological scale [24] with the aim of measuring the mental condition and characteristics of the user and clarifying the changes before and after the use of the system (namely the effect).

4.1.2 Solution Part

The solution part presents the set questions in order and is proceeded by the process that the user answers to reduce the stress. In the first half (Table 2), first of all, ask the user to remember the stress that the user is holding in accordance with the question and make aware of how much stress it is. Next, comparing that stress to color and form, encouraging the perception of physical discomfort by making imagination as if you are approaching yourself. Furthermore, by specifying the part and type and expressing the degree of stress as a numerical value (%), prompting the focus of consciousness towards discomfort in the body.

In the second half, it will try to reduce stress in accordance with the questions of the light image method and representative face image method (Table 3) against the focused physical disorder.

Table 1. Mental characteristic check test

Scale	Contents	Number of questions	Score range
Self-esteem	The degree of whether the image for himself is good and accepted positively. If self-esteem is high, it is easy to think that you can deal with stress even if there is stress, and feeling of anxiety and depression are less likely to occur. (Self-esteem scale developed by Rosenberg [21] and translated into Japanese by Munakata et al.[22])	10	0-10
State-Trait Anxiety Inventory(STAI)	It tends to fall into anxiety. The degree of vague anxiety that reflects the individual's past experience rather than state anxiety that changes over time [23]	20	20-80
Self-rating Depression Scale(SDS)	Evaluation of depression symptoms including mood, appetite, sleep [24]	20	20-80
Health counseling necessity	Health counseling Required degree	10	0-20
Self-repression behavioral trait	Behavior characteristics that suppresses one's feelings and thoughts	10	0-20
Difficulty to feel emotion	Even if feel a painful thing, you tend not to be emotional, and tend to endure yourself	10	0-20

Table 2. First half of solution part

Order	Question
1	Please remind me again what you are concerned about now
2	What is it like? Please choose (Choose from 34 sources of stress such as your future, family health etc.)
3	How much is that degree? Please choose (Choose from 3 stages "not so" to "very much")
4	Does that stress comparable to color? (Choose from red, brown, black, gray, purple, navy blue, light blue)
5	If you compare the stress to the shape? (Square, rugosum, muddy, fluffy, pointed, flat, selected from spheres)
6	Close your eyes, thinking about where this thing comes and imagining this image, where do you feel strangeness in your body?
7	How is that strangeness? (Choose from throbbing, cold, heavy, dull, sore, tight, numb, stretch)
8	What is the stress level of current discomfort? (answer from 0%~100%)

Table 3. Second half of solution part

Order	Question
1	The part that feels that discomfort is healed by which color light is being protected?
2	Please choose a comfortable face that came into your eyes. Do you have anyone who smiled easily?
3	Looking at that face, what percentage of stress is the same as before? (Answer from 0%~100%)
4	What kind of character are you going to be when you see these people?
5	If such a personality, in the situation of stress, how can you handle it? It's okay with what you came up with intuition.
6	What do you think is the result if you do that?
7	Who is the most interested of those who have chosen?
8	What message will you give me?
9	How will you feel?
10	How did you feel about the stress that first came up when you were watching all the faces of these people?
11	How has the degree of stress changed? (Choose from 3 stages "not so" to "very much")

5   Implementation of the Chat Bot Course

In the conventional self-mental care method, withdrawal of users is the biggest problem [25] [26]. Even in the SAT method, frequent stimulation of representative face images can improve the mental health improvement effect [4] [5], the practice of course repeating is important. To solve this problem, we devised a chat bot course using a chat bot with conversational guidance. In this research, we adopted LINE which is widely used as a chat tool in Japan and developed a self-mental care system for practicing a chat bot course.

5.1 System Configuration

Fig. 2 shows the configuration of this system. The numbers in the figure show the flow of data processing. As a chat tool, we provide a chat bot service on the LINE application of the most popular SNS service in Japan. A chat bot application server is built on a commercial HEROKU[3] server [27], and LINE server is provided by LINE. Use the Messaging API [28] for cooperation. The Messaging API is an application programming interface that allows data to be exchanged between the chat bot application server and the sending and receiving server of LINE.

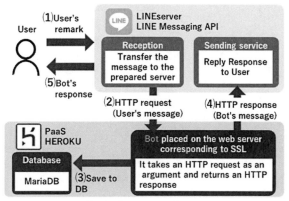

Fig. 2. System architecture

5.2 Start Screen

The user adds the LINE @ account of the chat bot. Select the added chat bot from the list on LINE's "Friends" screen and press the "Talk" button on the next screen to display the start screen (Fig. 3). The function menu at the bottom of the screen has three buttons, "Start", "Questionnaire", and "Help". Click "Start" to start the course. When " Questionnaire " is pushed, it transits to the web page screen (Fig. 4) of the mental characteristic check test which is the assessment section.

---

[3]"Heroku" is a registered trademark of Heroku, Inc.

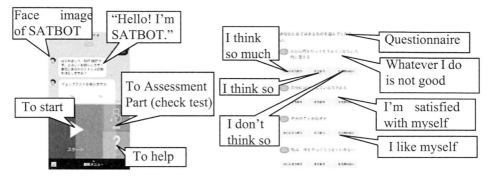

Fig. 3. The start screen   Fig. 4. The page of check test

5.3 Assessment Part

In the chat bot course, it is necessary to select and display a plurality of images from the image list, but since the display function of the chat screen of LINE is limited, in such a case, in the web page of a separate screen from the chat screen create. When the user selects a button with a URL link on the chat screen, it moves to the corresponding web page, and when the operation ends there, it returns to the chat screen. The mental characteristic check test conducted at the assessment part was made on this web page.

5.4 Solution Part

In this course, chat bot casts questions to users with balloons, just like having a chat with a friend. According to the flow of the first half of the solution part (Table 2), the user answers the question presented by the chat bot on the chat screen. First of all, recalling the stress scene (Table 2, Question 1) (Fig. 5), select from the list of prepared stress sources (such as things of own future, family health etc.) the one closer to the problem of the stress scene (Table 2, Question 3). Then choose from 3 options for the degree of stress. In the scene where stress is compared to color and shape (Table 2, Question 4), make a transition to a web page and make a selection from the image list. Returning to the chat screen, while recognizing the color and shape of the selected

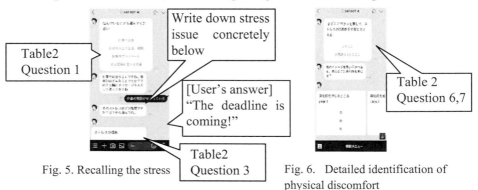

Fig. 5. Recalling the stress   Fig. 6. Detailed identification of physical discomfort

color, perceiving physical discomfort and specifying the part and type (Table 2, Questions 6, 7) (Fig. 6). Finally, answer by entering% of stress received by physical sense of discomfort in the text entry field.

Subsequently, questions are presented according to the latter half of the solution part (Table 3). The user is asked to select a light image (golden, green, peach, orange, blue, white, cream, yellow color, provided based on the optical image method) (Table 3, Question 1) and transit to the web page of the image list. From the image list, after selecting the image that can make an image that will heal physical discomfort, we return to the chat screen and the selected image is displayed (Fig. 7). Multiple images can be selected. After that, select a representative from the selected image and deepen the feeling of being protected by imagining speaking. Finally, it asked the user to answer how stress level against stress source confirmed in the first half has changed, and it ends.

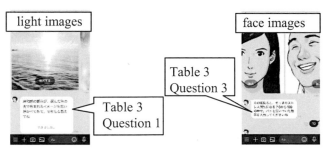

Fig. 7. The display for selected light image

Fig. 8. The display for the selected surrogate face representation image

6 Experiment

In this research, the evaluation experiment was carried out with the approval of the ethics review committee in Faculty of Library Information and Media Science, University of Tsukuba (Notification No. 29-137).

6.1 Purpose of the Experiment

Evaluate the stress reduction effect by implementing one chat bot course using smartphones and the motivation to use the course by the subsequent questionnaire survey. This will examine the effectiveness of using chat bots in self - mental care system. As a control group, use a web course created with only web pages without using chat bots.

6.2 Web Course

As for the web course, like the chat bot course, we developed it on the web page in order of the SAT method which converted into digital contents.

6.2.1 Start Page

When the user logs in using the ID and password on the login page, a start page is displayed (Fig. 9). Select the left button on the same page and go to the page of the Assessment part and select the other to move to the page of the solution part. After moving from this homepage, the user operates according to the instruction of the text displayed mainly at the top of each page.

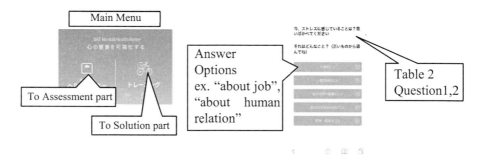

Fig. 9. The start page

Fig. 10. The page for re-calling stress

6.2.2 Assessment Part

As in the chat bot course, the mental characteristic check test is displayed in the assessment part (same as in Fig. 4).

6.2.3 Solution Part

According to the flow of the first part of the solution part (Table 2), on the web page, the user selects a button or the like prepared on the page to answer the question described in text at the top and responds. First of all, recalling the stress scene (Table 2, Question 1), select from the list of prepared stress sources (such as things of own future, family health etc.) the one closer to the problem of the stress scene. Then choose from 3 options for the degree of stress (Table 2, Question 3) (Corresponding to Fig. 5 of the chat bot course). Next, in a scene where stress is compared to color and shape (Table 2, Question 4), by selecting on the image list page of each color and form, imagining a place where it comes close, perceiving physical discomfort, (Table 2, Questions 6 and 7) (corresponding to Fig. 6). Finally, use the slider function to set the percentage of stress suffered by physical discomfort.

Subsequently, questions are presented according to the latter half of the solution part (Table 3). The user is asked to select from the list of light images (Table 3 Question 1),

110

and the image selected in Fig. 12 is displayed (corresponding to Fig. 7). Next, while having the feeling enveloped in this light image, a selection is requested from the list of representative face images, and the image selected in Fig. 13 is displayed (corresponding to Fig. 8). Using the slider function, you can set how much stress% changes when you are viewing images. After that, select a representative from the selected image and deepen the feeling of being protected by imagining speaking. Finally, it asked users to select how stress level against stress source confirmed in the first half has changed, and it ends.

The therapy process of the web course is basically same as the chat bot course, however, a user needs to read an instruction on each web page, choice an answer, and then push a button to move the next page manually. In other words, a user does not only feel comfortable by focusing on the therapy process but also need to think about what to do next.

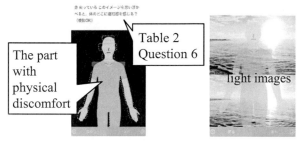

Fig. 11. The page for detailed identification of physical discomfort

Fig 12 Displaying light image

Fig 13 Displaying face image

6.3   Procedure

27 college students were selected as subjects, and randomly assigned to two groups, a chat bot course conducted experiment group and a web course running group (chat bot course: N = 15, male 6, female 9 Name, average age 24.80 years, SD = 1.57, web course: N = 12, male 6, female 6, average age 25.33 years, SD = 3.37). For each group, after explaining the SAT method, the contents of the experiment and the system, we started to use the system and conducted a questionnaire survey on motivation to use and finished the experiment.

6.4   Measurement

The evaluation of the motivation to utilize the system (the effect of improving the motivation to use) was evaluated using a questionnaire created based on the Technology Acceptance Model (TAM) which is a human behavior model that predicts and explains the usage behavior of the information system (7 levels of Likert scale) [29]. In this model, as factors leading users to use a system, Perceived Usefulness (PU), Perceived Ease of Use (PEOU), Attitude toward using (AU) and Behavioral Intention to use (BI) are measured.

6.5 Data Analysis

The score of the Likert scale of the question included in each factor of a questionnaire created based on TAM was added up and tested by Mann-Whitney's U test. Python's SciPy package was used for analysis. All tests used bilateral measurements.

7 Result

7.1 Motivation to Use the Courses

Looking at the results of analysis by Mann-Whitney's U test shown in Table 5, it was found that the average score of the chat bot course was high for all factors. In addition, a significant tendency was seen in the PU factor, and a significant difference was found in the factor of PEOU and factor of BI to use the course

Table 5. The score of the questionnaire based on the TAM model
(Chat bot course: N = 15, Web course: N = 12)

Scale	Average ± SD	p
PU (Perceived Usefulness)		
Chat bot course	24.73±6.09	0.078†
Web course	21.92±4.89	
PEOU (Perceived Ease of Use)		
Chat bot course	18.53±2.92	0.030*
Web course	17.33±1.44	
AU (Attitude Toward Using)		
Chat bot course	21.27±5.06	0.140
Web course	19.50±3.75	
BI (Behavioral Intention to Use)		
Chat bot course	16.00±3.09	0.027*
Web course	13.25±3.44	

Mann-Whitney's U test †:$p<0.1$, *:$p<0.05$,**:$p<0.01$

7.2 Discussion

Regarding the evaluation of the motivation to use the system by TAM, PEOU and BI were higher in the chat bot course than in the web course. In PEOU's "It's easy to learn to use this system", "I think it is easy to master this system," "I think it is easy to use this system" 3 total points and BI's "I will use this system in the near future", "I believe that the interest in this system will increase in the future", "Recommend to use this system for others" 3 total points, a significant difference was observed at the total points of the two question items. In addition, a significant trend was seen at the total point of the five question items of PU.

From the above, it was shown that the use of the chat bot in the self-guided mental healthcare series enhances the possibility of increasing the willingness to use, and it was able to confirm its effectiveness. As a future research subject, we will carry on continuing experiments to investigate stress reduction effect and actually verify whether the course will be used continuously.

8   Conclusion

In this study, the SAT method was converted to digital contents, a self-guided mental healthcare course and a system using a chat bot were developed. When the course is utilized as mental health measures of companies, it shall be considered that employees with various level of motivation in mental health efforts use the course. By using the chat bot, a user can carry out the course according to the automatic guidance of the chat bot without thinking what he/she should do next. There is a possibility that the chat bot can prevent users from lowering motivation to use. The results of the comparative evaluation experiment with an existing web course without a chat bot show the possibility that the use of the chat bot enhances user's motivation.

References

1. Asuki Nakanishi, et al.: A VR Self Mental Healthcare System by SAT-Based Method, IPSJ SIG Technical Report, vol, 2017-DCC-15, no.35, pp.1-8, 2017.
2. Tatsuya Ito, et al.: A Self-guided Mental Healthcare Digital Content for Smartphone VR Based on the Counseling Technique SAT Method, IPSJ SIG Technical Report, vol.2018-DCC-18, no.37, 1-8, 2018.
3. Tsunetsugu, M.: SAT therapy, KANEKOSHOBO, Japan, 2006.
4. Tsunetsugu, M.: The applicability of the simple edition of SAT method in promoting universal health, Journal of Health Counseling, 17, pp. 1-12, 2011.
5. Tsunetsugu, M.: Does SAT Re-scripting Expression Imagery Enable Us to Overcome Unendurable Hardships toward True Life Career? Journal of Health Counseling 15, pp.1-12 (2009).
6. Yoshihumi Tsuji: Development of a self-image focusing coping strategy aimed at improving psychological competitive skills. 2011. PhD Thesis. University of Tsukuba, Japan.
7. Kelley, Christina, Bongshin Lee, and Lauren Wilcox: Self-Tracking for Mental Wellness: Understanding Expert Perspectives and Student Experiences. Proceedings of the SIGCHI conference on human factors in computing systems. CHI Conference 2017, pp. 629–64
8. Wang Rui, et al: StudentLife: assessing mental health, academic performance and behavioral trends of college students using smartphones. Proceedings of the 2014 ACM International Joint Conference on Pervasive and Ubiquitous Computing, 2014, pp3-14.
9. "Mood Mint". http://www.biasmodification.com/, (view 2017-11-16).
10. F.B. Dickerson, et al.: The token economy for schizophrenia: review of the literature and recommendations for future research. Schizophrenia Research, vol.75, pp.405-416, 2005.
11. Jon Kabat-Zinn. An outpatient program in behavioral medicine for chronic pain patients based on the practice of mindfulness meditation: Theoretical considerations and preliminary results. General Hospital Psychiatry, 1982, Vol. 4, Issue 1, pp.33-47.
12. Rinske A. G: et al.: Standardized Mindfulness-Based Interventions in Healthcare: An Overview of Systematic Reviews and Meta-Analyses of RCTs, PLOS ONE.
13. "Headspace". https://www.headspace.com/, (view 2017-11-16).
14. Lindahl J.R., Fisher N.E., Cooper D.J., Rosen R.K., Britton W.B. (2017). The varieties of contemplative experience: A mixed-methods study of meditation-related challenges in Western Buddhists. PLoS ONE 12(5): e0176239.
15. Weizenbaum, J.: ELIZA: A computer program for the study of natural language communication between man and machine Communications of the ACM, 1966, 9 (1), pp.36-45.
16. "Facebook".https://www.facebook.com/, (view 2017-11-30).

17. "LINE". https://line.me/ja/, (view 2017-11-30).
18. Elmasri, D., & Maeder, A. (2016). A conversational agent for an online mental health intervention. Brain Informatics and Health: International Conference, BIH 2016, Omaha, NE, USA, October 13-16, 2016 Proceedings, pp. 243-251.
19. Gaffney, Hannah, et al. "Manage your life online (MYLO): A pilot trial of a conversational computer-based intervention for problem solving in a student sample." Behavioural and cognitive psychotherapy 42.6 (2014): 731-746.
20. Fitzpatrick, Kathleen Kara, Alison Darcy, and Molly Vierhile. Delivering Cognitive Behavior Therapy to Young Adults With Symptoms of Depression and Anxiety Using a Fully Automated ConverSATional Agent (Woebot): A Randomized Controlled Trial. JMIR Mental Health 4(2) (2017): e19.
21. Rosenberg, M.: Society and the adolescent self-image, Princeton New Jersey, Princeton University Press (1965).
22. Tsunetsugu, M., Takeshi, T., Yojiro, K., et al.: A comparative study on the family environment and mental health of Japanese and American youth, Scientific research report in Ministry of Health, Labour and Welfare, Japan (1987).
23. Spielberger, C.D.: STAI manual, Palo Alto, Calif, Consulting Psychologist Press, 1970.
24. Zung, W. K. K.: A self-rating depression scale, Archives of general psychiatry, 12, pp. 63-70 (1965).
25. Melville, K.M., Casey, L. & Kavanagh, D.J. (2010). Dropout from internet-based treatment for psychological disorders. Brit. J. of Clinical Psychology, 49, pp. 455-471.
26. Meyer, B., Ritterband, L. & Smits, L. (2010). The ins and outs of an online bipolar education program: A study of program attrition. Journal of Medical Internet Research, 12 (5).
27. Middleton, Neil, and Richard Schneeman. Heroku: Up and Running: Effortless Application Deployment and Scaling. O'Reilly Media, Inc. (2013).
28. "LINE Messenger API" https://developers.line.me/en/docs/messaging-api/overview/ (2017-11-30).
29. Davis, Fred D., Richard P. Bagozzi, and Paul R. Warshaw: User acceptance of computer technology: a comparison of two theoretical models. Management science 35.8 (1989) pp. 982-1003.

Smart Networking and Memory Systems

A.J. Han Vinck[1,2]

[1] University Duisburg-Essen, Germany
[2] University of Johannesburg, South Africa
han.vinck@uni-due.de

Abstract. We discuss the use of different types of memory systems. Error correcting codes improve the performance with respect to the life time of a memory. Special coding techniques are required to optimize storage capacity. We consider this problem from an information theory point of view. We start with the memory with defects and via write-once memory and flash, we end with the phase-change random access memory.

Keywords: memory, coding, write-once.

A smart network is a network where energy is transported controlled and supported by a parallel communication infrastructure. The problems in smart networking are very similar to problems in normal communication networking. As an example, connections between network nodes can be wireless and/or wired. In communication networks, optimization of throughput can be a goal. For a smart network, we consider the consumption-price management from a user point of view [1] as a problem. Based on the user prescribed consumption constraints coming from his own processes, we deal with a linear or convex programming task. We extended this model [2] to include batteries or memory. The inclusion of batteries could make users independent of the central control. This will be of great influence for future networks where a user can be almost completely independent of a utility. We can decide to store energy in the "cloud" as the utility or process it locally at the users. Furthermore, energy can be bought at a low price during low cost periods.

In communication networks we are dealing with large volumes of data to be stored. This can be done at a central facility (cloud) or locally. Efficiency, reliability, security and privacy are of concern. Problems might be easier to solve in a "private" memory system. Thus, memory will also be vital for efficient operation in communication networks. We consider the application of error correcting codes for some specific problems that can occur in data storage systems.

The application of coding for improved reliability in memory systems started with the work of Richard Hamming at Bell labs in 1946. He was annoyed by the fact the computer system stopped working after detecting an error in the memory. This happened during the weekend, which delayed his simulation results. The code used was a single parity check code with minimum distance 2 that detects one error. The extension to a 2D parity check code with minimum distance 4 enabled the correction of one error. Later, Hamming discovered his class of Hamming codes with minimum distance 3 and with higher efficiency. An interesting question is: how much longer can we work with a memory system if we store the information with an error correcting code that corrects errors up to halve the minimum distance. In [3] we consider this problem and under certain conditions, we show that the Mean Time to Failure of a memory of size N words of length n, an error correcting code of minimum distance D and a cell error probability p per time unit, is given by

$$MTTF(uncoded) \approx 1/npN,$$
$$MTTF(coded) \approx 1/npN^{1/(D-1)}.$$

For the $D = 3$ Hamming code, the gain in time is proportional to $N^{1/2}$. Hence, gain proportional to size of the memory. For large memory systems, the probability that the memory is without errors (defects) goes to zero. Without error correcting mechanisms the process yield will also go to zero. This leads automatically to the necessity of using error correcting codes.

Soft errors in a memory can be corrected by an error correcting code and restored into the memory. Hard errors, known as defects cannot be restored in a corrected way. These type of errors are permanent. For an error fraction p, the error correcting code has a maximum theoretical efficiency of $k/n = 1 - h(p)$, where k is the number of information bits and $h(p)$ the binary entropy function. For a defect matching code the maximum efficiency is $k/n = 1-p$. In practice, for short word lengths a practical method needs to be developed. We give an example in [3]. A practical problem, connected to the use of error correcting mechanisms, is that of delay. Processing data at reading or storing of information may cause unacceptable delays.

Flash memories can be used as permanent storage systems, since the size can be very large. Before storing information in a particular sector, the sector must be erased. To avoid this erase phase, we can store information in a Flash memory equivalent to storing information in a memory with defects. Increasing the capacity of a flash memory can be done by using multi-valued cells. We investigated the performance of Flash using the WOM mode in [4]. For T writes in a particular cell, we need T time instants for writing the information and T time instants for erasing the cells. The efficiency is thus ½ bit per writing cycle/cell. Using a binary WOM code, in T writing we can store about $\log(T+1)$ bits/cell. For $T = 2$, we store 1.58 bits in two writings instead of 1 bit in the standard writing with an erasure cycle. This theoretical result is rather surprising, but probably not very useful in practice.

The drawback of Flash memory is the writing and reading speed. Another drawback is the lifetime of a flash memory. Every access reduces the lifetime. These problem might be solved by using a new development in Phase-Change Random access memories (DRAM), [5]. A particular memory cell is heated in such a way that cell material is brought into an amorphous or crystalline state which changes the resistance of the material. Information theoretical methods can be used to estimate the capacity of the memory when only a limited number of bits can be changed.

Other methods for storing information are using optical and/or magnetic properties of the storage material. The problems are determined by the mechanisms of storing information.

References

1. A.Harutyunyan, A. Poghosyan and A.J. Han Vinck: Linear and convex programming problems in smart grid management. *WSPLC* 2010 (2010).
2. Omowunmi Mary Longe, Khmaies Ouahada, Suvendi Rimer, Hendrik C. Ferreira and A. J. Han Vinck: Distributed Optimisation Algorithm for Demand Side Management in a Grid-Connected Smart Microgrid. *Sustainability*, *9* (7), 1088 (2017).
3. A.J. Han Vinck and Karel Post: On the influence of coding on the mean time to failure for degrading memories with defects. *IEEE Transactions on Information Theory*, 35 (4), (1989).
4. A.J. Han Vinck and Hiro Morita: Codes over the ring of integers modulo m. *IEICE Trans. Fundamentals,* E81-A (10):2013–2018, (1998).
5. https://www.theverge.com/2016/5/17/11693054/ibm-phase-change-memory-breakthrough-ram-flash-storage.

Thoughts on Information-Theoretic Aspects of several Problems in Data Science[1]

Ashot N. Harutyunyan[1], Yanling Chen[2], and A.J. Han Vinck[2]

[1] VMware
aharutyunyan@vmware.com

[2] Institute for Digital Signal Processing, University of Duisburg-Essen
{yanling.chen;han.vinck}@uni-due.de

Abstract. We discuss information-theoretic contexts of several application-oriented data science problems. Largely motivated by intelligent and data-driven cloud management tasks in the industry, we specify several problem frameworks in view of information theory which can have also interesting algorithmic implications for those data science problems.

Keywords: Data science, information theory, data compression/quantization, information bottleneck, anomaly detection, typicality, rate-distortion.

1 Introduction

The technology of an intelligent and data-driven management of cloud computing infrastructures and applications is tasked with multitude of data science, machine learning, and AI problems. Some of earlier notes on this subject can be found in [1] and references therein. Those problem relate to anomaly detection and forecasting/prediction for time series and unstructured data (see [2,3]) sampled from enormously large IT systems in terms of various process indicators, change point detection, event correlation and problem root causing, intelligent workload placement and performance optimization, etc., strongly relying on statistical, machine learning, and AI solutions in near future to enable a cloud computing to be fully self-driving.

In [4]-[8] it is already well-recognized the value of the rate-distortion framework from information theory [9] in effective management of large data bases subject to preserving "relevant" (to the application) information content. We are going to expand on this and related contexts to address some problem formalisms to be explored further.

2 Atypicality is not Ignorable

Typicality argument is of central importance in Information Theory [9]. Optimal lossless compression of a Discrete Memoryless Source (DMS) X with distribution P^* is based on the Asymptotic Equipartition Property (AEP), with compression rate $H(P^*)$, the entropy of the source. Encoding only typical sequences [9] and ignoring atypical

---

[1] Collaboration of authors is supported by AvH Foundation.

sequences (having empirical distribution not "close" to P^*) introduces arbitrarily small ($\varepsilon > 0$) reconstruction error, asymptotically.

Optimal lossy compression with average distortion Δ is characterized by the rate-distortion function (as a minimization problem on the mutual information between input and reconstruction variables subject to expected distortion not higher than Δ). To achieve this bound asymptotically we need to take care (to appropriately encode) of only those messages that have empirical distribution "close" to source distribution P^*, again, ignoring the rest of messages.

At the same time, for the rate-distortion with error decaying [10] with a prescribed exponent $E > 0$, we have to take care of "Δ −covering" only for messages having empirical distribution P within KL-divergence E from P^*. It means that the "typicality radius" is not arbitrarily small or zero, it is E. This typicality radius increases with higher requirement on rate of error probability decay, we ignore less and less messages that are not "similar" to P^*. With $E \to \infty$ we take care of all messages and achieve zero-error compression rate which does not depend on the source distribution anymore.

The concept of the typicality radius can be applied to perform anomaly/outlier detection tasks (see the lecture notes on typical vs atypical [11]). In a non-asymptotic mode, we can declare outlying any message $x_n = (x_1, x_2, \ldots, x_n)$ that has an empirical distribution P_{x_n} beyond a preliminarily fixed radius $T \geq 0$ based on different distance measures (KL or total variation as in Fig. 1).

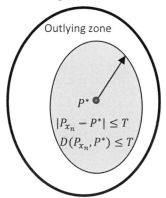

Fig. 1. Visualizing the typicality-based outlier detection with different "distance" measures.

In some data science applications, there is a need to loosely compress the data subject to preserving important/relevant/interesting patterns, meaning that the average reconstruction quality for all messages homogeneously is not valid. For instance, it is required to preserve anomalous patterns with high resolution but spare storage for "normal" or expected/typical behaviors (expected patterns can be characterized by their closeness to the "normalcy states" or distributions $P_{s_1}, P_{s_2}, \ldots P_{s_m}$ of the source). This is linking the data compression subject to a relevance criterion (see the information bottleneck concept [4]: quantize the data X so that to preserve its relevance (mutual information) to another correlated random variable Y) coming from an anomaly detection task. At the same time, there might be requirements to operate within some storage and its cost limits. This means that under these requirements we cannot ignore to encode the atypical sequences. Therefore, we have to operate in the "zero-error" mode, since otherwise, the role of atypical sequences in the mode of an error probability vanishes. Then we can think of rate-distortion settings, where the achievable quantization levels for typical and atypical patterns of the data source are different and optimized to cost functions subject to an overall storage limit.

Since now the atypicality coding rate $R_{AT}(\Delta_{AT})$ might even dominate the coding rate of typical sequences $R_T(\Delta_T)$, subject to fidelity requirements Δ_{AT} and Δ_T, $\Delta_{AT} \leq \Delta_T$, respectively, an interesting problem is to reveal the conditions when those coding rates are equal (an *equilibrium* holds). This means that we still allocate asymptotically the same storage for compressing the typical sequences subject to the prescribed distortion criterion while storing/restoring also all atypical messages. Such an equilibrium is not always attainable.

3   Compress more than Relevantly

Another data-science related formulation could be an extended information bottleneck method in view of privacy and security applications:
-   quantize variable X subject to an expected distortion less than Δ (preserve utility)
$$Ed(X; X') \leq \Delta$$
-   so that quantized version X' is still relevant to a variable Y (relevance) with mutual information
$$I(X; Y) \rightarrow max$$
-   but it maximally hides private information content in Z (privacy)
$$I(X; Z) \rightarrow min$$
Such an extended setting includes other models of prior art [5]-[8].

4   Compression with limited Data Processing Capabilities

Principal component analysis (PCA) or independent component/feature analysis (IC(F)A) can be utilized as lossy data compression methods for large data sets [12]-[13].

From information-theoretic perspectives such a goal might mean a task of describing the common information within the database. However, for big data sets with billions of attributes, PCA-like approaches are computationally hard. At the same time, identifying the most important subset of attributes that represents the whole database good enough in sense of its information content is another computationally hard problem. We can think of models that approximate such a task.

Assume we have n variables but able to jointly process only $k < n$ of them. How can we achieve the best quantization under such a constraint that maximizes the mutual information between the original and compressed sets of variables? With such a logic, we arrive at a communication model in Fig. 2 ($n = 3$, $k = 2$). A relevant reference is [14].

The problem is to find the best quantization strategy to maximize the mutual information between input and output variables:

$$I(X_1, X_2, X_3; Y_1, Y_2, Y_3) \rightarrow max.$$

In other words, characterize the achievability rates of this multi-terminal communication model with or without distortion criterion.

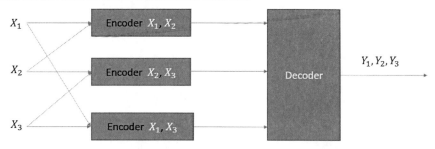

Fig. 2. Model of communication with limited data processing capabilities: $n = 3$ (variables), $k = 2$ (encoder/quantizer input limit).

5 Data Densification to capture Relevant Information

In other data science applications, an opposite problem to data quantization arises. Specifically, when the current monitoring/sampling rate of the process does not capture expected relevant information (for example, the investment I make with per 5-minute sampling of the data center indicators does not reveal enough information to predict my application degradations (in terms of its key performance indicators, like the response time), the relevant analytics engine is required to "densify the data", in other words, increase the sampling rate of monitoring flows to achieve such a goal. That algorithmically means that we need to increase the sampling rate until no further information gain is achievable.

Let us assume we monitor variables $X_1, X_2 \dots, X_n$ (time series or log source) sparsely, so instead of seeing their original joint distribution P^*, actually we see P, which is within some "distance" from P^*. Observing P does not give enough information regarding a relevant variable Y. Then we can think of an algorithmic approach to sample the variables with higher rate (not necessarily uniformly for every variable) to capture the relevant information, in other words, maximize the mutual information with Y, and perform it with fastest "path".

References

1. Harutyunyan, A.N., Poghosyan, A.V., and Grigoryan, N.M.: Experiences in building an enterprise data analytics. In: Proceedings of International Workshop on Information Theory and Data Science: From Information Age to Big Data Era, pp. 89-94, October 3-5, Yerevan, Armenia (2016).

2. Harutyunyan, A.N., Poghosyan, A.V., Kushmerick, N., and Grigoryan, N.M.: Learning baseline models of log sources. In: Proceedings of CODASSCA 2018, September 12-15, Yerevan, Armenia (2018).

3. Harutyunyan, A.N., Poghosyan, A.V., Grigoryan, N.M., Kushmerick, N., and Beybutyan, H.: Identifying changed or sick resources from logs, submitted to 4th International Workshop on Data-Driven Self-Regulating Systems (DSS 2018), September 7, Trento, Italy (2018).

4. Tishby, N., Pereira, F.C., and Bialek, W.: The information bottleneck method. In: Proceedings of 37th Annual Allerton Conference on Communication, Control and Computing, (1999).

5. Sankar, L., Rajagopalan, S.R., and Poor, H.V.: Utility-privacy tradeoffs in databases: An information-theoretic approach. IEEE Transactions on Information Forensics and Security 8(6), pp. 838-852, (2013).

6. Makhdoumi, A., Salamatian, S., Fawaz, N., and Medard, M.: From the information bottleneck to privacy funnel. Arxiv https://arxiv.org/abs/1402.1774, (2014).

7. Baggen, S.: On prediction using a data base. In: Proceedings 10th Asia-Europe Workshop on Concepts in Information Theory and Communications, June 21-23, Boppard, Germany (2017).

8. Kalantari, K., Sankar, L., and Kosut, O.: On information-theoretic privacy with general distortion cost functions. In: Proceedings of IEEE International Symposium on Information Theory, June 25-30, Aachen, Germany (2017).

9. Cover, T. and Thomas, J.: Elements of Information Theory, Wiley, (1991).

10. Haroutunian, E.A., Haroutunian, M.E., and Harutyunyan, A.N.: Reliability Criteria in Information Theory and in Statistical Hypothesis Testing. In: Foundations and Trends in Communications and Information Theory 4(2–3), pp. 97–263, Now Publishers (2008).

11. Han Vinck, A.J.: Information theory and big data: Typical or not typical, that is the question. In: Proceedings of Workshop on Information Theory and Data Science: From Information Age to Big Data Era, pp. 5-8, Oct. 3-5, Yerevan, Armenia (2016).

12. Harutyunyan, A.N., Poghosyan, A.V., and Grigoryan, N.M.: On compression of time series databases. In: Proceedings of 10th Asia-Europe Workshop on Concepts in Information Theory and Communications, June 21-23, Boppard, Germany (2017).

13. Poghosyan, A.V., Harutyunyan, A.N., and Grigoryan, N.M.: Compression for time series databases using principal and independent component analysis. In: Proceedings of IEEE International Conference on Autonomic Computing (ICAC), July 17-21, Columbus, Ohio, US (2017).

14. Lim, S.H., Feng, Ch., Pastore, A., Nazer, B., and Gastpar, M.: Towards an algebraic network information theory: Simultaneous joint typicality coding. In: Proceedings of IEEE International Symposium of Information Theory, June 25-30, Aachen, Germany (2017).

Design and Security Analysis of Novel White Box Encryption*

Gurgen Khachatrian[1] and Sergey Abrahamyan[2]

[1] American University of Armenia, Yerevan M. Baghramyan 40, Armenia
gurgenkh@aua.am
[2] Institute of Informatics and Automation Problems, P. Sevak street 1, Yerevan
0014, Armenia
serj.abrahamyan@gmail.com

1   Extended Abstract

Keywords: White-box cryptography, Encryption, Security analysis.

In many applications implemented in untrusted environments all operations with the secret key during an encryption operation are "obfuscated" in a way that while an attacker has access to all routines of operations, it will nevertheless be hard for him to determine the value of the secret key used during these operations. This kind of execution of encryption operation is called a White Box implementation.

In so called "black-box" encryption model cryptographic keys are protected via different methods such as passwords or in tamper-resistant modules. In this case the attacker of the system can see only inputs and outputs of the encryption engine and has no access to intermediate values inside the black box. In the white-box context an encryption routine is represented via lookup tables based on secret keys of the encryption which are accessible to the public in each of rounds.

The main purpose of these look-up tables is to hide cryptographic keys while performing correct encryption operations. As such white-box encryption allows anyone who has access to the white-box lookup tables to implement an encryption operation in the way that only the owner of a secret key can decrypt a result and get a valid plaintext. The security of the white-box encryption is the complexity of guessing a secret key or making a decryption operation with-out the knowledge of a secret key. In this way white-box look up tables can be considered as a Public key in the sense that anyone can encrypt a message, but only the holder of a secret key can decrypt it. Based on this idea the white-box encryption (or analogously, decryption) can find numerous applications where it would be much more efficient to use white-box encryption and symmetric decryption instead of computationally expensive public key operations. Subsequent paragraphs, however, are indented. The design of a secure cryptosystem robust in the context of white-box attack is a difficult task which has been addressed by many researchers in the last two decades. The academic study of white-box cryptography was initiated in [2, 3].

---

* Supported by American University of Armenia.

The existing implementations of white-box algorithms have been mainly based on AES block cipher, however, all the known systems have been broken mainly because of so called BGE attack [4, 5].

Attempts to securely implement AES white-box encryption were further continued in [9] (broken in [10]), [11]). However, these entire implementations share the same ideas and their cryptanalysis are mainly based on the BGE approach [4] described later in this paper. For example, implementation in [6] based on AES dual ciphers was claimed to be secure against BGE attack in the original paper, however another work in [8] has shown that the BGE attack can be applied with minor modifications to this implementation. In the paper [12] there was an attempt to design a secure white box algorithm based on SAFER+. However, our further analysis had shown some drawbacks in security analysis presented in that paper. In this paper we represent a modified white-box encryption based on SAFER+ algorithm and show that it is secure against different types of attacks including those that have been successful against AES white-box implementations.

The paper will be organized as follows: after introductory section 1, in the sections 2 and 3, black and white-box encryption rationale of SAFER+ will be represented. Section 4 is devoted to the detailed security analysis of SAFER+ white-box encryption. Section 5 will include results of the computational speed and memory requirements of SAFER+ white-box encryption. Our new design ends up with memory requirement for the white box implementation approximately 27 MB which is an acceptable level for current applications.

References

1   J. Massey, G. Khachatrian, M. Kuregian: Nomination of SAFER+ as a Candidate Algorithm for Advanced Encryption Standard (AES). Presented at the first AES conference, Ventura, USA, August 20-25, (1998)

2   S. Chow, P. Eisen, H. Johnson, P.C. van Oorschot: White-Box Cryptography and an AES Implementation. In 9th Annual Workshop on Selected Areas in Cryptography (SAC 2002), LNCS, vol. 2595, pp. 250–270. August15-16 (2002).

3   S. Chow, P. Eisen, H. Johnson, P.C. van Oorschot: A White-box DES Implementation for DRM Applications. In Proceedings of 2nd ACM Workshop on Digital Rights Management (DRM 2002), LNCS, vol. 2696, pp. 1–15, (2002).

4   O. Billet, H. Gilbert, C. Ech-Chatbi: Cryptanalysis of a White-box AES Implementation. In Selected Areas in Cryptography 2004 (SAC 2004), LNCS, vol. 3357. Springer, Berlin, Heidelberg, pp. 227–240 (2004).

5   T. Lepoint, M. Rivain: Another Nail in the coffin of White-box AES implementations. http://eprint.iacr.org/2013/455 (2013)

6   M. Karroumi, H Gilbert, Charaf Ech-Chatbi: Protecting white-box AES with Dual Ciphers. In: Rhee K. H., Nyang D. (eds) Information Security and Cryptology - ICISC 2010, LNCS, vol. 6829, pp. 292–310 (2010).

7   J. Bringer, H. Chabanne, E. Dottax: White Box Cryptography: Another Attempt. ePrint Archive https://eprint.iacr.org/2006/468 (2006)

8   Y. De Mulder, B. Wyseur , B. Preneel: Cryptanalysis of a Perturbated White-Box AES Implementation. In: Gong G., Gupta K.C. (eds.). Progress in Cryptology - INDOCRYPT 2010, LNCS, vol. 6498, pp. 278–291 (2010).

9. Y. Xiao and Xu. Lai: A secure implementation of white-box AES. In: 2009 2nd International Conference on Computer Science and its Applications, pp. 1–6 (2010).

10. Y. De Mulder, P. Roelse, B. Preneel: Cryptanalysis of the Xiao Lai White-Box AES Implementation. In: Knudsen L.R., Wu H. (eds): Selected Areas in Cryptography. SAC 2012, LNCS, vol. 7707, pp.34–49 (2012).

11. Y. De Mulder, P. Roelse, B. Preneel: Revisiting the BGE attack on B white-box AES implementation. Cryptology ePrint Archive, Report 2013/450. https://eprint.iacr.org/2013/450.pdf.

12. G. Khachatryan, M. Karapetyan: White-box encryption algorithm based SAFER+. Proceedings of the Workshop on Information Theory and Data Science, Yerevan, Armenia. October 3-5, pp.77–89 (2016).

Secrecy in Communication Networks: Being Cooperative or Competitive?

Yanling Chen[1], O. Ozan Koyluoglu[2], and A. J. Han Vinck[1]

[1] Insititute of Digital Signal Processing, University of Duisburg-Essen, Germany
[2] Department of Electrical Engineering and Computer Sciences,
University of California at Berkeley, USA
{yanling.chen, han.vinck}@uni-due.de, ozan.koyluoglu@berkeley.edu

Abstract. Communication networks have had a transformative impact on our society as they have revolutionized almost all aspects of human interaction. The explosive growth of data traffic has led to an increased demand on improving the reliability, efficiency and security aspects of the systems. In this paper, we focus on the multiple access channel, a communication model where several transmitters communicate to a common receiver (e.g., a cellular telephone network) in the presence of an external eavesdropper. The goal is to explore the competitive yet cooperative relationship between the transmitters in order to obtain an efficient communication under a certain reliability and security guarantee.

Keywords: Communication networks · Multiple access channel · Secrecy.

1 Introduction

1.1 Ubiquitous communication in the era of Internet of Things

Over the last decades, wireless communication has transformed from a niche technology into an indispensable part of life. The combination of ubiquitous cellular phone service and rapid growth of the Internet has created an environment where consumers desire seamless, high quality connectivity at all times and from virtually all locations. Most traditional wireless systems are based on the cellular methodology, where the area to be covered is broken into geographical cells. A base station (or access point) is placed in each cell, and the wireless users in each cell communicate exclusively with the corresponding base station, which acts as a gateway to the rest of the network. The single cell model shown in Fig. 1, in which there is a base station and multiple mobile devices. When the base station is transmitting messages to the mobiles, the channel is referred to as a downlink or broadcast channel (BC). Conversely, when the mobiles are transmitting messages to the base station, the channel is referred to as an uplink or multiple-access channel (MAC). Both BC and MAC are two important branches in the extensive field of the multiple-user communication. In this paper, we will mainly focus on the MAC.

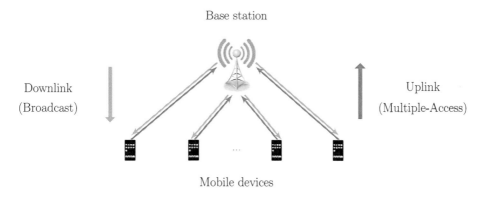

Fig. 1. Cellular channel model.

1.2 Previous studies on MAC

The study of MAC can be traced back to the classic papers from the 70s. For the discrete memoryless MAC (DM-MAC) with independent messages, Ahlswede [1] first studied the 2-transmitter and 3-transmitter cases and determined the respective capacity regions; whilst Liao [2] considered the general K-transmitter DM-MAC and fully characterized its capacity region. There are also many studies on different extensions of MAC, such as MAC with correlated sources [3–5] and the Gaussian MAC [6]. An extensive survey on the information-theoretic aspects of MAC was given in [7].

Another remarkable result on MAC is that the capacity region of a memoryless MAC can be increased by feedback, unlike the capacity of a single user memoryless channel. Especially, Gaarder and Wolf [8], Cover and Leung-Yan-Cheong [9], by providing examples of the binary erasure MAC and the Gaussian MAC, respectively, showed that feedback will enlarge the capacity region of the 2-transmitter MAC. Several general achievable rate regions for the 2-transmitter MAC with noiseless feedback (MAC-FB) were established by Cover and Leung [10], Carleial [11], Bross and Lapidoth [12], Venkataramanan and Pradhan [13]; a dependence balance based outer bound was provided in [14]; and constructive coding strategies that exploit feedback were discussed in [15–19]. Nevertheless, the capacity region of the 2-transmitter MAC-FB remains unknown in general, except for a special class, in which at least one input is a function of the output and the other input [20].

1.3 Secrecy over MAC: Transmitting confidential information

Nowadays, general awareness of user privacy in society has increased, leading to a greater focus on the protection of user metadata and communication. Inspired by the pioneering works of Wyner [21] and Csiszár and Körner [22] that studied the information theoretic secrecy for a point-to-point communication in the presence of an external eavesdropper, MAC with an external eavesdropper was

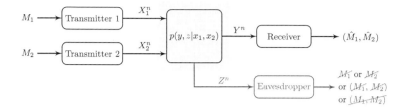

Fig. 2. 2-transmitter DM-MAC with an external eavesdropper.

first introduced in [23]. In particular, [23] focused on a K-transmitter Gaussian MAC with a degraded external eavesdropper and established several achievable rate regions subject to pre-specified secrecy levels; while a later work [24] extends the results of [23] to the general Gaussian MAC and general Gaussian two-way channel (TWC).

For the discrete case, a 2-transmitter DM-MAC with an external eavesdropper was considered in [25]. Note that the model in [25] took into account the generalized feedback that may enable cooperation between transmitters; and, a *joint* secrecy constraint (i.e., information leakage rate from *both* messages to the eavesdropper is made vanishing) was imposed at the eavesdropper. Achievable secrecy rate regions were derived in [25]. Additional studies include [26] and [27] that investigated MAC with a stronger secrecy criteria (i.e., the *amount* of information leakage from both messages to the eavesdropper is made vanishing). Nevertheless, for the general 2-transmitter DM-MAC (e.g., with an eavesdropper not necessarily degraded), the *joint* secrecy capacity region still remains open.

2 Secure communication over 2-transmitter DM-MAC

2.1 System model

In this paper, we focus on the 2-transmitter DM-MAC with an external eavesdropper, the model of which is shown in Fig. 2. As its name suggests, it consists of 2 transmitters, one legitimate receiver, and one passive eavesdropper, which is defined by the transition probability $p(y, z | x_1, x_2)$. The transmitter i, aims to send message m_i, to the legitimate receiver, where $i \in \{1, 2\}$. Define rate R_i at transmitter i by

$$R_i = \frac{1}{n} H(M_i), \quad \text{for } i = 1, 2, \tag{1}$$

where $H(\cdot)$ is the entropy function [28]. Suppose that x_i^n is the channel input at transmitter i, and the channel outputs at the legitimate receiver and eavesdropper are y^n and z^n, respectively. By the *discrete memoryless* nature of the channel (without any feedback), we have

$$p(y^n, z^n | x_1^n, x_2^n) = \prod_{i=1}^{n} p(y_i, z_i | x_{1,i}, x_{2,i}). \tag{2}$$

Over such a channel model, the goal is to achieve a reliable and secure communication. To do it, we first define a secrecy code. More specifically, a $(2^{nR_1}, 2^{nR_2}, n)$ secrecy code $\mathcal{C}_n$ for the 2-transmitter DM-MAC consists of

- 2 message sets $\mathcal{M}_1, \mathcal{M}_2$, where $m_i \in \mathcal{M}_i = [1 : 2^{nR_i}]$ for $i = 1, 2$;
- 2 encoders each assigning a codeword x_i^n to message m_i for $i = 1, 2$; and
- 1 decoder at the legitimate receiver that declares an estimate of (m_1, m_2), say $(\hat{m}_1, \hat{m}_2)$, to the received sequence y^n.

2.2 System requirements

Reliability at the legitimate receiver: Define the *average probability of decoding error* at the legitimate receiver by

$$P_e^n(\mathcal{C}_n) = \frac{1}{2^{n[R_1+R_2]}} \Pr\left\{ \bigcup_{i \in \{1,2\}} \{m_i \neq \hat{m}_i\} \mid \mathcal{C}_n \right\}. \tag{3}$$

Note that $P_e^n(\mathcal{C}_n) = \Pr\left\{ \{M_1 \neq \hat{M}_1\} \bigcup \{M_2 \neq \hat{M}_2\} | \mathcal{C}_n \right\}$ if M_1, M_2 are uniformly distributed over their corresponding message sets.

Secrecy against the eavesdropper: Suppose that the transmitters are aware of the presence of the passive eavesdropper. Briefly, we have the following scenarios:

- The secrecy of the messages is not of concern to both transmitters; or,
- The secrecy of the respective message is of concern only to one transmitter. In more details, we have the following possibilities:
  - Secrecy of M_1 is required, but not M_2. We define the *information leakage rate* of M_1 from transmitter 1 to the eavesdropper by

    $$R_{L,\{1\}}(\mathcal{C}_n) = \frac{1}{n} I(M_1; Z^n | \mathcal{C}_n), \tag{4}$$

    where $I(\cdot)$ is the mutual information function [28].
  - Secrecy of M_2 is required, but not M_1. We define the *information leakage rate* of M_2 from transmitter 2 to the eavesdropper by

    $$R_{L,\{2\}}(\mathcal{C}_n) = \frac{1}{n} I(M_2; Z^n | \mathcal{C}_n). \tag{5}$$

- The secrecy of the messages is of concern to both transmitters. In this scenario, we have the following two cases:
  - From end user point of view, each transmitter only cares about the secrecy of its own message. This is equivalent to limit

    $$R_{L,\{1\},\{2\}}(\mathcal{C}_n) = R_{L,\{1\}}(\mathcal{C}_n) + R_{L,\{2\}}(\mathcal{C}_n). \tag{6}$$

    In this case, the correlation information between M_1 and M_2 may be leaked to the eavesdropper, say $M_1 \oplus M_2$ but not M_1, M_2 individually.

- From the system designer's perspective, the information leakage of M_1, M_2 is considered jointly by defining

$$R_{L,\{1,2\}}(\mathcal{C}_n) = \frac{1}{n} I(M_1, M_2; Z^n | \mathcal{C}_n). \tag{7}$$

Imposing a limit on (7) implies limits on (4), (5) and (6) as well. As the limit becomes arbitrarily small, the correlation information between M_1 and M_2 may not be leaked to the eavesdropper in this case.

Cooperative or competitive transmission strategy at the transmitters: If there is no secrecy concern, the transmitters are competitive since they have to share the same channel resource. However, in case of a secure communication, the transmitters can be also cooperative since the transmission of one user essentially helps to hide the other user's message from the eavesdropper. Especially in case that only one message is required to be kept confidential from the eavesdropper, the other transmitter may

- use a deterministic encoder (which is conventionally used for DM-MAC without secrecy). The transmitter can compete in this case for the channel resource (i.e., being competitive); or,
- use a stochastic encoder (which is common in achieving information theoretic secrecy), helping to hide other transmitter' message from the eavesdropper (i.e., being cooperative).

Considering that secrecy does not come for free, we assume that the transmitter who demands secrecy for its message, will use the stochastic encoder. Thus,

- if there is no secrecy requirement from both transmitters, then both use deterministic encoders, i.e., being competitive;
- if only one transmitter demands secrecy for its message, then it uses the stochastic encoder, i.e., being cooperative; while, the other transmitter could be either cooperative or competitive;
- if both transmitters demand secrecy for their messages, (including both the individual or joint secrecy), then both use the stochastic encodes, i.e., being cooperative.

We remark here that the deterministic encoder can be considered as a special case of the stochastic encoder. Therefore, for the transmitter, being cooperative will be at least as good as being competitive in achieving the desired transmission rates. Recall the fact that being competitive is sufficient in achieving the capacity region in case of no secrecy constraints, i.e., being cooperative does not provide any gain in the reliable communication over MAC. However, the problem of our interest is, if there is any gain in secure communication over MAC for being cooperative; and if yes, how much is the gain?

Table 1. 2-transmitter DM-MAC with an external eavesdropper: under different secrecy constraints with both transmitters being cooperative.

		Rate region	Input distribution
$\mathcal{C}:$	No secrecy [28, Theorem 4.3]	$R_1 \le I(X_1; Y|X_2, Q)$ $R_2 \le I(X_2; Y|X_1, Q)$ $R_1 + R_2 \le I(X_1, X_2; Y|Q)$	$(Q, X_1, X_2) \sim p(q)p(x_1|q)p(x_2|q)$
$\mathcal{R}_{\{1\}}:$	$\{1\}$ − collective secrecy $\frac{1}{n}I(M_1; Z^n) \to 0$ [29, Theorem 1]	$R_2 \le I(V_2; Y|V_1, Q)$ $R_1 \le \min \left\{ \begin{array}{l} I(V_1; Y|V_2, Q) - I(V_1; Z|Q) \\ I(V_1, V_2; Y|Q) - I(V_1, V_2; Z|Q) \end{array} \right\}$ $R_1 + R_2 \le I(V_1, V_2; Y|Q) - I(V_1; Z|Q)$	$(Q, V_1, V_2, X_1, X_2) \sim p(q) \prod\limits_{i=1}^{2} p(v_i|q)p(x_i|v_i)$ such that $I(V_2; Z|Q) \le I(V_2; Y|V_1, Q)$
$\mathcal{R}_{\{2\}}:$	$\{2\}$ − collective secrecy $\frac{1}{n}I(M_2; Z^n) \to 0$ [29, Theorem 1]	$R_1 \le I(V_1; Y|V_2, Q)$ $R_2 \le \min \left\{ \begin{array}{l} I(V_2; Y|V_1, Q) - I(V_2; Z|Q) \\ I(V_1, V_2; Y|Q) - I(V_1, V_2; Z|Q) \end{array} \right\}$ $R_1 + R_2 \le I(V_1, V_2; Y|Q) - I(V_2; Z|Q)$	$(Q, V_1, V_2, X_1, X_2) \sim p(q) \prod\limits_{i=1}^{2} p(v_i|q)p(x_i|v_i)$ such that $I(V_1; Z|Q) \le I(V_1; Y|V_2, Q)$
$\mathcal{R}_{\{1\},\{2\}}:$	Individual secrecy [30, Theorem 1] $\frac{1}{n}I(M_1; Z^n) \to 0$ $\frac{1}{n}I(M_2; Z^n) \to 0$	$R_1 \le I(V_1; Y|V_2, Q) - I(V_1; Z|Q)$ $R_2 \le I(V_2; Y|V_1, Q) - I(V_2; Z|Q)$ $\max\{R_1, R_2\} \le I(V_1, V_2; Y|Q) - I(V_1, V_2; Z|Q)$ $R_1 + R_2 \le I(V_1, V_2; Y|Q) - I(V_1; Z|Q) - I(V_2; Z|Q)$	$(Q, V_1, V_2, X_1, X_2) \sim p(q) \prod\limits_{i=1}^{2} p(v_i|q)p(x_i|v_i)$
$\mathcal{R}_{\{1,2\}}:$	$\{1, 2\}$ − collective secrecy i.e., joint secrecy [30, Theorem 2] $\frac{1}{n}I(M_1, M_2; Z^n) \to 0$	$R_1 \le I(V_1; Y|V_2, Q) - I(V_1; Z|Q)$ $R_2 \le I(V_2; Y|V_1, Q) - I(V_2; Z|Q)$ $R_1 + R_2 \le I(V_1, V_2; Y|Q) - I(V_1, V_2; Z|Q)$	$(Q, V_1, V_2, X_1, X_2) \sim p(q) \prod\limits_{i=1}^{2} p(x_i|v_i)$

2.3 System throughput

If there exists a sequence of $(2^{nR_1}, 2^{nR_2}, n)$ codes $\{\mathcal{C}_n\}$ such that

$$P_e^n(\mathcal{C}_n) \le \epsilon_n \quad \text{and} \quad \lim_{n \to \infty} \epsilon_n = 0, \tag{8}$$

$$R_L(\mathcal{C}_n) \le \tau_n \quad \text{and} \quad \lim_{n \to \infty} \tau_n = 0, \tag{9}$$

then the rate pair (R_1, R_2) is said to be *achievable under the secrecy constraint defined by (9)*. Note that (8) is the *reliability constraint*; and (9) is the *secrecy constraint*. In particular, if $R_L(\mathcal{C}_n)$ in (9) is defined by (4), or (5), or (7), it corresponds to the $\mathcal{S}$-collective secrecy that is introduced in [29], for $\mathcal{S}$ being $\{1\}, \{2\}$ or $\{1, 2\}$, respectively. More specifically, (R_1, R_2) is said to be

1) $\{1\}$-collective secrecy achievable, if $R_L(\mathcal{C}_n)$ is defined by (4);
2) $\{2\}$-collective secrecy achievable, if $R_L(\mathcal{C}_n)$ is defined by (5);
3) individual secrecy achievable, if $R_L(\mathcal{C}_n)$ is defined by (6);
4) $\{1, 2\}$-collective or joint secrecy achievable, if $R_L(\mathcal{C}_n)$ is defined by (7).

Clearly, for given reliability and secrecy constraints, the union of all the achievable rate pairs gives the respective achievable rate regions, providing fundamental limits on the system throughput.

3 Discussions

3.1 Impact of different secrecy requirements

Recall that $\mathcal{S}$-collective secrecy is studied in [29], which includes all the instances of the above discussed secrecy requirements except the individual secrecy. Nevertheless, the individual secrecy has been studied in [30] together with joint secrecy for the 2-transmitter DM-MAC with an external eavesdropper. In addition, the capacity region in case of no secrecy constraint has been characterized [1] (see

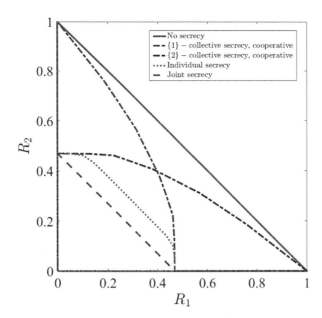

Fig. 3. Achievable rate regions for a binary multiplier 2-transmitter MAC with a degraded eavesdropper, with different secrecy constraints but cooperative transmitters. See [29, Fig. 2(b)].

also [28, Theorem 4.3]). Therefore, we could give a rather complete review on the achievable rate regions under different secrecy constraints.

For a fair comparison, we consider the optimistic case that both transmitter are cooperative in all scenarios. In Table 1, we provide the respective regions corresponding to the 5 different secrecy strengths (in which 4 secrecy constraints are as discussed above and the additional one is no secrecy constraint). In particular, we denote the $\mathcal{S}$-collective secrecy region to be $\mathcal{R}_{\mathcal{S}}$ for $\mathcal{S} \in \{1,2\}$, $\mathcal{S} \neq \emptyset$, $\mathcal{C}$ for the case of no secrecy, and $\mathcal{R}_{\{1\},\{2\}}$ for the individual secrecy rate region.

We provide a numerical illustration in Fig. 3, where we plotted all these regions for a 2-transmitter DM-MAC with an external eavesdropper, where the channel from (X_1, X_2) to Y is a binary multiplier MAC, and Z is a degraded version of Y through a binary symmetric channel (BSC) with crossover probability $p = 0.1$. Note that V_1, V_2 are taken as binary for the calculations. Not surprisingly, we observe that $\mathcal{R}_{\{1,2\}} \subseteq \mathcal{R}_{\{1\},\{2\}} \subseteq \mathcal{R}_{\{1\}}$ or $\mathcal{R}_{\{2\}} \subseteq \mathcal{C}$, where $\mathcal{R}_{\{1,2\}}$ is enclosed by (red) dashed lines; $\mathcal{R}_{\{1\},\{2\}}$ by (yellow) dotted lines; $\mathcal{R}_{\{1\}}$ and $\mathcal{R}_{\{2\}}$ by dash-dotted lines (blue for $\mathcal{R}_{\{1\}}$ and forest-green for $\mathcal{R}_{\{2\}}$, respectively); and $\mathcal{C}$ by (green) solid lines. Note that the inclusion relation of these regions is due to the correspondingly relaxed secrecy strengths. That is, more stringent is the secrecy requirement, smaller is the correspondingly achievable secrecy region. Another interesting observation is that $\mathcal{R}_{\{1\},\{2\}} \subset \mathcal{R}_{\{1\}} \cap \mathcal{R}_{\{2\}}$.

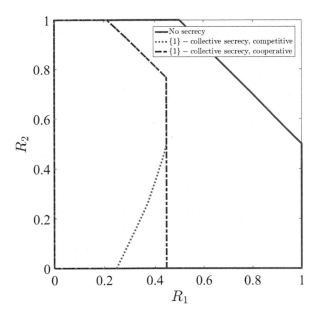

Fig. 4. Achievable rate regions for a binary input adder 2-transmitter MAC with a degraded eavesdropper, where transmitter 1 demands the secrecy but not transmitter 2. See [29, Fig. 2(a)].

In other words, $\mathcal{R}_{\{1\},\{2\}} = \mathcal{R}_{\{1\}} \cap \mathcal{R}_{\{2\}}$ does not hold. This implies that there are rate pairs achievable for either the secrecy of M_1 or the secrecy of M_2, but not the secrecy of M_1 and secrecy of M_2 simultaneously (i.e., individual secrecy).

3.2 Impact of transmitters being cooperative or competitive

Recall the fact that being cooperative does not provide any gain in the reliable communication over MAC (i.e., no secrecy requirement). However, we wonder if it is still the case in the secure communication over MAC.

Table 2. 2-transmitter DM-MAC with an external eavesdropper: $\{1\}$-collective secrecy.

	Competitive Transmitter 2, [29, (10) in Theorem 1]	Cooperative Transmitter 2, [29, (11) in Theorem 1]
Rate region	$R_2 \geq I(V_2; Z\|Q)$ $R_2 \leq I(V_2; Y\|V_1, Q)$ $R_1 \leq \min \left\{ \begin{array}{l} I(V_1; Y\|V_2, Q) - I(V_1; Z\|Q) \\ I(V_1, V_2; Y\|Q) - I(V_1, V_2; Z\|Q) \end{array} \right\}$ $R_1 - R_2 \leq I(V_1; Y\|V_2, Q) - I(V_1, V_2; Z\|Q)$ $R_1 + R_2 \leq I(V_1, V_2; Y\|Q) - I(V_1; Z\|Q)$	$R_2 \leq I(V_2; Y\|V_1, Q)$ $R_1 \leq \min \left\{ \begin{array}{l} I(V_1; Y\|V_2, Q) - I(V_1; Z\|Q) \\ I(V_1, V_2; Y\|Q) - I(V_1, V_2; Z\|Q) \end{array} \right\}$ $R_1 + R_2 \leq I(V_1, V_2; Y\|Q) - I(V_1; Z\|Q)$
Input distribution	$(Q, V_1, V_2, X_1, X_2) \sim p(q) \prod_{i=1}^{2} p(v_i\|q)p(x_i\|v_i)$ such that $I(V_2; Z\|Q) \leq I(V_2; Y\|V_1, Q)$	

Consider the specific case that transmitter 1 would like to keep its message secret from the eavesdropper; while transmitter 2 not. That is, transmitter 1 uses a stochastic encoder for the purpose of secrecy of M_1; while transmitter 2 may take a conventional deterministic encoder for being competitive for the same channel resource; or take a stochastic encoder for being cooperative to help to hide M_1 from the eavesdropper. According to [29, Theorem 1], we have two achievable regions corresponding to these two different transmission strategies at transmitter 2, and we provide them in Table 2.

Moreover, a numerical illustration is provided in Fig. 4, where we show the advantage of transmitter 2 being cooperative (in obtaining a larger secrecy rate region) by a concrete example. Consider the 2-transmitter DM-MAC with an external eavesdropper, where the channel from (X_1, X_2) to Y is a binary input adder MAC, and Z is a degraded version of Y with $p(z|y) = 1 - p$ for $z = y$ and $p(z|y) = p$ for $z = y + 1 \pmod 3$, where $p = 0.1$. In Fig. 4, we depict the respective achievable regions (with binary V_1, V_2 for the calculations), where the one enclosed by (magenta) dotted lines is for the case of transmitter 2 being competitive; and the one enclosed by (blue) dash-dotted lines is for the case of transmitter 2 being cooperative. The capacity region (without secrecy constraint) is also plotted for reference purpose, which is enclosed by the (green) solid lines.

As one can see in Fig. 4, in case of transmitter 2 being cooperative, the region is strictly larger than the case of transmitter 2 being competitive. In particular, a big gap in the achievable secret rate R_1 can be observed at $R_2 = 0$. The gap indicates that transmitter 2 can indeed help the secret transmission of transmitter 1 by sending random signals to jam the eavesdropper. (This is similar to the cooperative jamming observed in the Gaussian scenario [24], but as its counterpart in the discrete setting. More specifically, in this case, transmitter 2 have two ways of cooperation, one is to utilize codewords that carry randomization (bogus) messages and the other is to utilize additional noise in mapping codewords to channel inputs (channel prefixing)). Even in case that transmitter 2 uses a deterministic encoder, its transmission at low rates to some extent, could help transmitter 1 to achieve a larger secrecy rate. However, the advantage of using cooperative transmission strategy at transmitter 2, diminishes or even vanishes especially when R_2 is at high rates. This is because of the bounded sum rate capacity, due to the fact that the same channel resource is shared by both transmitters. This observation provides interesting insights into the competitive yet cooperative relationship between the transmitters in a secure communication, unlike their simple competitive relationship in a reliable communication.

4 Concluding remarks

In this paper, we review the secrecy results obtained for the 2-transmitter multiple access channel with an external eavesdropper. In particular, we discuss 5 secrecy strengths, from both the end user's perspective and the system designer's perspective. Both theoretical and numerical results are presented to show the impact of different secrecy requirements on the respective achievable rate regions (or in other words, the price paid for the required secrecy). Moreover, we look into the case where either competitive or cooperative transmission strategies can be employed at the transmitter who does not demand secrecy for its message. Unlike the reliable communication scenario where secrecy is not concerned, and it does not make any difference for the transmitters for being either cooperative or competitive, we show that in a secure communication over MAC, being cooperative can significantly enlarge the corresponding achievable secrecy region.

2-transmitter multiple access channel is a rather simple model, which has been extensively investigated and which results provide insights into the open problems in multi-use communications. For more extended and general results, one can refer to [29], where a class of collective secrecy was introduced and studied in the multiple access channel with arbitrarily many transmitters.

References

1. R. Ahlswede: Multi-way communication channels. *Akadémiai Kiadó*, (1973).
2. H. H.-J. Liao: Multiple Access Channels. Honolulu: *Ph.D. Dissertation*, University of Hawaii, (1972).
3. D. Slepian and J. K. Wolf: A coding theorem for multiple access channels with correlated sources. *Bell Syst. Tech. J.*, **52**(7), 1037–1076 (1973).
4. Te Sun Han: The capacity region of general multiple-access channel with certain correlated sources. *Information and Control*, **40**(1), 37-60 (1979).
5. T. Cover, A. Gamal, and M. Salehi: Multiple access channels with arbitrarily correlated sources. *IEEE Trans. Inf. Theory*, **26**(6), 648–657 (1980).
6. T. M. Cover: Some advances in broadcast channels. *Advances in Communication Systems*, **4**, 229 – 260 (1975).
7. E. van der Meulen: A survey of multi-way channels in information theory: 1961-1976. *IEEE Trans. Inf. Theory*, **23**(1), 1–37 (1977).
8. N. Gaarder and J. Wolf: The capacity region of a multiple-access discrete memoryless channel can increase with feedback. *IEEE Trans. Inf. Theory*, **21**(1), 100–102 (1975).
9. T. M. Cover and S. K. Leung-Yan-Cheong: A scheme for enlarging the capacity region of multiple-access channels using feedback. Dept. of Stat., Stanford Univ., Stanford, CA, *Tech. Rep. 17*, (1976).
10. T. Cover and C. Leung: An achievable rate region for the multiple-access channel with feedback. *IEEE Trans. Inf. Theory*, **27**(3), 292–298 (1981).
11. A. Carleial: Multiple-access channels with different generalized feedback signals. *IEEE Trans. Inf. Theory*, **28**(6), 841–850 (1982).
12. S. I. Bross and A. Lapidoth: An improved achievable region for the discrete memoryless two-user multiple-access channel with noiseless feedback. *IEEE Trans. Inf. Theory*, **51**(3), 811–833 (2005).
13. R. Venkataramanan and S. S. Pradhan: A new achievable rate region for the multiple-access channel with noiseless feedback. *IEEE Trans. Inf. Theory*, **57** (12), 8038–8054 (2011).
14. A. P. Hekstra and F. M. J. Willems: Dependence balance bounds for single-output two-way channels. *IEEE Trans. Info. Theory*, **35**(1), 44–53 (1989).

15. A. J. Vinck: Constructive superposition coding for the binary erasure multiple access channel. *Proc. 4th Symp. Information Theory in Benelux*, 179-188 (1983).

16. A.J. Vinck, W.L.M. Hoeks and K.A. Post: On the capacity of the two-user M-ary multiple-access channel with feedback. *IEEE Trans. Info. Theory*, **31** (4), 540-543 (1985).

17. A. J. Han Vinck: On the multiple access channel. *Proc. of the 2nd Joint Swedish-Soviet Int. Workshop on Info. Theory*, **54** (1), 24-29 (1985).

18. G. H. Khachatrian and S. S. Martirossian: Code construction for the T-user noiseless adder channel. *IEEE Trans. Inf. Theory*, **44** (5), 1953–1957 (1998).

19. G. Kramer: Feedback strategies for a class of two-user multiple-access channels. *IEEE Trans. Inf. Theory*, **45** (6), 2054–2059 (1999).

20. F. Willems: The feedback capacity region of a class of discrete memoryless multiple access channels. *IEEE Trans. Inf. Theory*, **28** (1), 93–95 (1982).

21. A. D. Wyner: The wire-tap channel. *Bell Syst. Tech. J.*, **54**(8), 1355–1387 (1975).

22. I. Csiszár and J. Körner: Broadcast channels with confidential messages. *IEEE Trans. Inf. Theory*, **24**(3), 339–348 (1978).

23. E. Tekin and A. Yener: The Gaussian multiple access wire-tap channel. *IEEE Trans. Inf. Theory*, **54**(12), 5747–5755 (2008).

24. E. Tekin and A. Yener: The general Gaussian multiple-access and two-way wiretap channels: Achievable rates and cooperative jamming. *IEEE Trans. Inf. Theory*, **54**(6), 2735–2751 (2008).

25. X. Tang, R. Liu, P. Spasojevic, and H. Poor: Multiple access channels with generalized feedback and confidential messages. In: *Proc. ITW 2007*, (2007).

26. M. Yassaee and M. Aref: Multiple access wiretap channels with strong secrecy. In: *Proc. ITW 2010*, Dublin, (2010).

27. M. Wiese and H. Boche: Strong secrecy for multiple access channels. In *Information Theory, Combinatorics, and Search Theory*, LNCS. Springer Berlin Heidelberg, **7777**, 71–122 (2013).

28. A. E. Gamal and Y.-H. Kim: *Network Information Theory*. New York, NY, USA: Cambridge University Press, (2012).

29. Y. Chen, O. O. Koyluoglu and A. J. Han Vinck: Collective secrecy over the K-transmitter multiple access channel. *IEEE Transactions on Information Forensics and Security*, **13** (9), 2279–2293 (2018).

30. Y. Chen, O. O. Koyluoglu and A. J. Han Vinck: On secure communication over the multiple access channel, In *Proc. 2016 IEEE International Symposium on Information Theory and Its Applications (ISITA)*, 355–359 (2016).

f-Divergence Measures for Evaluation in Community Detection

Mariam Haroutunian[1], Karen Mkhitaryan[1], and Josiane Mothe[2]

[1] Institute for Informatics and Automation Problems of NAS of RA,
1 P. Sevak, Yerevan, Armenia
iiap.sci.am
[2] IRIT, UMR5505 CNRS & ESPE, Univ. de Toulouse,
118 Route de Narbonne, TOULOUSE CEDEX 9, Toulouse, France
info@irit.fr

Abstract. Community detection is a research area from network science dealing with the investigation of complex networks such as biological, social and computer networks, aiming to identify subgroups (communities) of entities (nodes) that are more closely related to each other than with remaining entities in the network [1]. Various community detection algorithms are used in the literature however the evaluation of their derived community structure is a challenging task due to varying results on different networks. In searching good community detection algorithms diverse comparison measures are used actively [2]. Information theoretic measures form a fundamental class in this discipline and have recently received increasing interest [3]. In this paper we first mention the usual evaluation measures used for community detection evaluation We then review the properties of f-divergence measures and propose the ones that can serve community detection evaluation. Preliminary experiments show the advantage of these measures in the case of large number of communities.

Keywords: Community Detection · Information Theory · f-divergence · distance measures.

1 Introduction

The goal of community detection is to partition the given network into communities to understand its topological structure [1].

When a community detection algorithm is applied and the studied network is partitioned into communities, the output is a n dimensional random vector $X = (x_1, x_2, ..., x_n)$, where n is the number of nodes in the network and each $x_i \in \{1, ..., k\}$ element represents the community assignment of node i, where k is the number of communities $(i \in \{1, ..., n\})$.

In order to quantitatively assess the goodness of the derived network partition, it can either be compared with other partitions of a network or with pre-known ground truth [2, 4].In the literature of the domain it is mostly accomplished by using evaluation measures imported from clustering problems and information theory [2, 4, 5].

From the list of available evaluation measures, the application of information theoretic measures in community detection is more prospective because of their strong mathematical foundation and ability to detect non-linear similarities [3, 7].

Let $X = (x_1, x_2, ..., x_n)$ and $Y = (y_1, y_2, ..., y_n)$ be two different partitions of the network. We assume that community assignments x_i and y_i are values of random variables X and Y respectively with joint probability distribution $p(x, y) = P(X = x, Y = y)$ and marginal distributions $p(x) = P(X = x)$ and $p(y) = P(Y = y)$. Thus calculating the similarity of two network partitions can be viewed as comparing two random variables which is typical an encoding/decoding problem in information theory. Mutual information (MI) is a popular measure in information theory, measuring the mutual dependence of two random variables X and Y. It measures how much information about one random variable is obtained through the other random variable [6]. However MI is not a normalized measure making it unsuitable to quantitatively evaluate and compare different partitions. Several normalized variants of MI called normalized mutual information (NMI) were introduced by Yao [8], Kvalseth [9] and Strehl et al. [10]. Later Meila [11] introduced variation of information (VI) which unlike MI is a metric measure. Finally normalized variation of information (NVI) and normalized information distance (NID) were proposed by Kraskov et al. [12].

In [3], the authors performed an organized study of information theoretic measures for clustering comparison; it has been mathematically proved that NVI and NID satisfy both the normalization and the metric properties. Moreover, it was showed that NID is preferable since it better uses the $[0, 1]$ range. Despite the fact that NMI, NVI, NID have many advantages, some experiments challenge their effectiveness [3, 7].

According to Amelio and Pizzuti [13] normalized mutual information needs adjustment as it has unfair behavior especially when the number of communities in the network is large. The authors suggested to adjust the NMI by introducing a scaling factor which also compares the number of communities detected by an algorithm and the actual number of communities in the ground truth.

Another modification was suggested by Zhang [14] who claims that NMI is affected by systematic errors as a result of finite network size which may result in wrong conclusions when evaluating community detection algorithms. Relative normalized mutual information (rNMI) introduced by Zhang takes into account the statistical significance of NMI by comparing it with the expected NMI of random partitions.

An important class of information theoretic measures are so called f - divergences. These are measures of discrimination between two probability distributions. Their properties, connection inequalities and applications in information theory, machine learning, statistics and other applied branches were studies in many publications, see for example [15–18].

However, they have never been considered as community detection evaluation measures despite their properties that make them good candidate for this task. In this paper we investigate the properties of some f-divergences from community detection evaluation point of view. We think that some of them could serve as a good alternative to existing information theoretic measures in community detection evaluation framework.

The paper is organized as follows: we demonstrate some popular information theoretic measures in Section 2, show some f-divergence measures and discuss their useful properties for considering them in community detection evaluation in Section 3 and conclude in Section 4.

2   Information Theoretic Measures

Various measures are used in community detection problems to evaluate network's partition into communities, which are imported from other disciplines such as cluster analysis and information theory [2, 4, 5].

In recent years information theoretic tools were applied in various fields such as coding theory, statistics, machine learning, genomics, neuroscience etc. [6]. The same tools are also useful when in community detection since they provide a bunch of measures to compare network partitions. One of the basic measures is the mutual information between two random variables, which tells how much knowing one of clusterings reduces the uncertainty about the other. Mutual information of two discrete random variables is defined as [6]:

$$I(X;Y) = \sum_{y \in Y} \sum_{x \in X} p(x,y) \log \frac{p(x,y)}{p(x)p(y)} = H(X) - H(X|Y),$$

where $H(X)$ is the entropy of X and $H(X|Y)$ the conditional entropy of X given Y.

$$H(X) = -\sum_{x} p(x) \log p(x)$$

$$H(X|Y) = -\sum_{x,y} p(x,y) \log p(x|y)$$

Considering random variables as random community distributions of a network, it is used to compare network partitions.

To evaluate and compare community structures, it is highly desired that the measures satisfy two main properties: normalization property and metric property.

– **Normalization property**

A measure is normalized if the range of values it takes fall into a fixed interval. Normalized measures are easy to interpret and in community detection problems it is of paramount importance as it is necessary to quantitatively assess the similarity of a given partition with other partitions or with ground truth. In community detection evaluation most of the measures fall into intervals $[0, 1]$ or $[-1, 1]$.

– **Metric property**

A measure d is a metric if it satisfies the following properties:

– Non-negativity: $d(x, y) \geq 0$,
– Identity: $d(x, y) = 0 \Leftrightarrow x = y$,
– Symmetry: $d(x, y) = d(y, x)$,
– Triangle inequality: $d(x, y) + d(y, z) \geq d(x, z)$.

The metric property conforms to the intuition of distance [11] and it is important in the case of complex space of clusterings as many theoretical results already exist for metric spaces.

Based on the properties of MI, that is non-negativity and upper boundedness:

$$0 \leq I(X \cap Y) \leq \min\{H(X), H(Y)\} \leq \sqrt{H(X)H(Y)} \leq \frac{1}{2}(H(X) + H(Y)) \leq$$
$$\leq \max\{H(X), H(Y)\} \leq H(X, Y)$$

several normalized variants of NMI can be considered as similarity measures [3, 8–10]:

$$\mathrm{NMI}_{\mathrm{joint}} = \frac{I(X; Y)}{H(X, Y)}, \qquad \mathrm{NMI}_{\mathrm{max}} = \frac{I(X; Y)}{\max(H(X), H(Y))},$$

$$\mathrm{NMI}_{\mathrm{sum}} = \frac{2I(X; Y)}{H(X) + H(Y)}, \qquad \mathrm{NMI}_{\mathrm{sqrt}} = \frac{I(X; Y)}{\sqrt{H(X)H(Y)}},$$

$$\mathrm{NMI}_{\mathrm{min}} = \frac{I(X; Y)}{\min\{H(X), H(Y)\}}.$$

Based on the five upper bounds for $I(X; Y)$ also five distance measures can be defined as follows.

$$D_{\mathrm{joint}} = H(X, Y) - I(X; Y),$$
$$D_{\mathrm{max}} = \max\{H(X), H(Y)\} - I(X; Y),$$
$$D_{\mathrm{sum}} = H(X) + H(Y) - 2I(X; Y),$$
$$D_{\mathrm{sqrt}} = \sqrt{H(X)H(Y)} - I(X; Y),$$
$$D_{\mathrm{min}} = \min\{H(X)H(Y)\} - I(X; Y).$$

$D_{\text{joint}} = 2D_{\text{sum}}$ is known as variation of information (VI) introduced by Meila [11], it satisfies the properties of metrics but not the one of normalization. In [3] it was proved that D_{max} is a metric, while D_{min} and D_{sqrt} are not metrics.

Later Kraskov et al. [12] introduced normalized variant of variation of information called normalized variation of information (NVI) and normalized information distance (NID) which are both normalized and metric measures.

$$\text{NVI} = \frac{H(X,Y) - I(X;Y)}{H(X,Y)} = 1 - \frac{I(X;Y)}{H(X,Y)}$$

$$\text{NID} = \frac{\max(H(X), H(Y)) - I(X;Y)}{\max(H(X), H(Y))} = 1 - \frac{I(X;Y)}{\max\{H(X), H(Y)\}}$$

Vinh et al. [3] proved that NVI and NID are metrics.

3 f-Divergences and some Useful Properties

Definition:

Let $f : (0, \infty) \to R$ be a convex function with $f(1) = 0$ and let P and Q be two probability distributions. The f-divergence from P to Q is defined by

$$D_f(P \parallel Q) \triangleq \sum_x q(x) f\left(\frac{p(x)}{q(x)}\right).$$

Among others, f-divergences include well known notions from information theory listed below.

Kullback-Leibler divergence which is also known as relative entropy

$$D(P \parallel Q) = \sum_x p(x) \log\left(\frac{p(x)}{q(x)}\right),$$

is a f-divergence with $f(t) = t \log(t)$. Also $D(Q \parallel P)$ can be obtained from $f(t) = -t \log(t)$.

Total variational distance

$$V(P, Q) = \sum_x |p(x) - q(x)| = \sum_x q(x) \left|\frac{p(x)}{q(x)} - 1\right|,$$

is coming from the same f-divergence formula when $f(t) = |t - 1|$.

Hellinger distance defined by

$$H(P, Q) = \sum_x (\sqrt{p(x)} - \sqrt{q(x)})^2,$$

is a f-divergence with $f(t) = (\sqrt{t} - 1)^2$. The Hellinger distance is closely related to the total variational distance, but it has several advantages such as being well suited for the study of product measures.

Jeffrey divergence is the symmetrised Kullback-Leibler divergence

$$J(P \parallel Q) = D(P \parallel Q) + D(Q \parallel P) = \sum_{x} (p(x) - q(x)) \log(\frac{p(x)}{q(x)}),$$

that is obtained from $D_f(P \parallel Q)$ with $f(t) = \frac{1}{2}(t-1)\log(t)$.

Capacitory discrimination (also known as Jensen-Shannon divergence) is given by

$$C(P,Q) = D(P \parallel \frac{P+Q}{2}) + D(Q \parallel \frac{P+Q}{2}) = 2H(\frac{P+Q}{2}) - H(P) - H(Q)$$

which comes from $D_f(P,Q)$ with $f(t) = t\log(t) - (t+1)\log(t+1) + 2\log(2)$.

χ^2 ***divergence*** is a f-divergence measure,

$$\chi^2(P,Q) = \sum_{x} \frac{(p(x) - q(x))^2}{q(x)} = \sum_{x} q(x)(\frac{p(x)}{q(x)} - 1)^2,$$

where $f(t) = (t-1)^2$.

Bhattacharyya distance given by

$$d(P,Q) = \sqrt{1 - \sum_{x} \sqrt{p(x)q(x)}},$$

can be obtained from $D_f(P,Q)$, when $f(t) = 1 - \sqrt{t}$.

We considered the properties of above mentioned measure to decide how they can be applied for community detection evaluation. In fact, to compare two algorithms with network partitions X and Y we must evaluate the discrimination from P_{XY} to $P_X P_Y$.

First note that there is a well known property

$$D(P_{XY} \parallel P_X P_Y) = I(X;Y)$$

and hence **Kullback-Leibler divergence** being very useful in information theory is not interesting for our task.

It is obvious that the **total variational distance** $V(P,Q)$ takes values from interval $[0,2]$

$$0 \le V(P,Q) \le 2$$

and hence is normalized. It is proved that $V(P,Q)$ satisfies all metric properties. Consider,

$$V(P_{XY}, P_X P_Y) = \sum_{x,y} |p(x,y) - p(x)p(y)|,$$

142

it equals 0 when X and Y are independent, which means that as small is the variational distance as far are the two clusterings.

For **Hellinger distance** $H(P,Q)$ the following property

$$0 \leq H(P,Q) \leq V(P,Q)$$

shows that it is normalized too. It is also proved that $\sqrt{H(P,Q)}$ is a true metric. We are interested in

$$\sqrt{H(P_{XY}, P_x P_Y)} = \sqrt{\sum_{x,y} (\sqrt{p(x,y)} - \sqrt{p(x)p(y)})^2},$$

which as in the previous case tends to zero when X and Y are independent. **Capacitory discrimination** $C(P,Q)$ satisfies the following inequality

$$0 \leq C(P,Q) \leq V(P,Q),$$

thus taking values in $[0,2]$. It is proved that $\sqrt{C(P,Q)}$ satisfies the metric properties [19]. We shall consider the following measure

$$\sqrt{C(P_{XY}, P_X P_Y)} = \sqrt{D(P_{XY} \parallel \frac{P_{XY} + P_X P_Y}{2}) + D(P_X P_Y \parallel \frac{P_{XY} + P_X P_Y}{2})},$$

that can be used to compare clusterings as in the two previous cases.

For **Bhattacharyya distance** the following inequality is known

$$0 \leq d \leq 1,$$

and it is proved to be a metric. In this case

$$d(P_{XY}, P_X P_Y) = \sqrt{1 - \sum_{x,y} \sqrt{p(x,y)p(x)p(y)}},$$

being equal to 0 also when X and Y clusterings are independent.

Thus Total variational distance, Bhattacharyya distance, Hellinger distance and Capacitory discrimination are good candidates for community detection evaluation as they satisfy both normalization and metric properties.

4 Conclusion and Future Work

Researching information-theoretic measures and their properties we suggest Total variational distance, Bhattacharyya distance, Hellinger distance and Capacitory discrimination as promising candidates for evaluation tasks in community detection. In future we plan to investigate, evaluate and compare them on both real world and synthetic networks which may highlight the strong connections of f-divergences and community detection.

References

1. S. Fortunato: Community detection in graphs. Physics Reports **486**, 75–174 (2010)
2. J. Mothe, K. Mkhitaryan and M. Haroutunian: Community detection: Comparison of state of the art algorithms. Proc. of Intern. Conf. Computer science and information technologies, 252–256, Reprint in IEEE Revised selected papers, pp. 125-129 (2017)
3. N. X. Vinh, J. Apps, J. Bailey: Information Theoretic Measures for Clusterings Comparison: Variants, Properties, Normalization and Correction for Chance. The Journal of Machine Learning Research **11**, 2837–2854 (2010)
4. J. Malek, C. Hocine, C. Chantal, H. Atef: Community detection algorithm evaluation with ground-truth data. Physica A: Statistical Mechanics and its Applications **492**, 651–706 (2018)
5. Z. Yang, R. Algesheimer, C. J. Tessone: A Comparative Analysis of Community Detection Algorithms on Artificial Networks. Scientific Reports **6**(30750) (2016)
6. T. M. Cover and J. A. Thomas: Elements of Information Theory. Wiley Series in Telecommunications and Signal Processing (2006)
7. S. Wagner and D. Wagner: Comparing Clusterings- An Overview (2007)
8. Y. Yao: Information-theoretic measures for knowledge discovery and data mining. Springer, Entropy Measures, Maximum Entropy Principle and Emerging Applications, 115–136 (2003)
9. T. O. Kvalseth: Entropy and correlation: Some comments. Systems, Man and Cybernetics, IEEE Transactions **17**(3), 517-519 (1987)
10. A. Strehl, J. Ghosh: Cluster ensembles - a knowledge reuse framework for combining multiple partitions. The Journal of Machine Learning Research **3**, 583-617 (2002)
11. M. Meila: Comparing clusterings—an information based distance. Journal of Multivariate Analysis **98**, 873–895 (2007)
12. A. Kraskov, H. Stgbauer, R. G. Andrzejak and P. Grassberger: Hierarchical clustering using mutual information. EPL (Europhysics Letters)**70**, 2837–2854 (2005)
13. A. Amelio, C. Pizzuti: Is Normalized Mutual Information a Fair Measure for Comparing Community Detection Methods?. IEEE/ACM International Conference on Advances in Social Networks Analysis and Mining (2015)
14. P. Zhang: Evaluating accuracy of community detection using the relative normalized mutual information. Journal of Statistical Mechanics: Theory and Experiment **2015** (2015)
15. I. Sason, S. Verdú: f-divergence Inequalities. IEEE Transactions on Information Theory **62**(11), 5973–6006 (2016)
16. I. Csiszár, P. C. Shields: Information Theory and Statistics: A Tutorial. Foundations and Trends in Communications and Information Theory **1**(4), 417–528 (2004)
17. I. Sason: Tight Bounds for Symmetric Divergence Measures and a Refined Bound for Lossless Source Coding. IEEE Trans. on IT **61**(2), 701–707 (2015)
18. F. Topsøe: Some inequalities for information divergence and related measures of discrimination. IEEE Trans. on IT **46**(4), 1602-1609 (2000)
19. J. Lin: Divergence measures based on Shannon entropy. IEEE Trans. on IT **37**(1), 145–151 (1991)

Learning Baseline Models of Log Sources

Ashot N. Harutyunyan, Arnak V. Poghosyan, Nicholas Kushmerick,
and Naira M. Grigoryan

Office of CTO of Cloud Management, VMware
{aharutyunyan;apoghosyan;nicholask;ngrigoryan}@vmware.com

Abstract. Leveraging cloud management products to effectively control performance of IT applications and infrastructures inevitably leads to the issue of automatically identifying *baseline structures* (typical behavioral patterns) of measured data sets including log sources. Those structures can be utilized for a variety of purposes from anomaly and change detection, to characterization of the application or infrastructure state in large (for instance, high/low stress levels, sickness, overprovisioning, security threats, etc.). Particularly, VMware vRealize Operations Manager performs such an analysis for any time series metric of an IT object through its basic dynamic thresholding analytics, while building a similar capability for log analytics is challenging - the very high volume of log data makes machine learning extremely expensive. To overcome the learning complexity, we propose *random sampling* techniques. Our method allows for controlling the confidence of the learned model by tuning the sampling rate. In this paper, we focus on learning the baseline model of log sources in terms of the distribution of log event types generated by vRealize Log Insight. Moreover, our algorithms identify the *expected normal discrepancy* from such a baseline that the log source exhibits. We demonstrate the proposed approach by applying our prototype algorithms to different data sets.

Keywords: Automated log management, baseline model/structure, sampling with confidence control, binomial distribution, anomaly detection, state characterization, clustering, machine learning.

1   Introduction

With VMware's growing interest in application-aware cloud management and analytics, the log intelligence becomes especially import. VMware's cloud management solutions vRealize Operations (vR Ops) [1] and vRealize Log Insight (vR LI) [2] are the main platforms to empower the modern Software-Defined Data Center management with automated machine learning capabilities, self-tuning and optimization, and move forward into an AI-enabled autonomous management in the cloud computing market.

For vR Ops, the current state-of-the-art in terms of data analytics is based on dynamic thresholding [3] and capacity forecasting analysis for time series data of the environment objects.

vR LI supports two important machine learning features of 1) Event Types as similarity clusters of raw log data and the 2) Event Trends allowing to compare to selected time windows by their differences of corresponding event types. While vR Ops performs pattern detection for any metric data from data center objects and derives expected ranges of processes based on a complex time series analysis, accounting for change, trends, and periodicity, LI is lacking a similar capability to automatically identify the main behavioral patterns of the log source. It makes troubleshooting and pattern detection in log data mostly a query-based task with intensive user efforts to find problem root causes or track the application state in general.

In this regard, to have a much intelligent characterization of the application, identification of its *baseline model* or behavioral fingerprint from logs history is of exceptional importance. Intelligent proactive management of data centers and applications from logs perspective with building an accurate expert baseline requires a huge knowledgebase and extensive efforts. At the same time, it cannot be easily generalizable because of many factors coming from conditions of the IT ecosystem. Hence, machine identification of application baselines can be a powerful addition to any log analytics. Evidently, with such a fundamental structure then, the real-time anomaly detection and many other core tasks will be easily automated. By comparing the current log stream against its historically typical model, we'll be able to effectively describe the state of the application in real-time and efficiently identify issues and incidents (a new software bug, sickness, hardware failure, software upgrade, configuration changes, change in workload) related to various aspects of data center management (troubleshooting, performance monitoring, capacity planning, provisioning and configuration, compliance auditing, policy enforcement, etc.). This means that those structures should be enough informative to reveal the whole complexity of the log stream with sophisticated relationships between events.

Any method dealing with extracting and continuously updating baseline structures along the log stream requires an expensive unsupervised learning plan. Although alternative approaches applying meta-data analysis or quantification of log information bypass such a complexity (discussed in Section 2), however they address only a specific problem without structural characterization of the log source in general.

In this paper, we propose a random sampling technique to overcome the learning complexity of baselines subject to confidence level of the learned model based on binomial distributions. We focus on learning the baseline in terms of the probability distribution of event types that LI builds from the stream with similarity analysis of log messages. Moreover, our algorithms identify the *expected normal discrepancy* from such a baseline that the log source historically exhibits. Our prototype was applied to different data sets to validate and demonstrate the approach.

In Section 2 we motivate our research and discuss the related work. Section 3 describes our methods to identifying baselines of log sources and also demonstrateing their application to log data sets. In Section 4 we specify larger experimental plans and conclude in Section 5.

2 Motivation and Related Work

As we mentioned in the introduction, one approach to overcome the complex machine learning tasks for log data is to extract different meta-data properties from those sets and proceed with numeric data (time series) analysis (e.g. [4]) or build event correlation models (e.g. [5]). In particular, in our earlier work [4] we applied quantification of log data with information theory [6]. The quantified/extracted time series metric representing stream's Jensen-Shannon divergence over time was analyzed for change detection purposes. Although this kind of metric plus log analytics framework empowers the log intelligence with highly effective toolset of low complexity, but it remains an indirect method for behavioral analysis (without revealing the complete characteristics of the log source and hiding much of the content in logs).

In [4] we intensively utilized distributions of event types generated by LI in change point detection for a single source, sickness detection of a source within population of similar sources, as well as for an application topology discovery using hierarchical clustering. Below we are going to utilize LI's event types further to identify the sought baseline models for log sources.

Importance of baseline models for VMware's log analytics was first realized in [7], where authors applied information divergence measures to detect anomalies subject to a known/assumed baseline distribution of event types. The work was largely motivational for us to address the problem of automatic discovery of baseline distributions of log events.

For a short overview on Event Types by LI, let us mention that they are the main machine learning constructs of the product that represent abstract clusters of raw log events into similarity groups. With such a similarity grouping the product performs a dramatic data reduction, mapping thousands or millions of log messages into a manageable number of groups/types. Fig. 1 illustrates log data of a source for a 10-minute period as a bar chart of events of distinct types (in different colors). It highlights those distinct groups in a fractional view within each bar of the chart. Those fractions/rates in each bar (10 seconds) of the chart can be converted into relative frequencies or probability distributions of event types within the window. Then if we want to compare two log portions in term of their content we can apply information measures (or other similarity distances like *cosine*) to estimate their "difference".

Particularly, taking relative frequencies of event types observed in two log portions as probability distributions

$$P = (p_1, p_2, \ldots p_n) \text{ and } Q = (q_1, q_2, \ldots q_n)$$

of n different event types, we applied [4] Jensen-Shannon divergence varying between 0 and 1:

$$JSD(P, Q) = \frac{1}{2} D(P, M) + \frac{1}{2} D(Q, M),$$

where $M = \frac{P+Q}{2}$ and $D(P, Q)$ is the Kullback-Leibler divergence [6] between P and Q:

$$D(P, Q) = \sum_{i=1}^{n} p_i \log \frac{p_i}{q_i}.$$

Respectively, the cosine similarity is based on the angle between two vectors:

$$\cos(\theta) = \frac{\sum_{i=1}^{n} p_i q_i}{\sqrt{\sum_{i=1}^{n} {p_i}^2} \sqrt{\sum_{i=1}^{n} {q_i}^2}}.$$

For more details regarding event types, their probabilistic representation and application of information measures to anomaly, change, and sickness detection we refer the reader to the same papers [4,7].

Based on the above review, the proposed machine learning identification of baseline structures for log sources is a novel formulation.

Fig. 1. Bar chart representation of fractions of distinct event types by LI for each 10 seconds within a 10-minute window.

3   Identifying Baselines with ML

Our algorithms are based on random sampling employing the binomial probability distribution. This allows us to tune the confidence of our ML algorithms. Below we give a brief information about the binomial distributions.

3.1   Binomial Distribution and Sampling

The binomial distribution [8] with parameters n and p is the discrete probability distribution of the number of successes in a sequence of n independent experiments, widely used in probability theory and statistics. A single success/failure experiment is also called a Bernoulli trial or Bernoulli experiment and a sequence of outcomes is called a Bernoulli process. The binomial distribution is the basis for the popular binomial test of statistical significance. It is frequently used to model the number of successes in a sample of size n drawn with replacement.

The number of success (Yes) k versus failure (No) $n - k$ probability in n trials is given by the formula:

$$Prob(k \; success \; in \; n) = C_n^k p^k (1-p)^{n-k},$$

where p is the probability of success in a single trial.

Let us assume that the log source stays at its normal operational state most (99%) of the time. Instead of 99% can be another prior probability. This means that if we randomly sample some log portions during the progress of the stream, we'll get mostly normal (i.e., the success outcome) behavioral patterns of the log source (let us say in terms of its event types).

How many randomly sampled event type distributions are "enough" to verify if 99% of those distributions describe the normal mode of the log stream? The answer of the question can be given with the help of binomial distributions. Namely, if normal samples occur with probability 0.99 versus 0.01, then applying the binomial distribution (see the online calculator http://stattrek.com/online-calculator/binomial.aspx) we can measure how many sampled probability distributions of event types are "enough" to identify the "normal" (success) ones. Fig. 2 shows the calculator in action.

Probability of success on a single trial	0.99
Number of trials	5
Number of success	4
Binomial Probability: $P(X = 4)$	0.0480298005
Cumulative Probability: $P(X < 4)$	0.0009801496
Cumulative Probability: $P(X <= 4)$	0.0490099501
Cumulative Probability: $P(X > 4)$	0.9509900499
Cumulative Probability: $P(X >= 4)$	0.9990198504

Fig. 2. Results of the binomial distribution calculation for 5 trials with 4 "success".

It illustrates that from 5 distributions at least 4 are the normal patterns with confidence (cumulative probability) = 0.999. The number of necessary samples will evidently grow if we assume lesser probability of success, while guaranteeing the same level of confidence in our experiment/trial. In general, for a large number of samples collected, say, 10,000, we need to calculate the relevant quantiles of the binomial distribution https://keisan.casio.com/exec/system/1180573200. So, for the cumulative distribution equal to 0.999, with number of trials equal to 10,000 and the probability of success to be 0.99, we expect at least 9,868 sampled distributions representing the normal state of the log source which should be identified.

3.2 Algorithms and Experiments

As we mentioned in Section 1 and 2, when performing anomaly detection and other important tasks for a log source using LI, we face the problem of having a baseline model for the source as a typical characteristic of its historically normal behavior. More specifically, if the streams' current distribution of event types is largely deviating (as a matter of a distance measure) from the baseline, we can automatically raise an alert to the system administrator. We have already shown in [4] that in tasks such as anomaly, change, and sickness detection, the event types are invaluable "signatures" or "fingerprints" of log sources to rely on.

In this subsection, we describe our ML algorithms implemented in Python for identification of that baseline structure using LI's event types with random sampling. We describe two methods to perform such a learning task. The first method applies random sampling of log messages with confidence control of the inference. The sec-ond algorithm indicates the most generic and sophisticated solution to the problem although with much higher complexity.

Method I (with random sampling). How to identify the baseline distribution with the sampled 5 distributions in the example in subsection 3.1? The next question is then how to identify those 4 dominant (in terms of characterizing the state of the source) distributions out of 5?

Our solutions below indicate how to choose the baseline event type distribution and the related *normal discrepancy radius* of the stream that quantifies the tolerable "distances" of the observed event type distributions from this baseline as still within the expected behavior:

1. compute cosine similarity distances between all pairs of event type distributions (histograms) derived for each of sampled log portion;
2. compute average cosine similarity distance (ACSD) for each sample histogram from the rest;
3. rank sampled histograms in decreasing order of their ACSDs and pick up the top 4 (tries to identify the most similar subset of 4 distributions.);
4. pick up the histogram with minimum ACSD as the baseline (centroid) distribution;
5. if there are several histograms with min ACSD, compute Shannon entropy of those and pick up the one with maximum entropy value as a baseline distribution.

In an alternative implementation, the step 4 can be replaced with the maximum entropy principle applied to the top distributions directly to identify the most unbiased baseline distribution.

Shannon entropy [6] measures the uncertainty in a random variable defined by

$$H(P, a) = -\sum p_i \log_a p_i \leq \log_a n$$

and its binary version's plot is depicted in Fig. 3.

For a demonstration purposes, we performed a small experiment on an Apache server (consisting of web, email, and ftp services), a similar experiment described in [4] for sickness detection task within a population of peers. We emulated a stress or security attack (using ApacheBench test tool) on the web host with a high-rate service requests for a 5-minute duration, after observing it in a "normal" operational workload for half an hour. Then we sampled 5 different five log portions of 5-minute length that captured the stressed window (Sample 2) as well. For each of log portions (Samples 1-5 shortened to S1-S5) we computed the probability distributions of observed 25 event types within, which are shown in Table 1.

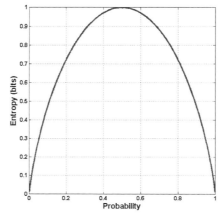

Fig. 3. Shannon entropy function for binary distribution and log base $a = 2$ with the maximum uncertainty (1) at probability = 0.5.

Then computing the ACSDs for each distribution from the rest, we get:
$$ACSD(S1) = 0.97, ACSD(S2) = 0.89,$$
$$ACSD(S3) = 0.96, ACSD(S4) = 0.97, ACSD(S5) = 0.97.$$

Table I. Five samples of log event types taken from a host for a 5-minute time range each.

LI's Event Types	Probabilities				
	S1	S2	S3	S4	S5
v4_18ca9254	0.03	0.02	0.03	0.03	0.03
v4_1a6ac047	0	0	0	0	0
v4_28077ade	0	0	0	0	0
v4_2f6e41a2	0.03	0.02	0.03	0.03	0.03
v4_36c81ef6	0.05	0.04	0.07	0.05	0.06
v4_393c8071	0.2	0.17	0.18	0.21	0.19
v4_59cd0174	0.03	0.02	0.03	0.03	0.03
v4_681f6046	0.05	0.04	0.07	0.05	0.06
v4_69475cc1	0	0.08	0	0	0
v4_6dd466a5	0.03	0.02	0.03	0.03	0.03
v4_71183f87	0	0	0	0	0
v4_802bd0d4	0.11	0.1	0.1	0.12	0.11
v4_87e0ca23	0.03	0.02	0.03	0.03	0.03
v4_88de5e12	0.03	0.02	0.03	0.03	0.03
v4_8ebbb638	0.03	0.02	0.03	0.03	0.03
v4_94680e71	0.03	0.02	0.03	0.03	0.03
v4_9d3e7bdd	0.03	0.02	0.03	0.03	0.03
v4_9fd2eafd	0.04	0.11	0.04	0.03	0.04
v4_a7f56e13	0.06	0.05	0.05	0.06	0.06
v4_a8a71825	0.03	0.02	0.03	0.03	0.03
v4_b610f232	0.03	0.02	0.03	0.03	0.03
v4_b9100c8f	0.05	0.04	0.07	0.05	0.06
v4_bafd4270	0.03	0.02	0.03	0.03	0.03
v4_bfebb8d	0.05	0.04	0.07	0.05	0.06
v4_f0533255	0.03	0.02	0.03	0.03	0.03

By ranking (step 4) samples/distributions in decreasing order of the distance measure, we pick up the following four having highest average similarity (this is the dominant similarity set representing the normal workload mode of the host):
$$ACSD(S1) = 0.97, ACSD(S3) = 0.96, ACSD(S4) = 0.97, ACSD(S5) = 0.97.$$

The chosen four distributions are the baseline "candidates". With this ranking, the anomalous Sample 2 indicated in red in Table I dropped from the "candidates" list.

Since there are three samples with the same score, we are going to identify the one with maximum uncertainty as the "safest" unbiased model for the baseline distribution. The entropies (in *nats*, $a = 10$) of sample distributions are:

$$H(S1) = 2.83,$$
$$H(S2) = 2.78,$$
$$H(S3) = 2.85,$$
$$H(S4) = 2.80,$$
$$H(S5) = 2.84.$$

And what is the best "candidate" to be the baseline? Applying the maximum entropy principle [10], it is the distribution that has the highest information uncertainty. Sample 3 (green column in Table I) has the maximum entropy distribution (Fig. 4) and is chosen to be the baseline for the log source.

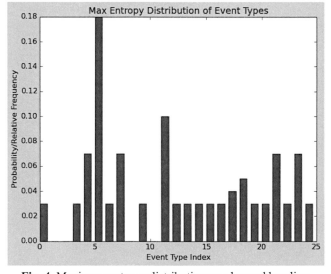

Fig. 4. Maximum entropy distribution as a learned baseline.

The final step is to derive the "normal discrepancy radius" of the baseline/source. This is the variance in ACSD that we observe in the top similarity subset of 4.

The *normal discrepancy radius* (R) then can be defined as the range of ACSD's in the "dominant" similarity set. In our experimental example, it is the following difference:

$$R = 0.97 - 0.96 = 0.01.$$

Method II (clustering of event type distributions without random sampling). In an alternative, highly complex implementation, without randomized sampling, with continuously measured and stored probability distributions/histograms of event types that contain all normal and abnormal patterns in the log stream, our algorithm performs the following steps:

1. calculate local outlier factors of all histograms using LOF algorithm [9];
2. pick up the "centroid" event type distribution as the histogram having the smallest LOF;
3. if those are several, the one that has the highest entropy;
4. compute the average and standard deviation of distances of all histograms from the centroid;
5. define the "normal discrepancy radius" of the log source from its baseline with 3-sigma rule, assuming that distances are distributed normally [11].

LOF is based on a concept of a local density (or similarity distance in our case), locality defined by k nearest (similar) neighbors. Those neighbors are employed to estimate the density. Based on this evaluation, outliers are detected as those distributions that have substantially lower density than their neighbors. The local density is estimated by the distance at which a point can be "reached" from its neighbors [9]. In a simpler implementation, the centroid can be the histogram having the minimum average distance from the rest of the histograms. The normalcy radius can be also linked to Chebyshev's inequality [12] without making the assumption of normality.

Fig. 5 pictorially supports the main ideas of Methods I and II.

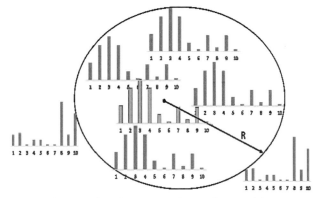

Fig. 5. Illustrating Baseline as a *Centroid Distribution* of the cluster and its *Normal Discrepancy Radius*.

Abnormality degree of baseline violation. We can measure the abnormality degree or criticality of alerts raised using the baseline. It is defined by how far is the run-time event type distribution from the centroid minus the discrepancy radius. So, if the normal operations are within 0.1-radius, a run-time distribution having distance=0.4 exceeds the tolerance by 0.3. Then we can use a scale to map those over-tolerance distances into a score range from "lowest" to "highest" (continuous or discrete). Alternatively, measure and communicate to the user how many times or by which percent the tolerance radius is exceeded.

It can happen that the event source operates in different modes and have different baseline characteristics accordingly (for example, the corresponding IT resource has high and low utilization modes). In such cases, k-means clustering [13] can be applied to derive relevant clusters and their centroids, and apply the above-mentioned normality assumption or Chebyshev inequality to extract the normal discrepancy radius for each of the clusters. This means that for the corresponding anomaly detection we identify in which mode the system operates and apply the relevant centroid baseline.

We conducted another controlled experiment as in [4], again choosing vR LI as our proof-of-concept application. We monitored LI's logs in INFO and DEBUG modes using another LI instance. This is a way to observe the application in two different stress modes (high and low). In those logging modes, our algorithm implemented in Python observes different event type distributions. Representative distributions are depicted in Figs 6 and 7, respectively.

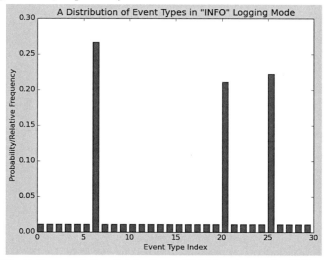

Fig. 6. Representative distribution in INFO logging mode of LI.

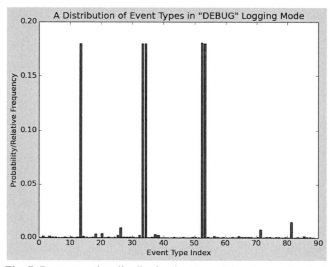

Fig. 7. Representative distribution in DEBUG logging mode of LI.

The graphs illustrate different number and rates of event types. Therefore, having detected possible workload modes of an application with complex clustering methods, then the sampling technique of Method I can be applied to derive the baseline for each mode individually.

4   Future Work

We plan to experiment with much bigger data sets. Particularly, within a large experimental setup we are going to learn baselines of ESXi hosts in various environments by applying our sampling concepts with confidence control in Method I and employ the learned structures in real-time anomaly detection. Then we'll be able to validate observed anomalies with the incident data regularly being reported by operations teams.

The live never-ending stream of ESXi events in large cloud infrastructures make a big volume. This means that even we observe a large number of different event types and hence deal with storage of large-size histograms, with the sampling techniques based on binomial distributions, the number of those histograms will be moderate. Therefore, feasibility of our implementation is not under risk because of algorithmic complexity.

5   Conclusion

We introduced the concept of *baseline models* for log sources employing LI's native constructs of Event Types and described algorithms to efficiently identify those structures using statistical sampling and machine learning. Baseline models are comprehensive for various analytical tasks in log management from real-time anomaly and change detection to other pattern detection problems. With controlled experiments, we demonstrated how the baselines are learned.

References

1. VMware vRealize Operations Manager:
   http://www.vmware.com/products/vrealize-operations.html.
2. VMware vRealize Log Insight:
   https://www.vmware.com/products/vrealize-log-insight.
3. Marvasti, M.A., Poghosyan, A.V., Harutyunyan, A.N., and Grigoryan, N.M.: An enterprise dynamic thresholding system. In: Proceedings of USENIX International Conference on Autonomic Computing (ICAC), pp. 129-135, June 18-20, Philadelphia, PA, USA (2014).
4. Harutyunyan, A.N., Poghosyan, A.V., Grigoryan, N.M., Kushmerick, N., and Beybutyan, H.: Identifying changed or sick resources from logs. Submitted to 4th International Workshop on Data-Driven Self-Regulating Systems (DSS 2018), September 7, Trento, Italy (2018).

5. Harutyunyan, A.N., Poghosyan, A.V., Grigoryan, N.M., and Marvasti, M.A.: Abnormality analysis of streamed log data. In: Proceedings of IEEE Network Operations and Management Symposium (NOMS), 7p., May 5-9, Krakow, Poland (2014).

6. Cover, T. and Thomas J.: Elements of Information Theory. Wiley, (1991).

7. Brown, D. and Kushmerick, N.: Anomaly detection using log summary divergence. A method for computing the similarity of two log message queries and its application in anomaly detection in distributed environments. Technical paper, VMware (2015).

8. Binomial Distribution: https://en.wikipedia.org/wiki/Binomial_distribution.

9. Breunig, M.M., Kriegel, H.-P., Ng, R.T., and Sander, J.: LOF: Identifying density-based local outliers. In: Proceedings of ACM SIGMOD International Conference on Management of Data, pp. 93–104, May 15-18, Dallas, TX, USA (2000).

10. Maximum Entropy Principle: https://en.wikipedia.org/wiki/Principle_of_maximum_entropy.

11. Normal Distribution: https://en.wikipedia.org/wiki/Normal_distribution.

12. Chebyshev inequality: https://en.wikipedia.org/wiki/Chebyshev's_inequality.

13. K-means clustering: https://en.wikipedia.org/wiki/K-means_clustering.

Logarithmically Asymptotically Optimal Testing of Statistical Hypotheses in Steganography Applications

Mariam Haroutunian, Evgueni Haroutunian, Parandzem Hakobyan and
Hovsep Mikayelyan

Institute for Informatics and Automation Problems of NAS of RA
{armar,evhar}@ipia.sci.am

Abstract. An information-theoretic model for steganography with a
passive adversary is considered. The adversary's task is to distinguish the
cover message from stegotext, which is the modified message with hidden
information. This task is interpreted as a hypothesis testing problem.
We are interested in the logarithmically asymptotically optimal testing
of statistical hypotheses for this model. We suggest the approach by
method of types and give the functional dependence of the reliabilities
of the first and the second kind errors. The proof gives the way of optimal
test constructing which is useful for real applications.

Keywords: Steganography · Information-theoretic security · Hypotheses testing · LAO tests · Error probability exponents (reliabilities).

1 Introduction

Steganography is the science of communicating by hiding information, i. e. by
embedding messages within other. Steganography means "covered writing" in
Greek. The goal of steganography is to hide the *presence* of a message and to
create a covert channel, while the main goal of cryptography is to hide the *content*
of a message. As in [1] we consider the model with *passive* adversary (who has
read-only access to the public channel) and use the standard terminology of
information hiding [2].

Two parties (Alice and Bob) are *users* of the stegosystem. Alice wishes to
send a hidden message over a public channel to Bob, such that the presence of
hidden information must be unnoticed to a third party (*adversary* Eve). Eve has
read-only access to the public channel. Alice can be *inactive* and send a covertext
C without hidden information or be *active* and send stegotext S. Covertext is
generated by a source according to a distribution P_C known to Eve. The stegotext
is computed from an embedding function and has the distribution P_S. We assume
that Eve knows also the embedding function and distribution P_S. The receiver
Bob and adversary Eve observe S. Bob has the exctracting algorithm, but Eve
does not know if Alice is active or not. The task of Eve is to decide if the data
was generated according to P_C or P_S, in other words she must solve the problem
of Hypothesis testing [3], [4].

The classical problem of statistical hypothesis testing refers to two hypotheses. Based on data samples a statistician makes decision on which of the two proposed hypotheses (H_1 and H_2) must be accepted. The procedure of statistical hypotheses detection is called test.The decisions can be erroneous due to randomness of the sample. The two errors that can be made in a decision are called the first type error for accepting H_2 when H_1 is true and the second type error for accepting H_1 when H_2 is true. The test is considered as a good one if the probabilities of the errors in given conditions are as small as possible. But they are interconnected, when we reduce the first one, the second one can get increased.

Frequently the problem is solved for the case of a tests sequence, where the probabilities of error decreased exponentially as 2^{-NE}, when the number of observations N tends to the infinity. We call the exponent of error probability E the *reliability*. In case of two hypotheses both reliabilities corresponding to two possible error probabilities could not increase simultaneously, it is an accepted way to fix the value of one of the reliabilities and try to make the tests sequence get the greatest value of the remaining reliability. Such a test is called *logarithmically asymptotically optimal* (LAO). Such optimal tests for two hypotheses were considered first by Hoeffding [5], examined later by Csiszár and Longo [6], Blahut [7], Longo and Sgarro [8] and others. The term LAO for testing of two hypotheses was proposed by Birge [9]. The problem of multiple hypotheses LAO testing was investigated by Haroutunian [10], [11], [12].

In this paper we study the functional dependence of exponents of the first and the second kind error probabilities of the optimal tests by the method of types [13] in the context of steganography.

For application of information-theoretical methods in probability theory and statistics we refer to ([12], [14], [15]).

The paper is organized as follows. In the next section the main notations and definitions are given. The main result is formulated and proved in the section 3 and we conclude in section 4.

2   Notations and Definitions

Here we present some necessary characteristics and results of information theory [3], [4]. We denote finite sets by script capitals. The cardinality of a set $\mathcal{X}$ is denoted as $|\mathcal{X}|$. Probability distributions (PDs) are denoted by Q, P. $\mathcal{P}(\mathcal{X})$ is the space of all PDs on finite set $\mathcal{X}$. Random variable (RV) which take values in finite sets $\mathcal{X}$ are denoted by X.

The Shannon entropy $H_Q(X)$ of RV X with PD Q is:

$$H_Q(X) \overset{\triangle}{=} -\sum_{x \in \mathcal{X}} Q(x) \log Q(x).$$

The divergence (Kullback-Leibler information, or "distance") of PDs Q and P on $\mathcal{X}$ is:

$$D(Q||P) \triangleq \sum_{x \in \mathcal{X}} Q(x) \log \frac{Q(x)}{P(x)}.$$

For our investigations we use the method of types, one of the important technical tools in Shannon theory [13]. The type Q of a vector $\mathbf{x} = (x_1, ..., x_N) \in \mathcal{X}^N$ is a PD (the empirical distribution)

$$Q = \left\{ Q(x) = \frac{N(x|\mathbf{x})}{N}, x \in \mathcal{X} \right\},$$

where $N(x|\mathbf{x})$ is the number of repetitions of symbol x in vector $\mathbf{x}$. We denote by $\mathcal{Q}^N(\mathcal{X})$ the set of all types of vectors in $\mathcal{X}^N$ for given N and the set of vectors $\mathbf{x}$ of type Q is denoted by $\mathcal{T}_Q^N(X)$.

We need the following frequently used inequalities [13]:

$$| \mathcal{Q}^N(\mathcal{X}) | \leq (N+1)^{|\mathcal{X}|}, \tag{1}$$

for any type $Q \in \mathcal{Q}^N(\mathcal{X})$

$$(N+1)^{-|\mathcal{X}|} \exp\{NH_Q(X)\} \leq | \mathcal{T}_Q^N(X) | \leq \exp\{NH_Q(X)\}. \tag{2}$$

If $\mathbf{x} \in \mathcal{T}_Q^N(X)$, then

$$P^N(\mathbf{x}) = \exp\{-N(H_Q(X) + D(Q||P))\}. \tag{3}$$

The security of the stegosystem is defined in the terms of relative entropy or Kullback–Leibler divergence between two distributions P_C and P_S.

Definition 1. ([1]) *A stegosystem is called perfectly secure against passive adversaries if*

$$D(P_C||P_S) = 0;$$

and a stegosystem is called ϵ –secure against passive adversaries if

$$D(P_C||P_S) \leq \epsilon.$$

Perfect security for a stegosystem parallels Shannon's notion of perfect security for a cryptosystem. Eve's capabilities of detecting an embedded message are obtained from the theory of hypothesis testing.

3 Formulation of Results

By observing data $\mathbf{x} = (x_1, ..., x_N)$, $x_n \in \mathcal{X}$ that was sent from Alice to Bob over the public channel Eve must decide if Alice was active or not. If Alice was not active, the data was generated by distribution P_C and if she was active it was generated by distribution P_S. Hence, Eve must accept one of two hypotheses $H_1 : P = P_S$ and $H_2 : P = P_C$.

Remark 1. The priority of hypotheses in the steganography context is important because it is more expedient not to miss the embedded message (the first kind of error to be small) than to decide that there is a hidden information in the data while in fact it is just a covertext (the second kind of error is not so risky).

The procedure of decision making is a non-randomized test $\varphi_N(\mathbf{x})$, which can be defined by partition of the set of possible messages $\mathcal{X}^N$ on two disjoint subsets $\mathcal{A}_l^N = \{\mathbf{x} : \varphi_N(\mathbf{x}) = l\}$, $l = \overline{1,2}$. The set $\mathcal{A}_1^N$ contains all data $\mathbf{x}$ for which the hypothesis H_1 is adopted, which in our context means that Eve decides that Alice was active and sent the *stegotext*. Correspondingly, the set $\mathcal{A}_2^N$ contains all $\mathbf{x}$ for which the hypothesis H_2 is adopted, i.e. Eve decides Alice was inactive and sent *covertext*.

The probability of the erroneous acceptance of hypothesis H_2 provided that H_1 is true, is the following:

$$\alpha_{2|1}(\varphi_N) = P_S^N(\mathcal{A}_2^N).$$

When hypothesis H_2 is true, but Eve accepted H_1 hypothesis then the error probability is defined as follows:

$$\alpha_{1|2}(\varphi_N) = P_C^N(\mathcal{A}_1^N).$$

The error probability exponents, called "reliabilities" of the infinite sequence of tests φ, are defined respectively as follows:

$$E_{2|1}(\varphi) \stackrel{\triangle}{=} \lim_{N\to\infty} -\frac{1}{N} \log \alpha_{2|1}(\varphi_N), \tag{4}$$

$$E_{1|2}(\varphi) \stackrel{\triangle}{=} \lim_{N\to\infty} -\frac{1}{N} \log \alpha_{1|2}(\varphi_N). \tag{5}$$

Definition 2. ([9]) *The sequence of tests φ^* is called logarithmically asymptotically optimal (LAO) if for given positive value of $E_{2|1}$ the maximum possible value is provided for $E_{1|2}$.*

We prove the following well known result [7] by the method of types.

Theorem 1. *If stegosystem is not perfectly secure in the sense that for distributions P_C and P_S, $D(P_C||P_S) > 0$ takes place, then for given $E_{2|1}$, $E_{2|1} \in (0, D(P_C||P_S))$ there exists a LAO sequence of tests, the reliability $E_{1|2}^*$ of which is defined as follows:*

$$E_{1|2}^* = E_{1|2}^*(E_{2|1}) = \inf_{Q:\, D(Q||P_S)\leq E_{2|1}} D(Q||P_C). \tag{6}$$

When $E_{2|1} \geq D(P_C||P_S)$, then $E_{1|2}^*$ is equal to 0 .

Remark 2. When $E_{2|1} \to 0$, then $E_{1|2}^* = D(P_S|P_C)$.

Proof. Let us consider the following sequence of tests φ^* defined by the sets

$$\mathcal{B}_1^N = \bigcup_{Q:\, D(Q\|P_S)\leq E_{2|1}} \mathcal{T}_Q^N(X),$$

$$\mathcal{B}_2^N = \bigcup_{Q:\, D(Q\|P_S)>E_{2|1}} \mathcal{T}_Q^N(X).$$

Now let us prove that the given $E_{2|1}$ is the reliability of error probability $\alpha_{2|1}(\varphi_N^*)$ of tests φ_N^*.

Using (1), (2) and (3), we can estimate $\alpha_{2|1}(\varphi_N^*)$ by the following way:

$$\alpha_{2|1}(\varphi_N^*) = P_S^N\left(\mathcal{B}_2^N\right)$$

$$= P_S^N\left(\bigcup_{Q:D(Q\|P_S)>E_{2|1}} \mathcal{T}_Q^N(X)\right)$$

$$\leq (N+1)^{|\mathcal{X}|} \sup_{Q:D(Q\|P_S)>E_{2|1}} P_S^N\left(\mathcal{T}_Q^N(X)\right)$$

$$\leq (N+1)^{|\mathcal{X}|} \sup_{Q:D(Q\|P_S)>E_{2|1}} |\mathcal{T}_Q^N(X)| \times P_S^N(\mathbf{x})$$

$$\leq (N+1)^{|\mathcal{X}|} \sup_{Q:D(Q\|P_S)>E_{2|1}} \exp\left\{NH_Q(X)\right\} \exp\{-N\left[D(Q\|P_S)+H_Q(X)\right]\}$$

$$\leq \exp\left\{-N\left[E_{2|1}-o_N(1)\right]\right\},$$

where $o_N(1) \to 0$ when $N \to \infty$.

For $\alpha_{1|2}(\varphi_N^*)$, we can obtain similar estimates:

$$\alpha_{1|2}(\varphi_N^*) = P_C^N\left(\mathcal{B}_1^N\right)$$

$$= P_C^N\left(\bigcup_{Q:D(Q\|P_S)\leq E_{2|1}} \mathcal{T}_Q^N(X)\right)$$

$$\leq (N+1)^{|\mathcal{X}|} \sup_{Q:D(Q\|P_S)\leq E_{2|1}} P_C^N\left(\mathcal{T}_Q^N(X)\right) \qquad (7)$$

$$\leq (N+1)^{|\mathcal{X}|} \sup_{Q:D(Q\|P_S)\leq E_{2|1}} \exp\left\{-ND(Q\|P_C)\right\}$$

$$= \exp\left\{-N\left(\inf_{Q:D(Q\|P_S)\leq E_{2|1}} D(Q\|P_C) - o_N(1)\right)\right\}.$$

Now let us prove the inverse inequality

$$\alpha_{1|2}(\varphi_N^*) = P_C^N\left(\mathcal{B}_1^N\right)$$

$$= P_C^N\left(\bigcup_{Q:D(Q\|P_S)\leq E_{2|1}} \mathcal{T}_Q^N(X)\right)$$

$$\geq \sup_{Q:D(Q||P_S)\leq E_{2|1}} P_C^N(\mathcal{T}_Q^N(X))$$

$$\geq (N+1)^{-|\mathcal{X}|} \sup_{Q:D(Q||P_S)\leq E_{2|1}} \exp\{-ND(Q||P_C)\} \tag{8}$$

$$= \exp\left\{-N\left(\inf_{Q:D(Q||P_S)\leq E_{2|1}} D(Q||P_C) + o_N(1)\right)\right\}.$$

Taking into account (7), (8) and the continuity of the functions $D(Q||P_C)$ and $D(Q||P_S)$ we obtain that $\lim_{N\to\infty} -N^{-1}\log\alpha_{1|2}(\varphi_N^*)$ exists and in correspondence with (6) equals to $E_{1|2}^*$.

The proof of the first part of Theorem 1 will be accomplished if we demonstrate that the sequence of the test φ^* is LAO, that is for given $E_{2|1}$ and every sequence of tests φ $E_{1|2}(\varphi) \leq E_{1|2}^*$ takes place.

Let us consider any other sequence φ^{**} of tests which for given $E_{2|1}$ is defined by partition of $\mathcal{X}^N$ to disjoint subsets $\mathcal{D}_1^N$ and $\mathcal{D}_2^N$ such that $E_{1|2}(\varphi^{**}) \geq E_{1|2}^*$. This condition is equivalent to the inequality

$$\alpha_{1|2}(\varphi_N^{**}) \leq \alpha_{1|2}(\varphi_N^*) \tag{9}$$

for N large enough.

Let us show that $\mathcal{D}_2^N \bigcap \mathcal{B}_1^N = \emptyset$. If $\mathcal{D}_2^N \bigcap \mathcal{B}_1^N \neq \emptyset$, then there exists Q' such that $D(Q'||P_S) \leq E_{2|1}$ and $\mathcal{T}_{Q'}^N(X) \in \mathcal{D}_2^N$ from which it follows that

$$\alpha_{2|1}(\varphi_N^{**}) = P_S^N(\mathcal{D}_2^N) \geq P_S^N(\mathcal{T}_{Q'}^N(X)) \geq \exp\left\{-N\left[E_{2|1} + o_N(1)\right]\right\}.$$

From $\mathcal{D}_1^N \bigcup \mathcal{D}_2^N = \mathcal{X}^N$, $\mathcal{D}_1^N \bigcap \mathcal{D}_2^N = \emptyset$ and $\mathcal{D}_2^N \bigcap \mathcal{B}_1^N = \emptyset$, follows that $\mathcal{B}_1^N \subseteq \mathcal{D}_1^N$. If $\mathcal{B}_1^N \subset \mathcal{D}_1^N$, then we have that $\alpha_{1|2}(\varphi_N^{**}) \geq \alpha_{1|2}(\varphi_N^*)$, which contradicts to (9). Hence $\mathcal{D}_1^N = B_1^N$, as well as $\mathcal{D}_2^N = B_2^N$. It is the same that $\varphi^{**} = \varphi^*$.

The proof of the second part of the Theorem 1 is simple. If $E_{2|1} \geq D(P_C||P_S)$, then from (6) follows that $E_{1|2}^*$ is equal to 0.

The theorem is proved.

4 Conclusion

The problem of logarithmically asymptotically optimal testing of statistical hypotheses for the steganography model with a passive adversy is solved by the method of types which gives the functional dependence of the reliabilities of the first and the second kind errors. The practical importance of the result for steganography applications is the way of constructing the optimal tests that will be implemented and experimented in our future work.

References

1. Cachin, C.: An information-theoretic model for steganography. Information and Computation, 192, 41-56, (2004)

2. Pfitzmann, B.:Information hiding terminology. In: Information Hiding, First International Workshop, Lecture Notes in Computer Science, vol. 1174, pp. 347–350. Springer (1996)

3. Blahut R.: Principles and Practice of Information Theory. Addison-Wesley, Reading, MA, (1987)

4. Cover, T., Thomas, J.: Elements of Information Theory. Second Edition, New York, Wiley, (2006)

5. Hoeffding, W.: Asymptotically optimal tests for multinomial distributions. The Annals of Mathematical Statistics. **36**, 369–401, (1965)

6. Csiszár, I., Longo, G.: On the error exponent for source coding and for testing simple statistical hypotheses. Studia Sc. Math. Hungarica. **6**, 181–191. (1971)

7. Blahut, R,.: Hypothesis testing and information theory. IEEE Transactions on Information Theory. **20** (4), 405–417, (1974)

8. Longo G., Sgarro, A.: The error exponent for the testing of simple statistical hypotheses: A combinatorial approach. Journal of Combinatorics, Information and System Sciences. **5** (1), 58-67, (1980)

9. Birgé, L.: Vitesses maximales de décroissance des erreurs et tests optimaux associeés. Z. Wahrsch. verw. Gebiete, **55**, 261–273, (1981)

10. Haroutunian, E.: On asymptotically optimal criteria for Markov chains. The First World Congress of Bernoulli Society, (in Russian). **2** (3), 153–156, (1989)

11. Haroutunian, E.: Logarithmically asymptotically optimal testing of multiple statistical hypotheses. Problems of Control and Information Theory. **19** (5-6), 413–421, (1990)

12. Haroutunian, E., Haroutunian, M., Harutyunyan, A.: Reliability Criteria in Information Theory and in Statistical Hypothesis Testing. Foundations and Trends in Communications and Information Theory. **4** (2-3), (2008)

13. Csiszár, I., Körner, J.: Information Theory: Coding Theorems for Discrete Memoryless Systems. Academic press., New York, (1981)

14. Kullback, S.: Information Theory and Statistics. New York: Wiley, (1959)

15. Csiszár, I., Shields, P.: Information Theory and Statistics: A Tutorial. Foundations and Trends in Communications and Information Theory, **1** (4), (2004)